George Orwell
on Screen

George Orwell on Screen

Adaptations, Documentaries and Docudramas on Film and Television

DAVID RYAN

Foreword by A. L. Kennedy

McFarland & Company, Inc., Publishers

Jefferson, North Carolina

ISBN (print) 978-1-4766-7369-1
ISBN (ebook) 978-1-4766-3313-8

LIBRARY OF CONGRESS CATALOGUING DATA ARE AVAILABLE

British Library cataloguing data are available

Front cover: John Hurt as Winston Smith in the
1984 film *Nineteen Eighty-Four* (Virgin Films)

Printed in the United States of America

*McFarland & Company, Inc., Publishers
Box 611, Jefferson, North Carolina 28640
www.mcfarlandpub.com*

For my friends and loved ones,
who are more equal than the others.

Table of Contents

Foreword by A. L. Kennedy

One of the less grim talking points of 2017 was the uptick in sales of *1984*, George Orwell's classic denunciation of totalitarianism, pitting love of Big Brother against love of Life, Liberty *and so forth*. In the intervening time we have been able to appreciate the size and frailty of *and so forth* to a degree that far-sighted and gleefully grim Orwell would have appreciated.

Completing *1984* was the last creative act in a life foreshortened by stress, injury, a working life plagued by poverty and a tendency towards bohemian self-harm, black tea and chain smoking. Despite chronic ill-health and a relatively late start as a writer, Orwell's output before his death at 46 was monumental, amounting to a waist-high stack of reviews, essays, letters, radio scripts and novels. A coddled and healthy author in an age of easy, computerized rewrites would be hard-pressed to produce so much and so much of great quality, insight, bleak humor and passionate humanity. Orwell's late nights and self-inflicted privations speak of an obsessional streak, and his startling commitment to the human project—fighting for the republic in Spain, endlessly helping young authors and needy cases, polemicizing on behalf of the powerless—has allowed some to find in him the qualities of a tall and whispering secular saint.

Orwell's passions and obsessions seem more than averagely apt to attract answering passions and obsessions among readers and among the necessary guardians of a literary life cut short. This can lead to factionalism and there are certainly rival camps of Orwellites, but at their best those who love and honor Orwell form an eclectic band of academics, enthusiasts, campaigners and readers, each personally and often rather gloriously inspired by the work. The Orwell Foundation, for example, runs a vibrant calendar of lectures and events and organizes, among other initiatives, the annual Orwell Prize for political journalism, the premier award for political writing in its widest, most challenging and beneficent sense.

Which brings me to this latest, rather glorious project of passion and entirely fruitful obsession. You will find David Ryan's *George Orwell on*

Screen is an astonishingly comprehensive record of, as we might guess, film and television adaptations of Orwell's work. You may be surprised by the humor here, although those familiar with Orwell's deadpan asides and animal-based quips will feel mightily at home. Ryan provides unmistakable affection and a dogged, almost miraculous accumulation of detail that, along with remarkable anecdotes and literary asides, will please the most ardent fan of Orwell and Orwell biography. Those who come for the media studies may be thoroughly engaged by the ghostly figure of Orwell, emerging from a mass of research. Those who come for an Orwell fix may stay for an oblique record of a decline in television production standards and commitment to quality drama on both sides of the Atlantic. All this, plus Richard Burton and some farting rats.

Ryan happily narrates how his gradual slide into Orwell-obsession became a full-blown book after 25 years of research. Beginning by reading *Animal Farm* at school (something which can extinguish any young readers' enthusiasm) Ryan was embraced by the Orwell Society and moved on to dinner with actor Ronald Pickup—who once played Orwell, carefully perfecting his hoarse, soft, Etonian locution—and then a trip to Jura, where Orwell completed and then rewrote *1984*, along with Orwell's son Richard Blair. (Orwell's real name was Eric Blair.) Ryan is an enthusiastic narrator, injecting just enough of his investigative travails and serendipities to enliven what might have been simply a dry list into an agreeable artistic adventure.

We move from Orwell's own dramatic adaptation of *Animal Farm* in 1947 to a surprise pick of usually dapper and debonair David Niven as the first Winston Smith in 1949, with a side mention of Lorne Greene, homely and cheerful star of *Bonanza*, as the Inquisitor in an early CBS version. Characteristic of Ryan's style, we also learn CBS was so anti-sex that they insisted writers rename Big Brother's Junior Anti-Sex League.

The BBC's ground-breaking 1954 TV version of *1984*, directed by the great Rudolph Cartier, remains of the days when a political drama could genuinely shock without being prurient, and without giving rise to wholesale calls for the UK's currently tottering public broadcaster to be mobbed with flaming pitchforks at sunset. (Although its shocking effect might conceivably have led to the death of a Herne Bay beauty queen of the previous decade. Ryan's talent for digging out bizarrely wonderful details strikes again.) The pitchforks might still have been out had viewers known that the rats used in Room 101's torture were happy, fat and rampantly gay.

We move on to learn that the CIA-backed a Cold War animation of *Animal Farm*, and that the film was famously hated by Romanian dictator Nicolae Ceaușescu and therefore screened on New Year's Day 1990—something which would surely have pleased Orwell.

We discover that David Bowie, among others, pondered a *1984* musical. (It's surely only a matter of time before London's musical-obsessed West End follows up on its recent, highly successful stage version with something more family friendly and toe-tapping.) And there's a bittersweet mention of David Attenborough as masterful and inspiring controller of BBC 2.

A description of the BBC's novel production of *Keep the Aspidistra Flying* will remind you of scriptwriter Robin Chapman's genius and the possibility that television drama once didn't have to involve multiple casualties or medical emergencies.

Ryan doesn't just deal with dramatic productions; he also looks at long-forgotten documentaries. The very idea of Jack Bond's Orwell documentary—with Malcolm Muggeridge interviewing Orwell's second wife, Sonia Orwell, long-time friend Cyril Connolly and sister Avril Dunn—is mind-bending. The fact that it's preserved and yet virtually unknown is heart-breaking. The fact that Muggeridge was a happily voluntary crewmember somehow delights me. And I was even more delighted by Connolly's quoted comment on Orwell's famously Eyoreish nature: "It's a bracing pessimism, a feeling that once you admit the worst, everything's a bit more fun all round."

And Colin Blakely was, of course, the perfect TV drama casting to play George Bowling—a character cursed with dense suppressions and an anxiously soapy neck. I want to see that version of *Coming Up for Air*. In fact, any sane and savvy broadcaster should online boxset and schedule the hell out of every Orwell-related drama Ryan lists. And throw in the documentaries, because why not? I want to see them all and I'm sure others would too. I would even hold my breath during the missing 7 minutes of the 1965 BBC version of *1984* Ryan cites from the National Library of Congress. I imagine only a European terrestrial network like Arte might attempt anything like an true Orwellathon, but who knows what digital possibilities may emerge if one Armageddon or another doesn't catch up with us first.

Ryan introduces U.S. audiences, perhaps for the first time, to the work of veteran broadcaster, Melvyn Bragg. The UK media scene was once generous enough to let him make arts TV, particularly *The South Bank Show*, a weekly examination of anything and everything, which opened up my small-town life to the arts. *Omnibus* and *Arena* used to be BBC forces to be reckoned with. Ryan summons up his culture shock, as he watches Bragg's 1971 Orwell documentary, which formed part of the *Omnibus* strand. Bragg was just in time to an apparently vanished tribe—proud, articulate, self-educated trade unionists, dressed in their Sunday best and sitting in bookcase-laden living rooms. When was the last time someone like that appeared on television?

Speaking of director Frank Cvitanovich's *The Road to Wigan Pier (A Musical Documentary)*, Winifred Smith of Corringham, Essex, is quoted as saying, "To the present generation, those bitter years are of little interest outside academic research…. But fate plays ironic tricks…. That which has happened once may happen again." Something many of us wake up thinking.

The Crystal Spirit: Orwell on Jura emerges as one of the finest dramas. The delight of renowned dramatist Alan Plater's sharp, deft dialog meeting sharp, dying Orwell on Jura. Plater is quoted in the comment, "We can't and mustn't play the traditional game of demonstrating how day-to-day contacts and incidents influenced the form and content of the book." I would hope that could be tattooed on every biographer and literary critic's forehead. Ronald Pickup, playing Orwell, is noted as placing a call to translator Michael Meyer, who knew Orwell, in order to produce an admirable approximation of Orwell's voice. The piece was broadcast in 1983 and never rescreened. It lost out in the year's TV awards to *An Englishman Abroad*, Alan Bennett's drama about Guy Burgess, filmed in my famously grim hometown, in the absence of accessible Russian locations.

We then move on to the 1984 festival of dystopia, which seemed, even at the time, entirely un-prescient, far too late. A five-part BBC documentary on Orwell, which began in December, showed the last of the BBC's glory. "It was the early days of [arts strand] *Arena*," director Nigel Williams is quoted as saying. "The BBC in those days was a massive program-making organization, all of which was finished really by [nineties director-general] John Birt and Margaret Thatcher, not necessarily in that order. In those days you would just suggest an idea and make it. As it developed, the films got longer and longer and longer and we ended up doing five, because you could do that in those days. Originally it was one film." It is possible to experience very Orwellian moments of furious gloom while reading this book—something which seems only right.

And, as we glide along we are treated to the passing image of Orwell and Stevie Smith making love in a park, unable to keep tall George's head down and out of the headlights…. There's James Fox as a strangely appropriate Orwell and, again Ryan's research is glorious, a *Guardian*-reading part-time clown and comedian just back from entertaining troops in the Falklands, plays Big Brother in a 1984 production of *1984*. We learn that Michael Radford's *1984* involved Richard Burton managing end-stage alcoholism, and that same film put John Hurt into Room 101 with farting rats. This version, one of the few accessible Orwell dramas, is "enjoying" a new success in the U.S.

Ryan passes us beyond Alan Plater's next Orwell drama, *A Merry War*, and the difficulties of shooting—in the filmic sense—a barn full of animals for the 1999 *Animal Farm*, introducing us to Dipendragod the (unscathed) elephant cast in *Shooting An Elephant*. Ryan notes a 2003 *South Bank Show* documentary amidst a wealth of continuing interest and responses to Orwell, albeit in muzzled times worthy of Big Brother. Lateral and surreal approaches are attempted, there's an opera, a work by Northern Ballet, a sense that Orwell will continue to provoke and inspire—and continue to be a safe bet for at least a halfway decent audience share.

I hope this book gets the praise and attention it deserves and may it inspire that retrospective season I long for. I'm glad David Ryan had the pleasure of viewing so much forgotten material, but I'd like us all to be able to share that pleasure. I think that would be in the spirit of meeting *in the place where there is no darkness*.

A.L. Kennedy is an award-winning author, journalist and comedian, and associate professor of creative writing at University of Warwick. Her 2017 lecture "Orwell with women" was included in the Orwell Lecture series, given annually by the Orwell Foundation since 1989.

Preface

The book you're holding has been in the works for 25 years, I guess, though I've been acquainted with George Orwell since 1983, when I read *Animal Farm* at school. I was 15 when the year 1984 came along and remember the media's agonized chin-stroking at the time; later that year, I read *Nineteen Eighty-Four*, which impressed me tremendously but not enough to make me a card-carrying Orwell aficionado.

For that, we need to fast-forward to the beginning of my career. It's 1992 and I've been hired as a cub reporter at *The Hexham Courant*, an old-fashioned, rural weekly newspaper in Northumberland, England. In the nearest city, Newcastle-upon-Tyne, I've moved into an apartment, where one of my roommates is a teacher called Eamon McManus. I don't remember the exact conversation we had, but Eamon lends me a book, *The Penguin Essays of George Orwell*, and suggests I read its first gem: *Why I Write*, from 1946. If you're familiar with Orwell's essays, you'll appreciate why I was hooked.

All my life, I've had another passion: movies. I'd say "vintage TV shows" too, if it weren't for the fact that when I was growing up, they weren't necessarily vintage. Driven by the demons that Orwell pinpoints so thrillingly in *Why I Write*, I also dreamed of becoming an author. But the brainwave I had—to combine TV, movies and Orwell in a book that drew on my quarter-century in journalism—didn't happen until 2015.

It seemed straightforward at first. The movie website IMDb listed about a dozen adaptations of Orwell's novels, which I thought I'd critique for a self-published ebook. Such a book would have been too repetitive, frankly, as most of the dramatizations were of *Nineteen Eighty-Four*. Somewhere along the line, I thought of widening its scope to include documentaries and dramas about Orwell. And what about the people who made them? A niche subject, for sure, but I felt confident I was just the man to explore it. On top of my knowledge and interests, I'd been part of the London media scene and had countless showbiz interviews under my belt.

Christopher Morahan, a distinguished director who'd made three BBC plays in 1965 under the umbrella title *The World of George Orwell*, granted me my first interview for what was very much a speculative project. For that, I'm exceedingly grateful, and was dismayed to hear that Mr. Morahan died in 2017. I must also mention Shirley Rubinstein, who's been supportive from the very start. In 2000, she and her husband, the scriptwriter Alan Plater, welcomed me into their London home for a newspaper interview. Alan, whose work forms the basis of two of my chapters, died in 2010, but Shirley's list of contacts—and her suggestion that I consult his archive at Hull History Centre—proved invaluable. It seemed I was on to something after all.

Nonetheless, I had nagging doubts. Would I even be able to see some of these rare shows? Once again, pieces of the puzzle fell into place. I asked the British Film Institute about Morahan's *1984*, missing for decades but found in the U.S. Library of Congress in 2010. Might I be able to watch it? Quite easily, as it turned out. Across the UK, the BFI runs a series of "Mediatheque" lounges, offering free access to a kind of archival YouTube (which isn't YouTube, I hasten to add). As well as the 1965 *1984*, the playlist included *The Road to the Left*, *The Crystal Spirit: Orwell on Jura*, *1984: Designing a Nightmare* and more. Fortuitously, the BFI held a London screening of *The Road to Wigan Pier (A Musical Documentary)* in March 2016.

Ronald Pickup, whose performance as Orwell in *The Crystal Spirit* earned him a BAFTA nomination for best actor, bought me a meal and reminisced about one of his favorite jobs. Julia Goodman, an actress-turned-businesswoman who'd played Orwell's second wife in *The Road to 1984*, had an off-air VHS copy of the TV movie and invited me over to discuss it. Most of those involved in the fifties and sixties productions are no longer with us, but here and there I'd strike gold—for instance, tracking down actor Clive Elliott (from Morahan's *Keep the Aspidistra Flying*) to a retirement home in Des Moines, Iowa.

Shortly after embarking on this project, I joined the Orwell Society and met Orwell's son, Richard Blair. In June 2016, we were among two dozen members to visit Jura, the isolated Scottish island where Orwell wrote *Nineteen Eighty-Four*. This is, as you'd expect, a literary society, and over a meal one evening, I found myself sitting next to Professor Jean Seaton, chair of the UK's answer to the Pulitzer, the Orwell Prize. When I joked that I was writing "the least intellectual Orwell book ever," Jean protested. "No, no, this is important," she said. By studying popular interpretations of Orwell, made for mass-market consumption, it could be argued that I was breaking new ground.

I'm a journalist, not an academic, but there's a scholarly aspect to this endeavor. I've spent many hours in the British Library, poring over books, magazines and newspapers to learn just how the popular press reacted to Orwell's posthumous fame. On top of that, I've visited the BBC Written Archives in Caversham, where archivist Matthew Chipping handed me production files from the fifties and sixties. Having interviewed the charming Robin Chapman—who wrote 1965's *Keep the Aspidistra Flying* and *Coming Up for Air*, both sadly lost—I was delighted to read his teleplays on one of Caversham's microfilm machines. With Robin's kind permission, I've reproduced several quirky extracts that enhance Orwell's stories for the small screen: they're 95 percent Chapman and can't be found anywhere else.

DJ Taylor, the Orwell biographer and all-round good guy, described his *South Bank Show* tie-in documentary, screened in 2003, as "another brick in the Orwell path." I feel the same way about this book, which chronicles the history of Orwell on screen for posterity.

All that remains is to acknowledge my other contributors and to mention that for stylistic reasons, everyone is quoted in the present tense. So thank you, Susan McKenzie, for giving me a rare glimpse into the making of *Studio One's 1984*; Allan Clack, for your wonderful tale of Big Brother coppers in Churchill's London; Professor Tony Shaw, for your insights into 1950s Cold War politics and culture; Vivien Halas, for a renewed appreciation of your parents' *Animal Farm* cartoon; Michael Anderson (who died just over a month ago, aged 98) for answering my email about *1984*; Jack Bond, for our beers in Soho; John Glenister, for volunteering anecdotes about *Coming Up for Air* as well as *The Crystal Spirit*; Jane Merrow, for your memories of *Theatre 625* and your memorable turn in *The Prisoner's Schizoid Man* episode, a favorite of mine; Madeline Smith, for telling me about your husband David Buck at a sci-fi convention (even though none of it made it into the book); Lord Bragg, for your essay on *The Road to the Left*; Bob Davenport, for songs at Islington Folk Club and stories about *The Road to Wigan Pier*; Sir Jeremy Isaacs, for answering my questions on the hoof at the BFI; Norman McCandlish, for the mental image of John Cleese playing Orwell; Simon Wilson, for help with the Plater archive in Hull; Nigel Williams, for being so candid about the *Arena* documentaries; Mark Mason-Jones, for the hospitality you and your wife Julia showed me; Janet Dale, for being an Orwell devotee and, like Julia, an onscreen Mrs. Orwell; Simon Perry, for being so thorough and so positive, even though *Nineteen Eighty-Four* caused you some grief in the eighties; Keir and Louise Lusby, for inviting me into your home and letting me play with Winston Smith's coral paperweight; Jean Seaton, Stephanie Le Lievre and Jeremy Wikeley at the Orwell Foundation (formerly the Orwell Prize) for letting me quote to my heart's content from Jean's Mike Radford interview; David Cann, for being so affable; Bob Bierman, for pointing me in the right directions; Peter Shaw, for the down-to-earth quotes about *A Merry War*; John Stephenson, for a fascinating conversation about *Animal Farm* and Jim Henson's Creature Shop; Chris Durlacher, for coffee, chat and *A Life in Pictures*; Mark Littlewood, for the *Orwell: Against the Tide* DVD and notes; Tony Grace, for a perspective on the Spanish Civil War; Peter Gornstein, for his sci-fi treatment of *Shooting an Elephant*; JP Rothie, for his trad version; Marshall Peterson, for sharing *Four Episodes from 1984*; the BFI, for converting VHS copies of *Beautiful Lies* and *Down and Out in Paris and London* to digital, for my benefit; Stuart Davies of Paper Zoo Theatre Company, for confirming what a nice guy John Hurt was; Fiona Kieni-Judd, for interviewing Hurt so brilliantly in 1985, aged 16, and saying much the same as Stuart in an email; my editor, Natalie; and Richard Blair, Quentin Kopp, Les Hurst, Neil Smith, Desmond Avery, Jennifer Custer, Richard Lance Keeble and the rest of the Orwell Society for your support, advice and encouragement.

Thank you, everyone. It's been doubleplusgood.

Introduction

In January 1950, Eric Blair was on the verge of death. He'd been many things in his 46 years: a schoolboy on a scholarship to Eton; a self-loathing British imperial policeman in Burma; "George Orwell," the gonzo journalist who'd become a bum in order to write about it; the Depression-era polemicist who'd taken the road to Wigan Pier on behalf of the Left Book Club; the volunteer soldier in Spain, shot in the neck by one of Franco's fascists and hunted by communist death squads; a Second World War propagandist on BBC radio; and, towards the end, a widower and single parent in North London.

He was also, of course, one of the greatest writers and visionaries of all time—not that many people knew it then. His genius as an essayist, the abiding power of his plain English prose and his status as a revered founding father of British political journalism are almost beyond dispute these days. But as one of his foremost admirers, the journalist Christopher Hitchens, put it in 2006, Orwell "never had a steady publisher, a steady job, a steady place to live; was always ill, was always poor, was always censored."

Were Hitchens still alive, one might quibble with this argument. Putting money matters to one side, his hero's last two novels—*Animal Farm* and *Nineteen Eighty-Four*, published in 1945 and 1949 respectively—had, at the very least, put Orwell's name on the map. Broadly speaking, though, the point is a sound one. Gangling, lugubrious, chain-smoking Orwell was the archetypal struggling writer—and succumbed to a tubercular illness just as wealth and fame came knocking.

In his lifetime, Orwell's books had made it to the radio as full-cast dramas. His own adaptation of *Animal Farm*, satirizing the Russian revolution, went out on the BBC in January 1947, produced by his friend Rayner Heppenstall. Within weeks of *Nineteen Eighty-Four* hitting the shelves, NBC University Theater brought the Orwellian police state graphically to life in August 1949, casting David Niven as the rebel Winston Smith.

As Cold War paranoia intensified, this democratic socialist's impeccable anti–Soviet credentials stood him in good stead. It could indeed be argued that the right-wing establishment made his name for him, giving us three onscreen *Nineteen Eighty-Four*s and a CIA-sponsored *Animal Farm* cartoon in the fifties alone.

In 1965, the BBC mounted three plays under the umbrella title *The World of George Orwell*. Along with a *Nineteen Eighty-Four* remake, it committed the author's third and fourth novels—*Keep the Aspidistra Flying* and *Coming Up for Air*—to videotape, only to wipe the master tapes in one of its periodic purges.

Almost two decades later, the year 1984 seemed too good a marketing opportunity to miss, bringing us a visceral, bleak, sexually charged film of the novel courtesy of writer-director Michael Radford. On top of that, two television dramas recapped the author's life and a slew of documentaries made it to the screen.

Since then, actual adaptations have been few and far between. In the late nineties, we had a light-hearted *Keep the Aspidistra Flying—A Merry War* in the States—and a TV movie of *Animal Farm*, made with *Babe*-style animatronics. All we've seen this century are two shorts, both of them based on the essay *Shooting an Elephant*.

Still, there's hope. In 2015, *The Economist*'s sister magazine, *Intelligent Life*, reported that the Orwell industry was growing almost by the day. Edward Snowden's revelations about government surveillance in cyberspace gave *Nineteen Eighty-Four* (the novel) a shot in the arm, propelling it into the Amazon bestseller lists. The election of President Donald Trump did likewise, prompting *The Hollywood Reporter* to call it "the hottest literary property in town."

From time to time, studio executives dust off their copies of the book and ponder another remake. The same goes for *Animal Farm*, which at the time of writing is being developed by actor-director Andy Serkis for the performance-capture technology treatment. The aim of the book you're reading is to chronicle the adaptations, docudramas and standout documentaries to date.

Given that Orwell's UK copyright expires in 2021, it's exciting to think that the Eric Blairite cause can only grow stronger.

1

Studio One: 1984 (1953)

It's easy to mock the screen debut of Orwell's last masterpiece, *Nineteen Eighty-Four*. Produced by the CBS network with a New York cast and crew, and screened live as part of the *Studio One* anthology series in 1953, this bare-bones, 50-minute dramatization looks primitive to the 21st-century viewer. But to do so is to sell the drama short. In an age when owning a 17-inch black-and-white set was a privilege,[1] *Studio One* was a shining example of America's "golden age of television." TV's pioneers were on an exhilarating journey, crafting a whole new art form with the meager resources at hand. So, to find out what made the show so ground-breaking, let's step back in time—not to 1953, or even to 1984, but to November 1987.

Manhattan's Museum of Broadcasting, now known as the Paley Center for Media, set out to honor the five-time Emmy Award-winning series,[2] which from 1948–58 produced 467 Monday-night plays.[3] The result was a *Studio One* seminar, chaired by one of its regular writers, Loring Mandel.[4] The graying panelists lined up on stage had been raised in an America without television—a concept that modern audiences found hard to grasp, said fellow screenwriter Tad Mosel. In the fifties, live TV drama counted as a prestigious event. Seeing a play in their living rooms made the audience feel proprietary about the actors and the writers, to the extent that strangers would phone Mosel next day to discuss his work.

Of course, early TV had been primitive, even laughable at times. Director Lela Swift spoke ruefully of an overrunning *Studio One* mystery, yanked off the air before the denouement; of stagehands crouching on their hands and knees after being caught on camera; and of an actor jumping out of a skyscraper window, only to stand up and walk away, in shot.

Typically, a show used three cameras. On the DVD box set *Studio One Anthology*, actor William Shatner likens them to prehistoric monsters that "breathed" via internal cooling fans.[5] But at the seminar, Betty Furness—who'd been spokeswoman for the show's sponsor, Westinghouse—was anything but sentimental. In her early career, she'd acted in movies and seen

Scenic designer Kim Swados (left) and director Paul Nickell (right) join actors Norma Crane and Eddie Albert for a CBS photoshoot to publicize *Studio One*'s *1984*.

cameras gliding smoothly along dolly tracks. On TV, the cameramen kicked their machines and ran after them.

By Mandel's reckoning, writers would work for the show every seven weeks, on average: an absurdly short period in which to pitch an idea to the producer, have it accepted by the sponsors and write a teleplay. This creative rollercoaster frightened and thrilled Mosel. "This medium had been dumped on the world and nobody quite knew what to do with it," he said, but a youthful scribe who'd work cheap and had stamina could pretty much do what he wanted.

Needless to say, there were caveats. For one thing, sponsors such as Westinghouse, an electrical goods company, could be maddeningly capricious. When the show adapted Rudyard Kipling's *The Light That Failed* in 1949, the men in suits demanded a change of title. They compromised in the end, by agreeing that it should be read aloud rather than shown.[6]

Then there was the blacklist of alleged communist sympathizers,[7] which in practical terms amounted to a telephone in a drawer, associate producer Charles "Chiz" Schultz told the seminar. Week after week, the casting director would dial a one-digit number and read out a list of actors. To each name, an anonymous official would say either "yes" or "no."[8]

Perhaps, in this political environment, the decision to stage *1984* was an astute contribution to the "Red scare" gripping America. Or perhaps, as its director claimed many years later, the message was altogether subtler.

Hitting the Big Time

A strength of the one-hour anthology format, a mainstay of post-war U.S. programming,[9] was that it offered writers and directors a chance to find their feet and move the medium forward. Worthington "Tony" Miner, for instance, was said to be the first TV director to convey a character's inner thoughts by playing pre-recorded lines on to the set.[10] In his day job as CBS drama supervisor, Miner transferred *Studio One* from the radio and went on to produce four acclaimed TV seasons: that's 140 plays, ranging from pared-down Shakespeares to a 1949 *Mary Poppins*.[11] He set Charlton Heston, the show's most dashing and charismatic repertory actor, on the road to stardom[12]; and when rival network NBC poached him in 1952, his shoes proved enormously difficult to fill.

Several placeholder producers later, the series found its moorings with newcomer Felix Jackson, who earmarked Orwell's four-year-old novel as the basis for a relaunch. Perhaps Stalin, the tyrant most associated with Big Brother, inspired the play when he died in March 1953. It's also conceivable that Jackson—an ex-journalist and playwright from Hamburg, born Felix Rafael Joachimson in 1902[13]—wanted to make a point about Nazi Germany, which he'd escaped in the thirties for Hollywood.[14]

Throwing every resource he could muster at the sixth season's opener, scheduled for 21 September, he assembled the largest company American TV had ever seen[15]: in ballpark figures, 50 actors and a crew of 100. Two weeks ahead of the air date, *The New York Times* reported that to muffle the noise they were making, he'd ordered them to sole their shoes with felt.[16] With two staff directors to choose from, Jackson settled on Paul Nickell— a surprise in some respects, as co-worker Franklin J. Schaffner had a current affairs background and had worked on documentary series *The March of Time*.[17] Schaffner is best remembered today for helming *Planet of the Apes* (1968) and winning an Oscar for *Patton* (1970).

"I have never been so nervous in my life," Nickell told Mandel in October 1987, at another Museum of Broadcasting event.[18] To him, the show seemed almost too unwieldy to manage, with a cast of what felt like thousands. To play Winston Smith—"the everyman," Nickell calls him in the interview—he hired 47-year-old Eddie Albert, a TV stalwart who'd written and acted in America's first teleplay[19] in 1936. After numerous auditions—perhaps as many as a dozen—Norma Crane, aged 24, launched her career on screen by playing Julia, his lover and partner in rebellion. The plum role of Smith's nemesis, "the inquisitor" O'Brien, went to Lorne Greene, destined to find fame as Old West patriarch Ben Cartwright in NBC's *Bonanza*.

With so much riding on Jackson's first show, Nickell was nervous, even though the script by William Pettigrew Templeton (a London playwright who'd grown up in the slums of Glasgow, Scotland) was a solid one. At his lowest ebb, he asked his producer to replace him, arguing that Schaffner was a better fit. "And in his very quiet little manner, Felix said: 'You will direct the show.'"[20]

Basic Instinct

For all its limitations—like ignoring the manipulation of language, a central theme of Orwell's—the play has much to recommend it. Its tense, claustrophobic script is a model of economy. Shadowy sets recall German expressionism. The actors turn in dignified, memorable performances. And in just four minutes, Templeton and Nickell sketch out Orwell's nightmare to startling effect.

A painted title card of a silhouetted couple embracing, watched by three sinister pairs of eyes,[21] makes way for a spinning globe, emerging from darkness. The discordant, quasi-militaristic music of the title sequence fades out, to be replaced with the sound of marching boots. An unseen, stentorian announcer—CBS newsman Don Hollenbeck—delivers a measured but forceful introduction. This, he says, is a story about the future. Not the spaceships-and-aliens kind: the immediate future.

The tone is preachy at first. If we allow the freedoms of speech, thought or religion to be eroded, warns Hollenbeck, "then what happens to the people in this story will happen to us." Here, then, is Orwell's nightmare world: the warring, despotic superstates, Oceania, Eurasia and Eastasia[22]; the two-way telescreens that pump out propaganda and stifle dissent; and a twisted culture of falsifying history to satisfy the ruling Party.

Rather appropriately, the first we see of Oceania is a telescreen in the darkness—it's reminiscent of a modern flatscreen, with a swirling heat pattern for a screensaver. The camera pulls back to reveal a poster: "Big Brother is watching you." But if you're expecting a Hitler/Stalin figure, forget it. The hairless, freakishly distorted cartoon face looks like something *Mad* magazine has commissioned from Picasso. In a half-in-shadow office building composed of daises and flights of steps, a glum-faced, weedy, middle-aged man in overalls enters the picture. As Outer Party member Winston Smith, a downtrodden drone at the Ministry of Truth, Albert brings a hangdog air of weariness to Orwell's flawed hero.

There's no suggestion he's in the London of the novel, by the way—nor indeed of Britain being a satellite state of America, "Airstrip One." Most of the characters have North American accents, although the telescreen in Smith's apartment, which monitors his every action, sounds clipped and mid–Atlantic[23]: it's Robert Culp, adopting an affectedly English accent in only his second TV role.[24] At one point, this voice of repression applauds an organization of celibate women who'd rather plow their energies into Big Brother's one-party state. In the book and in every adaptation since, it's called the Junior Anti-Sex League. On prudish CBS, it's the Anti-Love League.

Secreting himself in an alcove hidden from the telescreen, Smith stages his own private insurgency, scrawling "Down with Big Brother" in the pages of an antique diary—but there's a knock at the door. It's bovine neighbor Parsons and his prepubescent, obnoxious daughter Selina, a fanatical member of the Youth Spies. The novel features two Parsons children: a boy of nine and a sister two years his junior. It's interesting to note that Templeton and other adapters have placed the spiteful little girl center-stage.

Dropping Selina off at a meeting, the duo retire to a hostelry, the Chestnut Tree Cafe. At the next table are minor celebrities Jones and Rutherford, whom Big Brother has just appointed to his Inner Party circle. Smith, however, has earthier interests, watching with badly concealed lust as young activist Julia sweeps by in her dungarees, gallic peaked cap and Anti-Love League sash.

As Parsons, under his breath, warns Smith not to let his expressive face give away too much, the Gestapo-like Thought Police clamp their hands on Jones and Rutherford's shoulders, leading them away to who knows what. Reeling from the arrest he's just seen, Smith calls on an antiques shop in the proletarian district—known here as the people's quarter[25]—run by Charrington, a dapper old Englishman[26] who remembers life before the rule of the Party. More to the point, he has an upstairs room with no telescreen installed.

Next day at work, revising back issues of *The Times* newspaper to reflect the current Party line, Smith stumbles upon a photo of Jones and Rutherford, who have been written out of history since he last saw them. His supervisor, O'Brien, smiles to himself as Smith, fearing for his life, splutters his apologies and tosses it into his desktop incinerator. Praising him as "a valuable man," the bear-like apparatchik in the military-style shirt offers Winston his home address and directs a long, meaningful gaze at him. These days, we'd say it was homoerotic.

The whole department stops work for the Two Minutes Hate, a daily bonding ritual in which the masses, future Oscar-winner Martin Landau among them, hurl vitriol at film of an exiled "arch-traitor" dispensing ugly truths about Oceania. "Cassandra," or Emmanuel Goldstein as he is in the novel, is to all intents and purposes Lev Bronstein, the Russian revolutionary better known as Leon Trotsky. Smith's colleague Syme—one of Orwell's pivotal characters, who in print boasts of helping to destroy the language—is reduced in these scenes to a bit part: a slight, balding man, blinking behind owlish spectacles. Most of the time, Templeton concentrates on Parsons instead, making him an all-purpose neighbor, drinking buddy and confidante.

The hate session reaches it climax with a near-religious display of devotion as chanting workers fall to their knees before an image of "BB." Afterwards, pretending to lose her balance, Julia thrusts a note into Winston's hands, professing her love for him. In act two, they hook up in the countryside (another basic studio set), where he tentatively caresses her face, kisses her full on the lips, embraces her desperately, drops to his knees and buries his face in her torso. In a play that conspicuously skirts the word "sex," it's a powerfully suggestive scene.

Emboldened, but resigned to the possibility of being captured and tortured, the lovers continue to meet illicitly in the room above Charrington's shop,[27] where Julia casts off her dungarees for a plunging, off-the-shoulder white dress. "In this room, I'm going to be a woman," she says. The mood is shattered, though, when a rat—or at any rate, a squeaky sound effect—triggers Smith's most deep-seated childhood phobia.

Believing O'Brien to be part of a resistance movement, the couple call on him at home. Switching off his telescreen for a few minutes (a perk of Inner Party membership), the charismatic bigwig confirms as much and arranges that Cassandra's counter-revolutionary book should be delivered to Smith. But it's a trap. At the lovers' next rendezvous, a concealed telescreen announces that the game is up—and as his goons bludgeon Winston to the floor, Thought Police agent Charrington crows: "Your education is about to begin."

The third act is set in the Ministry of Love. Winston is sitting in a holding cell when suddenly, guards throw Parsons in with him. The neighbor, who's boasted of his daughter's eagerness to inform on others, has been hoist with his own petard, as Selina overheard him saying: "Down with Big Brother," in his sleep.

O'Brien enters, not as a prisoner but as a captor. Taking Smith to a dimly lit torture chamber, he subjects him to electric-shock treatment in an effort to break his spirit. Holding up four fingers, he demands that, should the Party wish it, Winston see five. There's no medieval-style rack,[28] like the one in the book, nor for that matter any electrodes. It's just two men in a darkened room—one standing, threatening, dominant, with a voltmeter; the other seated, cowering, writhing in pain and begging for mercy.

The running length won't allow for philosophical discussions, so some of Orwell's iconic lines—like O'Brien's vision of the future as "a boot stamping on a human face"—fail to materialize. Still, despite all the threats, Winston has not betrayed Julia. Not yet. To achieve this, O'Brien condemns him to Room 101, where "the worst thing in the world" awaits: in Smith's case, a gruesome death by rats. It's a curious scene, this one, and oddly minimalistic. We don't see any rodents, for a start. Instead, O'Brien manhandles Winston, pushing him through a door marked "101"[29] and watching impassively as the squeaking drives him insane.

"Do it to Julia, not me," screams Winston.

His mental collapse—his acceptance and love of Big Brother in the final sentence of the book—has always been tricky to convey on screen, and this version barely tries. "You will be able to devote your whole life," says O'Brien, looking down on a gibbering wreck, "to loving no one but Big Brother."

Their relationship destroyed, Julia and Winston meet one last time. He's in the Chestnut Tree Cafe, writing 2 + 2 = 5 on a sheet of paper when she enters. They're open about their mutual betrayal—and as Julia departs, a song starts up. We've heard it before, during Jones and Rutherford's arrest. A woman's voice, mournful. "Under the spreading chestnut tree, I sold you and you sold me."

Something to Say

By any measure, the play was an outstanding success. Seen in 8.7 million homes—a 53 percent share of the market—it was the highest-rated *Studio One* broadcast of 1953.[30] The press enjoyed it too, more or less, with Jack Gould of *The New York Times* applauding Jackson's "boldness." Though one false move could have rendered it "a grotesque space opera," it was, he wrote, "a masterly adaptation that depicted with power, poignancy and terrifying beauty the end result of thought control…. The new TV season has come alive."[31]

The New Yorker, which rarely had a good word to say about television,[32] joined in the chorus of praise. Calling the play "stunning," its critic Philip Hamburger trilled: "It is hard to believe that as splendid a production should be played only once." Templeton's script caught "the chill terror" of the book; Kim Swados and Henry May's sets were "stark and triumphant expressions" of a police state[33]; and Norma Crane was "exceptional" in a top-flight cast. She "made me, for one, believe that she was literally fighting for the very right to think and breathe and remain human." It felt like she was speaking for every person on Earth who was suffering under a cruel government, wrote Hamburger.[34]

Broadcasting-Telecasting magazine, since renamed *Broadcasting & Cable*, thought it was "video fare at its very best, convincingly acted, artfully directed and imaginatively staged." *Variety* wasn't quite so enthusiastic, grumbling that the play was nowhere near as believable as the novel: "Taken out of the context of the book and judged as a television production, however, *1984* was a shocker that was vividly and deftly handled."[35] In *The Billboard*, Bob Francis considered it an "opulent, well-directed production," though the script was "cluttered with fantastic, pseudo-scientific devices" that made it "more ridiculous than moving."[36]

Two weeks after transmission, *Life* magazine ran a picture spread featuring rehearsal photos and three cartoons by Abner Dean, previously used for *Life*'s review of the novel in 1949. "Technically forbidding, the play took four months to prepare," the magazine reported, praising it as "brave and stimulating."[37] It's telling, writes Orwell scholar John Rodden, that publisher Henry Luce was a fervent anti-communist and prominent Republican.[38] "Increasingly, Orwell was being taken in some quarters of the popular press as an exponent of Luce's conservative, anti-socialist politics."[39]

In what remained of 1953, the show continued to generate stories in the U.S. media. Interviewed by Val Adams of *The New York Times* in October, Jackson batted away accusations that his drama had been too gloomy. "To me, a morbid play is one that looks at a bad situation from one side only and offers no solution," he said. "In *1984* we prefaced the show by saying that this could happen to you if you don't guard your freedom."[40]

As the year drew to a close, *Variety* reported that movie producers were eyeing *Studio One*'s most successful plays for development. One in particular, the ex–RKO chief Peter Rathvon, was drawing up plans to shoot *1984* in Italy.[41] Through the expedient of pointing a camera at a monitor—known as "kinescoping" in the States and "telerecording" in the UK—CBS retained a copy of the telecast, not for posterity's sake, but for broadcast in other U.S. time zones in the hours that followed its airing in New York.

Nickell, who taught at the University of North Carolina[42] from 1968–81, used to field questions from students about what his best show was. He left them to decide for themselves, but maintained for the rest of his life that *1984* was the most important.

Interviewed in 1987, he said that after the broadcast, his next-door neighbor in Bronxville, New York, refused to speak to him for about three weeks. "She said she'd never been so depressed in her life. She and her husband had just returned from South America and said: 'Paul, it's exactly the way it is down there.'" When the sponsor phoned Jackson to say the play had kept his wife awake all night, Nickell took it as a compliment.

An audience member at the seminar asked him about the blacklist. Had he tried to draw a parallel between the thematic material of the novel and rampant McCarthyism? Not really, he replied. "That was what I wanted to come out subconsciously."

The play's narrator, Don Hollenbeck, would never have a chance to reminisce about it. Hounded by anti-communists for his work on a "pinko" newspaper in the forties, and depressed by health and marital problems, the 49-year-old gassed himself in the kitchen of his New York apartment the following June.[43]

Susan McKenzie, who as nine-year-old Susan Hallaran played Youth Spy Selina Parsons, remembers the frightening tone of the script to this day. "I worked for the director, Paul Nickell, many times and he was wonderful," she says. "I know it made an impact on me because I remembered what it was about, even though I was so young. I watched the Army-McCarthy hearings[44] a year later with my mother and remember what a terrible witch-hunt it was.... It reminded me of *1984* and of the Hitler Youth."[45]

Studio One: 1984

Winston Smith: Eddie Albert
O'Brien: Lorne Greene
Julia: Norma Crane
Charrington: Noel Leslie
Parsons: Truman Smith
Female telescreen voice: Midge Donaldson
Male telescreen voice: Robert M. Culp
Cassandra: Victor Thorley
Syme: Peter Ostroff
Singer: Janice Mars

Selina: Susan Hallaran
Man in cell: Fred Scollay
Prison officer: Vincent Vanlynn
Narrator: Don Hollenbeck
Written for television by: William Templeton
Director: Paul Nickell
Producer: Felix Jackson
Settings: Kim Swados and Henry May
Music: Alfredo Antonini

2

Nineteen Eighty-Four (1954)

If *Nineteen Eighty-Four* is a distorted vision of a demoralized, bankrupt UK in the immediate post-war years, as many contend,[1] then the British Broadcasting Corporation's 1954 adaptation is the closest we'll come to a contemporaneous, site-specific staging of it.[2] An austere, quietly devastating masterpiece, humming with political insights, it remains one of the most revered TV dramas in history.[3] On the domestic front, it also created a new kind of media phenomenon: the television scandal.

By the early fifties, TV was more than just a minority pastime for the well-off. In the post-war era, transmitters had sprung up across the country and, spurred on by the coronation of Elizabeth II in June 1953, the number of households with a set had mushroomed. In 1947, the government issued 14,560 TV licenses (which, by law, set owners had to buy); six years later, the figure was 3.2 million.[4]

In 1953, Orwell's estate held talks with three interested parties about the screen rights to his last novel: the U.S. network CBS (see chapter 1), movie producer Peter Rathvon (see chapter 4) and the UK's monopoly TV and radio service, the BBC.[5] The corporation's drama department commissioned a script from aristocrat's husband and ex-Spitfire pilot Hugh Falkus,[6] which was eventually rejected by producer/director Rudolph Cartier.[7]

Since television was live and recording techniques primitive, in no real sense were the BBC and CBS competing. Rathvon's movie proposal was another matter and after much wrangling about trade shows and transmission dates—not to mention script approval from Orwell's widow, Sonia—the BBC agreed that it would stage two identical productions in December 1954.[8] For the best part of a year, Cartier and scriptwriter Nigel Kneale hammered this hugely ambitious play into shape for the *Sunday-Night Theatre* slot, supervised by Cecil McGivern, the BBC's controller of TV, and Michael Barry, head of its drama department.

Cartier, who'd go on to be a TV legend, was a formidable figure: a Viennese Jew who'd worked with Billy Wilder, Emeric Pressburger and Sam

Spiegel before fleeing Nazi Germany in 1935.[9] In the summer of 1953, his first major hit with Kneale, *The Quatermass Experiment*, had caused a sensation. This six-part science-fiction serial, about a rocket scientist who accidentally unleashes a monster from space, had typecast them, in Kneale's words, as "future specialist creatures."[10]

"The more difficult and improbable it was, the more keen [Cartier] was to do it," the writer told BBC TV's *The Late Show* in 1990. Cartier, on the same program, remembered McGivern calling him into his office and saying: "I liked your science-fiction very much. Would you like to do Orwell's *Nineteen Eighty-Four?*"[11]

The scale of the drama was daunting, as Kneale explained to his biographer in the early 2000s. "We read the book and we were appalled by the sheer complexity of it—but it was wonderful, obviously wonderful. How difficult to get that into a live studio, though!" The problem was "that it was a big story with a lot of characters and a lot of scenes. Just to get it on, live, was a horror. I wrote a script which is very complicated, even for me."[12]

Cartier, who'd been a subscriber to America's *Life* magazine when it was hyping the novel as an anti-communist tract in 1949,[13] informed a studio manager in August 1954 that this would be one of the BBC's most ambitious drama productions to date, involving roughly three times as much preparation, filming and research as usual.[14] As Winston Smith, the Austrian cast 41-year-old Peter Cushing, who'd impressed him as a Russian nobleman in the BBC play *Anastasia* the previous year.[15] For Julia, he sought out Yvonne Mitchell (13 years more mature than Orwell's 26-year-old fantasy figure), who'd shone as Cathy in Kneale and Cartier's *Wuthering Heights*, earning her the Top TV Actress of 1953 accolade.[16] O'Brien was to be played by the urbane, charismatic stage actor Andre Morell, who in February 1953 had fronted another of Cartier's Sunday-night plays, *Is It Midnight, Dr Schweitzer*, about the recent Nobel Peace Prize winner.[17] That same year, he'd turned down the role of Professor Bernard Quatermass, though he'd relent for 1958's *Quatermass and the Pit*, the third and best serial in the trilogy.

Though the production was mostly studio-bound, Cartier incorporated film sequences to improve the dramatic flow. Moreover, he demanded a bespoke musical score, rather than take the easy route of playing stock gramophone records. But his request in late September for a budget of £3,250 floored television drama organizer Norman Rutherford, who shot back that he was "astounded." As far as he was concerned, the production had long been budgeted at £2,500.[18] Eight days later, Cartier's team put in a detailed estimate of £3,260, of which £1,500 was to be spent on artists' fees, £750 on design, £500 on film and £250 on copyright.[19] Grudgingly, Rutherford agreed to £3,000, tops.[20]

The first indication that the play might upset viewers came on 22 October, when set designer Barry Learoyd sent a handwritten letter to Barry, the head of drama. Every time he looked at the script, he said, he felt a "feeling of nausea." While admitting it was none of his business, he suggested that for ethical reasons, the play should be called off.[21]

For a production lasting 107 minutes—two hours if you include the interval—the team prepared nearly 11 minutes of film footage. On 10 and 11 November, they shot inserts at the BBC's Alexandra Palace studios of, among other things, the Two Minutes Hate, Emmanuel Goldstein's speech, cubicles at the Ministry of Truth, Smith and Syme in the cafeteria and Room 101's rats. Winston and Julia's outdoor rendezvous, arranged for 18 November near the BBC's Lime Grove studios, was rescheduled because of bad weather, adding to Cartier's costings. The next two days were partly devoted to prole sector scenes—shot (according to Cushing) on the site in Wood Lane, White City, where BBC Television Centre was set to be built.[22]

By the end of the month, Cartier was arguing about money again. Given that the play had 22 sets, 28 actors and 25 extras, he told his bosses, a margin of error was inevitable. Not only had artists' fees gone up, but composer John Hotchkis, "after a lengthy battle," had demanded 17 musicians rather than the 12 he'd budgeted for.[23]

The first performance from Lime Grove studio D[24] was scheduled for 8:30 p.m. on 12 December, after the panel game *What's My Line*, with a repeat the following Thursday at 9:30 p.m. Kneale set the scene in the BBC's listings magazine, the *Radio Times*, hailing Orwell's originality (in Newspeak, he was "doubleplusungoodthinkful") and reminding readers of the novel's shock value. "It was the setting down of a nightmare—our own age gone mad, gone bad," he wrote.[25] With hindsight this reads ironically, though he couldn't have know this at the time. Collectively, the British were days away from losing their minds.

Sunday, 12 December

As a shadowy hand jabs at a panel of buttons, launching a nuclear strike,[26] the play's narrator describes *Nineteen Eighty-Four* as "one man's alarmed vision of the future." Years later in London—capital of Airstrip One in the superstate Oceania[27]—a colossal white pyramid looms over what remains of Westminster. It is the Ministry of Truth, emblazoned with three gargantuan slogans: "War is peace," "Freedom is slavery," and "Ignorance is strength."

From a porthole-like window, Winston Smith gazes up from the Records Department. He is a gaunt, diffident man, dressed in overalls bearing his name and number, KZ-6090 Smith W.[28] When a telescreen—a large, round monitor set above a small, circular surveillance camera—scolds him for lingering too long, he scurries back to his desk, clutching the replacement valve he'd been seeking for his Speakwrite machine.

With dazzling elegance and economy, Kneale establishes that:

- Winston is a wimp and a drudge. As he redrafts old newspaper reports to make the ruling Party look infallible, his genteel but menacing supervisor, O'Brien, looks on in approval.
- In his heart of hearts, he's a rebel, all the same. Granted, he throws himself into the Two Minutes Hate, shrieking abuse at Goldstein, the counter-revolutionary[29]—but when it's time to worship the Party figurehead, the words "I hate Big Brother" flash across his mind.
- The Party is molding language to its own ends. In one of the more unsettling scenes, Smith visits the cafeteria with his colleague Syme, played with noxious relish by Donald Pleasence. The squat, bald, slimy lexicographer gloats about his work on the Newspeak dictionary, destroying words in their thousands so that "thoughtcrime" is literally impossible. Accused of clinging to "Oldspeak," Winston murmurs to himself: "To be or not to be." We're abolishing the verb "to be," smirks JX-2159 Syme B.
- Smith's neighbors are just as brainwashed. Unblocking a sink for the wife of Tom Parsons, a co-worker who lives in the same apartment block, he rides out threats from the couple's hateful, paranoiac daughter, who sees everyone as a potential traitor. Her indoctrinated brother, reading about "ca-*pit*-alists" in a history book, thinks that life before the Party was all about rich men lording it over the populace.
- Yet not even the traditional family is safe. Visiting Winston's apartment, Parsons[30] notices that a space intended for a bookcase is out of the telescreen's range, prompting Smith to change the subject hurriedly (throughout the play, the constant nervous glances at the telescreen are to treasure). The men discuss their duty to marry and reproduce, and the Party's long-term aim of rearing test-tube babies in state-run institutions. When Winston says he's separated from his wife, Parsons asks if they married for love: "That's called sexcrime today." As soon as he's gone, Winston's "Down with Big Brother" rebellion can start.

The story's sexual elements, which must have been a shock to viewers weaned on drawing-room comedies and the like, come to the fore again when Winston pays a visit to a prole sector pub. Across the room, three cocky young men leer at Jason Flinders' novel *One Night in a Girls' School*: an illicit thrill, or so it seems. Asking questions about the Britain of old, Winston draws a blank with a wizened old man. At a neighboring junk shop, he tries again with Charrington, the proprietor, who sells him a snow-globe paperweight[31] and shows him up to his disused spare bedroom. Dropping in on the Chestnut Tree Cafe, Smith runs into Syme, who babbles that he's under investigation. The last we see of him, he's a terrified wreck on the verge of being arrested.

The following day is a hectic one at the Ministry of Truth's Fiction Department, where DK8567 Dixon J—Julia, whose surname isn't stated in Orwell's book—operates the Pornorite Mk 6 novel-writing machine, "Jason Flinders." While a government-manufactured ditty, *It Was Only a Hopeless Fancy*, plays in the background, O'Brien gives a tour of the facility to a high-ranking official and reads an extract from the state-approved soft porn. Julia screams—it looks like she's caught her arm in the mechanism—and as a matronly colleague guides her away for treatment, slips a love note into Winston's hand.

Compared to *Studio One*'s, the liaison in the countryside seems terribly British—but as the couple watch Hate Week celebrations from the window of Charrington's room later on, Kneale slips in a line from Orwell's novel that still sounds daring today. Activities like these, says Julia, are "simply sex gone sour."

And so we wind towards the meeting with O'Brien, Winston's excitement at the contents of Goldstein's book (he clasps Julia's knee suggestively as he's reading it) and the lovers' arrest by Charrington's Thought Police. With a brutality that's alarming even now, one of the thugs drags Julia through a door and coshes her over the head.

Subjected to electric shocks in a tilting, coffin-shaped casket—so much more unnerving than *Studio One*'s chair—Smith emerges a broken man, weeping from O'Brien's cruel and degrading treatment. He's weak, filthy, dressed in rags and literally gap-toothed, because Cushing (who lost three teeth to abscesses in 1946[32]) has taken out his dental plate.

Room 101's rat contraption—a transparent helmet, connected to the vermin's cage by a rubber tube—is gruesome enough to make Winston's betrayal of Julia entirely plausible. And that voice at the end, warbling *Underneath the Spreading Chestnut Tree* as the visibly aged pair swap weary recriminations in the cafe? It's Cushing, surreptitiously serenading himself. With no cash available for a singer, Cartier had cast him in that role too.[33]

Monday, 13 December

If they'd watched from the very beginning, no one could claim that sensitive viewers weren't warned about the play: twice, as a matter of fact. "More than anything else," cautioned the BBC announcer, "this story is a warning, an imaginative picture of the sort of world that might come into being when man should lose all that he believes to be right and just. As such, it is a strange picture, sometimes alarming."[34]

But this wasn't enough for Lt Colonel JLB Leicester-Warren, principal of Tabley House, a school for boys aged 13–18 in Knutsford, Cheshire. Having invited senior pupils to watch the play, he'd switched off the set in high dudgeon midway through. Next day, he composed an indignant missive to the BBC's head of religious broadcasting, the Reverend Peter Hamilton. The play was obscene and revolting, he argued. It "struck at the root of everything a respectable school tries to teach" and didn't help his efforts to inculcate "a decent Christian spirit" in the boys.[35]

As it turned out, the lieutenant-colonel was far from alone in his views. This outrage over a TV program was a novelty as far as the press was concerned and before the day was out, editors were milking the story for all it was worth.

True, there were sober appraisals in some of the morning editions. An unidentified critic in *The Times*, judging the play purely on artistic merit, came to the conclusion that it was "not so much Orwell's vision as a pictorial simplification of it." Vivid it may have been, but ignoring the book's sense of irony and trimming back the ideological musings had robbed the story of at least half its power.[36] Peter Black in the *Daily Mail* enjoyed the "atmosphere of secrecy and decay" and the "forceful control and moving underplaying" of Cushing—but was Sunday night, with the largest family audience of the week, a wise time to screen it?[37]

The Manchester Guardian's radio critic thought it brilliant, "both technically and in the acting."[38] *The Daily Telegraph* found it hard to imagine "a novel being more faithfully, or effectively, adapted for television…. Cartier completely understood his audience—and his medium."[39] But on the front page of London's *Daily Herald,* Philip Phillips accused the BBC of overstepping the mark. In furious calls to the newsroom, readers had called it "filthy, rotten, immoral" and "far worse than a horror comic." "Behind a background of groans and shrieks, beatings up, kickings by jack-booted men and torture scenes of a kind never before seen on TV, this nightmare story of Britain in 1984 played out," wrote Phillips. "The fact that it was superbly acted by all concerned only made the horror worse."[40]

In a front-page splash, the *News Chronicle* spoke of hundreds of viewers bombarding the BBC with complaints. Edna Burgess, of Holborn in London, contacted the paper to say: "I trembled with fear as I watched. It was not fit for ordinary decent-minded human beings. It was nothing but unoriginal bits of horror put together." Frederick Poate, who'd been watching with Canadian friends in Woking, wasn't happy either: "None of us is particularly squeamish, but we found the torture scene where a man was being given electric shocks in a coffin more than we could stand."[41]

David Holloway's review on page three, while littered with words such as "triumph," "compelling" and "magnificent," made no bones about how repulsive he'd found it. "I think it may have been too much for many people to bear, but to have mutilated it would have been unfair to Orwell," he wrote. "I never want to see this play again. I shall try to forget it, but I know I never shall."[42]

The communist *Daily Worker*, renamed the *Morning Star* in 1966, also led on the controversy. Journalist Alison Macleod reported that phone lines to the BBC had been jammed. "It's all these complaints they're having," sighed a switchboard operator. In a tizz about Ingsoc, Orwell's English socialist police state, Macleod slated the narrative as "anti-human" and balked at the message that, subjected to the right kind of torture, any one of us could betray our nearest and dearest. She sneered at "the sight of Peter Cushing and Yvonne Mitchell defiantly taking a roll in the hay for freedom" and agreed with the BBC's warning "that the play was not suitable for children or old people. They might have added 'or anyone in between.'"

Tuesday, 14 December

Within 24 hours, Fleet Street was overcome with hysteria. "Wife dies as she watches" screeched the headline on page one of the *Daily Express*, breathlessly reporting that Beryl Kathleen Mirfin, a 40-year-old "local beauty queen of 1936" from Herne Bay in Kent, had suffered a heart attack at home. Mrs. Mirfin, incidentally, suffered from high blood pressure. Could the BBC have killed her? Unlikely, said her widower in the seventh paragraph. "My wife enjoyed TV," he told the paper. "I don't think the play itself caused her to collapse."[43]

Inside, it ran an interview with Cartier headlined: "Repentant? No, I am PROUD!" Admitting he was "staggered" that the BBC had been bold enough to stick with the play, he said "it was right and wise to put this terrible vision before the largest possible audience. As a warning." The script, he commented, was so wonderful that he didn't change a line; the actors too were in raptures. In fact, the hopeless ending was the whole point of it. "Our job was to shake, and if we have succeeded in shaking half the nation then we have done the job we set out to do."[44]

A repeat broadcast, planned for Thursday night and also performed live, would proceed without cuts, reported the *Daily Sketch*. "My desk is deep in congratulations and the score is now about 50–50 between viewers who liked it and those who didn't," it quoted Cartier as saying.[45] The *Sketch's* resident provocateur, "Candidus," offered further congratulations, reminding offended viewers that "IT WAS MEANT TO SHOCK PEOPLE." Saluting "one of the great, grim masterpieces of the age," he raved: "In putting this thing over, the BBC achieved heights of brilliance in presentation that television has never known before."[46]

"Magnificent," was the official comment from the BBC. "And what is magnificent on Sunday must also be magnificent on Thursday. There were a great number of complaints, it is true, but they are only a tiny proportion of our vast viewing audience."[47] Tellingly, the irate calls started ahead of the interval, before any actual horror.[48] "I think some of these people who ring us up do it just for the hell of it," said a BBC official.[49]

The *Daily Herald*—which in time would mutate into *The Sun*, a Rupert Murdoch-owned, BBC-bashing tabloid—ran a supportive editorial entitled "Don't chain the BBC." "It would be deplorable if the BBC never had the courage to depart from the innocuous entertainment which is its staple offering," it opined.[50] In the same vein, the *Daily Mirror* wrote: "It is absurd to think that television must be run simply for the people who can't stand anything stronger than [children's show] *Muffin the Mule*." The Sunday play had carried two separate warnings for nervous people. "There was a time-honoured remedy for them: SWITCH OFF."[51]

Over at the *Daily Mail*, journalist Peter Black penned a mini-biography, "Honest Orwell did not write to horrify," which painted the author as a gentle, quixotic, almost saintly figure. It included several quotes from Sonia, who stressed that her husband had been a loyal Englishman and a socialist. Black's piece was scrupulously fair, informing readers that *Nineteen Eighty-Four* was not about communism per se, but all forms of totalitarianism. "He did not want to horrify people," said Sonia. "He wanted to make them think and reflect."[52]

Investigating the *Studio One* adaptation, *The Manchester Guardian* claimed that reaction across the Atlantic had been "almost completely favourable and laudatory."[53] Going one better, the *Express* spoke to CBS executive Hubbel Robinson, who boasted of a 90 percent positive reaction and unanimous praise in the press.[54]

Wednesday, 15 December

It was time for parliamentary correspondents to enter the fray. "Commons split over 'Sunday sadism,'" reported the *Daily Mail*.[55] "BBC attacked and applauded," *The Manchester Guardian* chimed in.[56] *The Times* was more muted, running the story fourth in its Political Notes column under the heading "Controversy over 1984."[57] What happened, essentially, was this. Without mentioning *Nineteen Eighty-Four* by name, five Conservative members of parliament (or Tory MPs, as they're known) signed the following motion in the House of Commons: "That this House deplores the tendency, evident in recent BBC television programmes, notably on Sunday evenings, to pander to sexual and sadistic tastes."

Within hours, four socialists and a Tory had tabled an amendment: "That his House deplores the tendency of honourable members to attack the courage and enterprise of the British Broadcasting Corporation in presenting plays and programmes capable of appreciation by adult minds on Sunday evenings and other occasions." A second Tory amendment expressed gratitude "that freedom of the individual still permits viewers to switch off."

Still not satisfied, six Tories put down a second motion: "That this House applauds the sincere attempts by the BBC to bring home to the British people the logical and soul-destroying consequences of surrendering their freedom and calls attention to the fact that many of the inhuman practices depicted in the play *Nineteen Eighty-Four* are already in common use under totalitarian regimes."

The *Daily Worker* rolled its eyes. In a front-page editorial, it denounced Orwell's story as "a Tory guttersnipe's view of Socialism" and accused its right-wing rivals of making a clumsy about-turn. On Monday morning, journalists had considered the play "a stupid, dull horror comic." But by the evening, they had remembered that *Animal Farm* and the "rotten" *Nineteen Eighty-Four* were the Old and New Testaments of intellectuals who'd sold out to capitalism. They were, in short, milking the controversy for ideological ends.[58]

By this stage, the story had acquired a playful tone in the popular press. After much speculation about his real-life identity, Big Brother turned out to be Roy Oxley, a 49-year-old senior art director at Lime Grove. Singled out for fame by Nigel Kneale, the father-of-two had put on a uniform and a fake mustache for his photoshoot, earning one-and-a-half guineas for his troubles.[59] "He's such a kind and gentle man," his 39-year-old wife Jean told the *Daily Sketch* from their home in Twickenham, Middlesex. Michael, their seven-year-old, and daughter Jill, 14, had not been allowed to watch.[60]

Oxley—the kind of man who helped his wife with the washing up, according the *Daily Herald*—could seen the funny side of friends and relatives calling him big-headed.[61] In the days before obsessive PR management in the media, he was also free to speak his mind about the production. "I don't care for the sort of entertainment given in Mr. Orwell's play," the *News Chronicle* had him saying, next to a photo of the family playing snooker. "I think it was too frightening."[62]

Back at the BBC, Cartier was growing jumpy about the more excitable souls who'd been in touch. Unnerved by threatening phone calls and letters, he asked security to confirm it would be laying on extra studio attendants on Thursday.[63]

In the evening, flagship current affairs show *Panorama* hosted a debate between head of drama Michael Barry; *Daily Sketch* radio critic Jonah Barrington (who'd hated the play); Malcolm Muggeridge, Orwell's friend and fellow journalist; and Alderman Herbert Sheppard, a 42-year-old local politician and insurance broker from Tunbridge Wells, Kent. To Brits, "Disgusted, Tunbridge Wells" is a light-hearted term, meaning "angry, stuffy conservative firing off a letter." But *Panorama* editor Michael Barsley was confident he'd found a broad-minded man. As he confided to the *News Chronicle*: "I'm told he voted for Sunday cinemas in his town."[64]

On camera, Sheppard tore into Barry for serving up "sheer, stark, unadulterated horror"[65] and warned that programs of this nature could lead to "a tremendous increase in crime."[66] That the play had been produced on a Sunday just before Christmas was a further insult.[67]

Even royalty was talking about Orwell. At a VIP event across town, the BBC's television liaison officer,[68] DK Wolfe-Murray, chatted with Prince Philip, who said that he and the new Queen had admired the play and its message.[69]

Thursday, 16 December

On the day of the live repeat, the *Daily Mirror* ran a plea from a "desperate housewife" still traumatized by Sunday night's events. Elizabeth Orwell, of Shooter's Hill in Woolwich, was married to a man called George who worked in shipping. Unfortunately for them, he was the only George Orwell in the London phone book, which meant that rather than enjoying a day of rest, they'd endured a prolonged hatefest.[70]

The same morning, weekly magazine *The Listener* hit the stands, carrying a review by Philip Hope-Wallace that, given its copy deadline, was ignorant of the fuss the play had caused. Demonstrating an irreverent view of Orwell that seems almost sacrilegious now, Hope-Wallace theorized that this "marvellous journalist" had next to no concept of what made people tick. The play was, he groaned, a "serious (but often unintentionally comic) pamphlet against the enemies of humanity."[71]

In its leader, *The Times* took a radically different view. Congratulating the BBC on its bravery, it noted with some prescience that the dramatization's impact underlined "the tremendous possibilities of television." For five years, the novel had given the intelligentsia food for thought. Now, thanks to the broadcasters, millions were discussing its themes.[72]

Returning to her soapbox, Alison Macleod of the *Daily Worker* vented her frustrations about right-wing papers' sudden deification of "Honest Orwell." "Honest? I dispute it. The man who christened his hero 'Winston' had an eye on the main chance—in this case, the Tory-reading public," she wrote. At least on TV, she added, "viewers were becoming more and more clearly aware that Socialist countries are not joyless haunts of terror."[73]

Rubbishing Wednesday night's *Panorama*, the *Daily Herald* bemoaned the fact that all four participants "were gabbling together so that they became incoherent." After nine minutes of squabbling, it reported, the TV personality Gilbert Harding had scolded them for their vacuity: "You just went yackety-yackety-yack…. You should have talked sense."[74]

Shortly before 9:30 p.m., Michael Barry took to the airwaves to introduce the repeat performance. The play, he told viewers, was neither disgusting nor immoral[75]: "It is grim and frightening, and at times shocking in the sense that we are all shocked when brought face-to-face with man's inhumanity to man." He conceded that the story lacked hope, blaming the novelist's terminal illness when he wrote it.[76] "I think Orwell would want us to find through our own resources, and our own hearts and minds, that hope and belief in mankind that is not there in the play."[77]

For viewers in Aberdeen in the far north-east of Scotland, this must have been a bewildering experience; their transmitter had gone live only days before. Solemnly, Barry asked them to consider "whether those sitting at home with you should see this play."[78] Message over, the picture cut to a fish tank for a few minutes while technicians repaired a faulty camera.

In the first 40 minutes, 115 viewers phoned Lime Grove, 88 of them in support of the BBC. On the Sunday, 65 percent of callers had been critical, the *Daily Mail* reported. In what may well have been an inaccurate story (see below), it added that in London, pubs with TVs did a roaring trade while cinemas saw attendances drop by 300 on average.[79]

Aftershocks, Audiences and Aussies

In the calm that followed the storm, the media took stock of Orwell and his message. *The Listener*'s Philip Hope-Wallace reassessed the play, judging it a clever, humorless adaptation that "somehow lost the satirical chill" of the novel. Yet Orwell himself would have loved the controversy and the bold realization of his book by Barry Learoyd. "Certainly the canteen scene, so reminiscent of the one which he used to visit [as a BBC producer in the war], would have struck him as a miracle of verisimo."[80] The same magazine's Reginald Pound, summing up 1954 in the issue that followed, had harsh words for television audiences in general. They were, in essence, dreary slobs incapable of paying attention to complicated literary concepts. "Add to it the fact that most people, again, are about as humourless as Eric Blair, alias George Orwell, himself was—I write from personal transactions with him—and you approach possibilities containing cause for concern and even alarm."[81] Whatever that means.

Publisher Edward Hulton, writing in his magazine *Picture Post*, thought his friend Orwell "would perhaps have been hurt" by the outcry: "He wrote his book as a satire—and a warning. But I doubt if he would have wished to harrow people with actual scenes of torture on the screen."[82] Elsewhere in the same issue, Orwell's successor as literary editor of *Tribune*, TR Fyvel, agreed that his illness had added to *Nineteen Eighty-Four*'s gloominess. "I think this is true, probably not for the structure of the book, but for its black mood; and its lack of the humour of Orwell's other books."

In a column for the *Daily Worker*, penned long before his distinguished career in TV, Scottish journalist Llew Gardner was less charitable. Orwell was "sick in body and mind," he declared, "an embittered man who could never forgive himself for his failure to be born a member of the ruling class." And the amateur psychology didn't stop there. "He hated humanity and he hated himself," claimed Gardner.[83]

It's commonly thought that the repeat was a ratings behemoth, racking up the biggest audience since the coronation, in the *Daily Mail*'s words.[84] Yet the BBC's figures tell a different story. According to its Audience Research department, 19 percent of UK adults watched the play on Sunday, compared to 7 percent on Thursday. Narrow this down to people with a TV set at home, and the figures are 63 percent and 23 percent respectively.[85] In an exhaustive piece for the British Television Drama website in 2014, journalist Oliver Wake stated that the BBC of 1954 estimated the adult population to be 37.6 million.[86] That means 7.1 million watched the premiere and 2.6 million the repeat[87]—a far cry from the nearly 20 million who tuned in for the coronation at its peak.[88] Cartier said as much in 1991: "Everybody who wanted to see it had seen it on the Sunday. So practically the smallest audience I ever had was on the repeat."[89]

The BBC's Reaction Index—a yardstick for how much viewers liked a show—gave the respective broadcasts 39 and 54 out of 100,[90] well below the average of 65 for plays that year.[91] According to the broadcaster's report, "about a third of viewers on Sunday reacted violently against it, its horror tending to blind them to its moral."[92]

Throwing up its hands, the Australian media published lurid stories from the mother country in the weeks that followed. One London–based writer for the *Queensland Times* saw sadism at work, wailed that "the whole play was soaked in a hopeless sadness" and signed off: "Anyhow, see what you're letting yourselves in for when you start television?"[93] Undeterred—or more likely encouraged—the country's *Lux Radio Theatre* staged an audio adaptation in Sydney, flying Vincent Price in from Hollywood to play Winston Smith.[94]

British radio saw an opportunity too, as the writers of comedy *The Goon Show* capitalized on the madness. The result, transmitted by the BBC Home Service on 4 January 1955, was a half-hour spoof, *Nineteen Eighty-Five*.[95] Spike Milligan and Eric Sykes' script recasts the show's regular protagonist, Neddy Seagoon (Harry Secombe), as 846 Winston Seagoon, a put-upon worker at the Big Brother Corporation, or BBC. Following a "Hate Half-Hour" against the Independent Television Army's stereotypically Jewish boss—in the real world, commercial television was months away—Seagoon falls for 612 Miss Fnutt (Peter Sellers), who runs the Pornograph Machine in the Forbidden Records Department.

In the background lurks the sinister Vision Master Ronnie Wallman (Sellers again), who tortures Seagoon into signing a BBC contract by playing him sped-up light entertainment shows. There's a Parsons parody too—213 Eccles, played by Milligan—whose catchphrase "It's good to be alive in 1985!" is wheeled out periodically for easy laughs. The show was so popular that the Goons performed it again on 8 February.

More to the point, the phrase "Big Brother is watching you" was everywhere. Retired Metropolitan Police sergeant Allan Clack, who's a member of the Orwell Society, says that London coppers like his dad used to announce it from their squad cars as a joke. Unlike the Goons on the radio, however, their commanders failed to see the funny side and ordered them to cut it out.

Screen and Screen Again

The play's second performance survives, recorded for posterity in the same primitive manner as *Studio One*. Cushing always considered it a disappointment, believing the uproar had drained the life from it.[96] "To me, it lost the edge," he said.[97]

"It was a question of lying low after that one," Kneale told the science-fiction magazine *Starburst* in 1979. "Nothing like it had ever hit television before. They tended to use three-act stage plays and you got little intervals between the acts. Very well done and beautifully acted, but a little sedate." He, on the other hand, had tailored the narrative to TV, almost as if he were writing a film script. "That was new. And, I suppose, if one started writing in those terms, immediately the thing had far more impact."[98]

He relived the furor later, with his biographer: "Peter Cushing had to disconnect his telephone. I had to hide. We all had to get out. The BBC said: 'Don't answer the phone until further instruction.'"[99]

For Cushing and Pleasence, the future lay in horror movies. The play—or to be precise, the rats of Room 101—also furnished Cushing with one of his favorite anecdotes, recounted in his 1986 autobiography. "A rat catcher's services were petitioned, and he procured two dirty grey, scraggy-looking specimens in time for the final rehearsal, and left them on the set," wrote the star. "Snug in their bed of straw, they basked in the warmth from the arc lamps, ate bits of cheese which sympathetic members of the unit kept dropping through the bars of their cage, to their surprise, and they certainly enjoyed an unexpected break from the dank sewers of London.

"So great was their comfort that when the moment came for them to leap at my throat, yellow teeth bared and snarling, there they were, snuggled together, content with this new existence, satiated with food, and fast asleep. They were sacked on the spot, and a minion dispatched post haste to the nearest pet shop to purchase a couple of tame ones, which were white, and had to be dyed dark brown by the make-up department."

To make the rats suitably ravenous, staff were warned not to feed them under any circumstances. "This achieved the desired effect, but just before we were due on the air,[100] hunger got the better of them." Shrieking and squeaking, they "had to be removed into a separate studio, with a camera and microphone all to themselves. When their great moment arrived, morsels of nourishment were dangled tantalisingly above their heads, out of shot, making them leap up and down as if on invisible pogo sticks, snapping viciously. At a given signal from the floor manager, I reacted to their attack without even seeing it. For this piece of emoting by remote control, playing one of the greatest heroes in literature, I became known as 'The Horror Man of the BBC.'"[101]

Bernard Wilkie, who with Jack Kine comprised the BBC's special effects department, told a similar tale, only this time with a sexual element. "The warmth of the studio and perfume of their make-up woke them up and encouraged them to copulate with unrestrained vigour," he wrote in his autobiography, *A Peculiar Effect on the BBC*. "We did eventually get the shot, but how Peter Cushing and Andre Morrel (sic) didn't collapse with laughter I shall never know. It can't be easy to act out naked fear while peering at two gay rats having it away like knives."[102]

Wound Up Tight

For fans of vintage British TV, Wilkie's hilarious, self-deprecating book (published 13 years after his death, in 2015) is a goldmine of reminiscences. In particular, the chapter on *Nineteen Eighty-Four* conveys the tension and excitement of live drama beautifully: "In darkened living rooms, viewers watched their screen with mounting disbelief, shutting their eyes to the horror, but unable to switch it off. In the studio the mood was electric."

During the days of miserable TV budgets, when "even the actors were paid only nominal fees," he and Kine "had become adept at creating props from scrap materials and household utensils." The small surveillance cameras on the show's three telescreens, for example, consisted of "big glass lenses (salvaged from scrapped roadside oil lamps) with rotating lights behind them." These were pocket flashlights, "strapped to the spindles of old-fashioned, spring-wound gramophone motors.... Full wound, the motors would turn the small circles of light for about ten minutes."

In the minutes leading up to Winston and Julia's arrest on the Sunday, Wilkie and Kine mislaid the winding handle. "There are three degrees of panic—mild, frightening and absolutely terrifying. Ours went off the scale. Without that handle, all three telescreens would come to a stop—including the vital one that had to be revealed during one of the most dramatic sequences in the plot. For a split second he and I stared at each other in disbelief, then we took off! Heedless of the need for silence, we ran around the studio like charging bulls, thrusting aside actors awaiting their cues and tossing costumes, props and equipment into the air. I remember scrabbling around Peter Cushing's feet while he was actually delivering his lines. Being a true professional he showed no surprise.... We found it in the nick of time, nestling on a ledge."[103]

Writing for *Cult TV* magazine in 1997, Wilkie added an amusing coda. "On camera," he wrote, "Cushing and Mitchell were acting out their roles, appearing to be petrified as the cupboard door swung open. Behind the set Jack, genuinely scared, was winding like a demented organ grinder."[104]

Shock, Horror

Julia's Pornorite machine, writes Wilkie in his book, "was an impressive looking prop with control knobs and levers and with a large revolving print roller mounted on the top. Yvonne Mitchell, who had to operate this machine, was supposed to look round in an unguarded moment and get her hand trapped in the works." Since the roller was a cardboard tube painted silver, the actress was never in any danger. "But it didn't seem that way to Jack. He was controlling the machine off-stage and had to kill the switch the moment Yvonne became trapped."

During the final rehearsal, Mitchell "thrust her arm deep into the casing and *screamed*." Afraid that she'd touched an unshielded electric motor, Kine hurtled across the studio and pulled her arm free. She hissed at him in astonishment. "What the fuck are you doing, Jack? Can't you see I'm acting?"[105]

Trailing behind this is the snowglobe anecdote, rehashed and very probably embellished by members of the crew down the years. Remember, the paperweight that catches Winston's eye makes two appearances, in the antiques shop and again in Charrington's upstairs room. Unfortunately, at the end of the final run-through on the Sunday, it was left on the shop counter and never seen again. After killing the lights, Cartier implored the thief to return it, no questions asked. When this didn't work, the story goes that a junior assistant stage manager rushed home to borrow her kid sister's paperweight.[106]

"It arrived with only a short time to spare," according to Wilkie,[107] who was commendably restrained about the whole story. The yarn that Kneale used to tell is more outrageous. "Come the scene in question," writes his biographer, "Cushing found himself handling a paperweight with a Mickey Mouse design, and delivering the line 'My word, what a beautiful thing—Victorian, no doubt?' with a straight face."[108]

A New Life

In all seriousness, Orwell scholar John Rodden views 12 December 1954 as the moment the author's reputation was "launched." *Studio One's 1984* may have been a conversation-starter, but it hadn't rocked America in quite the same way. "Complicating the British response," comments Rodden in his book, *George Orwell: The Politics of Literary Reputation*, "was the still-palpable presence of Orwell felt by British intellectuals. The immediate memory of the man among his acquaintances, unresolved disputes about his political position during his final years, and his radiance as an intellectual youth hero: all these factors influence the course of the BBC controversy."[109]

Acknowledging the Conservative press's support for the play—from an abridged serialization in the *Daily Express* to *Daily Mail* editorials about communism's "beastliness"—Rodden points to the "immediate and enormous impact on sales of *Nineteen Eighty-Four*." In mid–1954, weekly sales of the Secker & Warburg hardback edition stood at 150. A new Penguin paperback edition had also just been published. "During the week following the first telecast, 1,000 hardback and 18,000 paperback copies were sold. *Nineteen Eighty-Four* was catapulted into what the book industry has since dubbed 'supersellerdom.' Equally significant, the sale of Orwell's *oeuvre* was permanently boosted."[110]

Added to which, a movie of Orwell's previous novel was weeks away.

Nineteen Eighty-Four

Winston Smith: Peter Cushing
O'Brien: Andre Morell
Julia: Yvonne Mitchell
Syme: Donald Pleasence
Emmanuel Goldstein: Arnold Diamond
Parsons: Campbell Gray
Mrs. Parsons: Hilda Fenemore
Parsons girl: Pamela Grant
Parsons boy: Keith Davis
Woman supervisor: Janet Barrow
First youth: Norman Osborne
Second youth: Tony Lyons
Third youth: Malcolm Knight
First man: John Baker
Second man: Victor Platt
Barman: Van Boolen
Old man/thin prisoner: Wilfrid Brambell (credited as Wilfred Brambell)
Mr. Charrington: Leonard Sachs
Waiter: Sydney Bromley
Canteen woman: Janet Joye

Guard: Harry Lane
Narrator: Richard Williams
Other roles (uncredited) played by: Lola Willard, Jessie Ball, Malya Nappi, Nelly Griffiths, Margaret Dickie, Edwin Finn, Paul Machell, Charles Reynolds, Neil Heayes, Norman Leony, Kathleen Macaulife, Maisie Macfarquhar, Hilary Sesta, Jack Zolov, Jeffry Gardiner, George Herbert, Bart Allison, Howard Green, Dermot Macmahon, Sheldon Allen, Robert Hargreaves, Harry Hearne, Charles Price, Stephen Scott
Adapted as a television play by: Nigel Kneale
Produced by: Rudolph Cartier
Designer: Barry Learoyd
Models and effects by: Bernard Wilkie and Jack Kine
Incidental music composed and conducted by: John Hotchkis

3

Animal Farm (1954)

The animated *Animal Farm*—"based on George Orwell's memorable fable," as the opening credits have it—was fondly regarded for decades as an adroit, family-friendly interpretation of his satire on the Bolshevik revolution. As Britain's first feature-length cartoon, it is not just a landmark work, but a testament to the ambition and tenacity of its creators, John Halas and Joy Batchelor. By building a cottage industry almost from scratch, the married couple transformed a seminal political novel into mass entertainment for all ages. But as we've known for sure since the nineties, this most English of stories relied on another, more shadowy player: the United States' Central Intelligence Agency, which bankrolled the film as a Cold War propaganda tool.

The book, published in August 1945, three months after VE Day, is a blatant reworking of 20th-century Russian history. Instead of Marx and Lenin, its ideologue is Old Major, a venerable prize boar who inspires his fellow livestock to revolt against humanity. But dreams of an egalitarian utopia turn sour when the pigs at the top of the hierarchy—led by the egomaniacal Napoleon, in effect a porcine Joseph Stalin—turn out to be as cruel as the hated bipeds, if not more so. Orwell, an avowed democratic socialist, had seen Stalinist terror up close during the communist purges in Spain—and though it's not wholly faithful to the novel, Halas and Batchelor's film, under the guidance of U.S. intelligence, at least reflects his hatred of the communist establishment.

"I think you've got to be eight, really, to appreciate it,"[1] says Vivien Halas, who was nine when her parents' movie came out. Her father, a poster artist and protégé of the animator George Pal, was a Hungarian migrant in London before the war; her mother, one of the few female illustrators in thirties Britain. "They did whatever they could to find work around the advertising agencies, and then they got asked to work with the agency J. Walter Thompson. When the war broke out, it was taken over by the government—by the Central Office of Information—and they found themselves making information films, propaganda films, things like that."

In which case, why did they make *Animal Farm*? "Well, they were asked. Just after the war, they were doing films for the Marshall Plan, the reconstruction of Europe, and they made a film called *The Shoemaker and the Hatter*, which was all to do with lowering trade barriers in Europe. The people who were working on that were part of a documentary film unit in America and there was somebody called Louis de Rochemont who'd been making films for Time Life, newsreel films called *The March of Time*. He kind of invented the genre of docudrama by re-enacting things to look like the real thing, but they kind of were helped along…

"He heard about my parents, he'd seen their work and he was thinking of making *Animal Farm*. Sonia Orwell, Orwell's widow, had sold the rights to the American government—a couple called Carlton Alsop and Finis Farr, who were part of a kind of funding unit for the arts to promote American culture in Europe and around. That, they kind of later on morphed into the CIA. They had the funding and they asked Louis de Rochemont. He didn't want a Disney thing—he wanted something a little more, I don't know, European-friendly—and so he asked my parents if they would think about it and do a storyboard and if they thought it would make a good film. They were absolutely delighted because, although not many people knew about Orwell at that time, they did and he was one of their heroes. Also, he had been working at Bush House in Aldwych [producing wartime propaganda for BBC radio]. They probably never knew each other but at the same time my parents were working out of Bush House, making their films during the war. There are all kinds of links there. People all knew each other."

Since Russia was occupying post-war Hungary, it's safe to assume that Halas approved of Orwell's satire. "Oh, absolutely. I think they saw it as more than just the Russian revolution. It was their way of feeling better about the whole Second World War and the fact that a lot of his relatives had been taken off to concentration camps.[2] Some got back, some were killed and I think he felt a little bit—well, I won't say guilty exactly, but uncomfortable with the fact that a lot of his family had suffered and he was here in England. He was very helpful to people. He used to send my grandmother food parcels and we had a Hungarian cousin come and stay with us when he escaped in [the uprising of] '56. My father helped him on his way to Canada."

The Secret Service

Before considering the film itself, it's useful to note that years before its production, UK government officials bought the rights to produce an

In a pivotal scene from Halas and Batchelor's *Animal Farm*, the exploited, neglected beasts of Manor Farm prepare to raid a barn full of food (copyright Halas & Batchelor, 1954).

Animal Farm strip cartoon, targeted at the developing world. University of Hertfordshire history professor Tony Shaw, author of *British Cinema and the Cold War*, says: "It's interesting to see that, for instance, the British government had an organization called the Information Research Department, which was a propaganda unit it set up in 1948, working through the Foreign Office to produce anti-communist material and to place anti-communist material within Britain but predominantly overseas. You can see through their files that they're very keen to project and take further *Animal Farm* and then *Nineteen Eighty-Four*."

In 1949, Orwell passed a list of suspected communist "fellow travelers" to this very department. "From a very early stage, the British Foreign Office and the CIA are promoting the distribution and sale of *Nineteen Eighty-Four* and of *Animal Farm*," says Shaw. "They would have been and were popular books without any government involvement, but the sponsorship and distribution of those two books as we go through the 1950s, I think is very interesting—and then the production of the movies helps to cement Orwell's reputation. None of the government involvement makes Orwell—

Orwell made himself—but it certainly helps to expand the influence of those two books in particular."[3]

In her 1999 book, *Who Paid the Piper?*, British journalist Frances Stonor Saunders blew the lid off the CIA's involvement in Halas and Batchelor's cartoon. Studying declassified U.S. government files, she concluded that its agents were "sort of the executive producers."[4] What's clear is that shortly after Orwell's death in 1950, two members of the CIA's psychological warfare workshop—writer Finis Farr and his friend Carlton Alsop, formerly a film producer and Hollywood agent[5]—set out for England to negotiate *Animal Farm*'s film rights with Sonia. The way Stonor Saunders tells it, the duo, under orders from future Watergate conspirator Howard Hunt, clinched the deal by arranging for Sonia to meet her idol, Clark Gable.[6] Not everyone finds this plausible, however. In his 2007 book *Orwell Subverted: The CIA and the Filming of Animal Farm*, history professor Daniel J. Leab of Seton Hall University, New Jersey, casts doubt on Hunt's involvement. He also suggests that the Gable story may have been a joke on the part of the Americans, or even the "flighty" Mrs. Orwell herself.[7]

Whatever the case, the agency found a front in Louis de Rochemont. According to Shaw, the producer approached Halas and Batchelor because (i) they were smaller and cheaper than U.S. animation studios, (ii) they were renowned for their wartime propaganda films, (iii) some Hollywood animators were thought to be subversives and (iv) the studio's British character would deflect attention away from the Americans. During production, he writes, the couple grew more aware of the project's political nature, "but there is no evidence that they (or their colleagues) knew of the precise origins of the film."[8]

For a UK studio, this was an unprecedented venture. In his tie-in nonfiction book of 1954, *The Animated Film*, author Roger Manvell pegs *Animal Farm* as only the 26th feature-length animated movie in history (a figure that includes "puppet films"). Manvell credits Soviet stop-motion director Alexander Ptushko with the first of these—1935's *The New Gulliver*—with Walt Disney's *Snow White and the Seven Dwarfs* blazing a trail for cartoons in 1938. By his reckoning, 15 of the first 25 were American, another four were French and two were Russian. Italy, Germany, Spain and Denmark had one apiece.[9]

"There were rooms full of preparatory drawings and various versions of storyboards," says Vivien Halas. "The script [by Batchelor] was written at least nine times. It was really, for them, the most interesting and important film that they did. They were really glad to have something to get their teeth into."

A Painstaking Process

The film took three years to make, running massively overbudget and a good 18 months late. In his remarkably thorough book, Leab writes that John Halas put the final cost at £179,000: about $500,000 at the contemporary exchange rate.[10] Press releases in 1951–52 had put the projected budget at £80,000.[11]

Manvell's book explains the production process in detail, starting with a break-down chart listing the novel's characters and their relationships to one another. At this early stage, figures on the periphery, such as Mollie the vain white pony, fell by the wayside. From here, Halas and Batchelor drew up a tension chart, showing how the drama and excitement would rise and fall from scene to scene.[12] Joy Batchelor's draft script, or first treatment, came next.[13] With the aid of a colleague, Philip Stapp, the couple prepared a picture book of the film, made up of 350 drawings plus text. By the end of week 16, they and a team of four artists had put together a storyboard,[14] filling the walls of two rooms.[15] And as the storyboard grew, a shooting script took shape, involving 18 sequences and roughly 1,000 background paintings.[16] The finished product, all 75 minutes of it, would require 300,000 man-hours and two tons of paint.[17]

In terms of animators, Vivien Halas says that "the studio grew from under 20 to just under 100 at the time. They weren't all working on *Animal Farm* because they kept going with other productions as well." As luck would have it, two other British studios had just closed their doors, leaving a ready-made pool of staff. One of the firms—owned by animation veteran Anson Dyer, who'd recently retired—had escaped the German bombing of London by moving to Stroud, a Gloucestershire market town 106 miles away. Halas and Bachelor bought a three-storey Victorian house there to complement their three offices in the capital.[18]

Film journalist Iain F. McAsh, who died in 2012, was a trainee clean-up artist and inbetweener on the film, filling in the gaps between the senior animators' key drawings. Writing in 2001 for *The Veteran*, a magazine for UK cinema and TV industry retirees, he reminisced about his time as the studio's youngest employee. McAsh joined the studio in London straight from school in September 1952, aged 17. At that stage, *Animal Farm* had been in production for a year, and as he worked by hand at a circular drawing board mounted on a light box, he felt excited to be part of Britain's answer to *Snow White*.

"While the main Halas and Batchelor studio was in Soho Square," wrote McAsh, "feature production and the commencement of *Animal Farm* meant the hiring of around 100 more artists, along with the need of moving to larger premises." A three-storey house at 2 Westbourne Terrace offered extra space—and with Paddington Station nearby, the team could send rushes to Stroud by train. The production demanded 300,000 drawings, each of which had to be traced on to celluloid sheets for inking. With opaque paints, the artists could then add color to each of the "cells." In his later years, one of McAsh's fondest memories was of animating the birds. "From our drawing boards, we would try to entice local pigeons on to our window sills so we could study them more closely," he recalled.[19]

While production was in full swing, British magazine *Picturegoer* paid a visit to Westbourne Terrace. The resulting two-page spread, "The amazing things that went on in this house," is intriguing to say the least, though it's understandably naive about de Rochemont. This "Hollywood intellectual," it seems, so admired *Robinson Charley* (a cartoon from 1948 about the UK's economy) that within days of seeing it, he was making Halas and Batchelor an offer they couldn't refuse. American investment aside, conditions in the carpetless Victorian property were modest, with animators working cheek by jowl. A contingent of them visited a farm for inspiration, the article reports, and for months, a scale model farmyard occupied a corner of Halas's office. In addition, the team made plastic wood models of three of the major characters: Napoleon, the tyrannical pig; Boxer, the trusting, conscientious carthorse; and his cynical best friend, Benjamin the donkey.[20]

For a while, Disney-trained John Reed served as animation director, lending the film his Hollywood expertise and adding whimsical touches such as a cute yellow duckling. But this led to bad blood, according to Leab. Fending off accusations of "Americanization" from at least one prominent colleague, Reed left the company in acrimonious circumstances.[21]

Faced with spiraling costs, Halas and Batchelor discarded plot elements and supporting characters. A list of seven commandments, central to the novel, was cut to five.[22] Modern-day histories of the film speak of frustrating delays and endless wrangling over Batchelor's rewrites; in fact, according to Leab, CIA men "scoured the script for any nuances that might undermine their political agenda."[23] In his efforts to placate them, de Rochemont asked an uncredited American script doctor, John Stuart Martin, to rework the film's narration.[24]

The biggest stumbling block was the book's ending, in which, famously, the ruling pigs become indistinguishable from the human beings they replaced. As Stonor Saunders told a BBC radio show in 2014, documents in the Washington archives highlight objections to Orwell's fuzzy symbolism. "So in the film, the ending is changed so that the other animals rebel against their sort of porcine Politburo…. What you have effectively is a counter-insurgency and it ends on this high note, this hopeful note, which I think would have appalled Orwell."[25]

Moments before they drive him off the farm, the tyrannical Farmer Jones bursts in on his livestock in a rage (copyright Halas & Batchelor, 1954).

From Page to Screen

The novel's first scene takes place at night, in a barn on Manor Farm, England. At a meeting of all the animals, venerable pig Old Major talks of an inspirational dream he's had. Drunken farmer Jones is a tyrant, like all human beings, he says. Freed from mankind's shackles, the creatures could share the fruits of their labor and enjoy long, productive lives. With terrific zest, they sing Beasts of England, the anthem of their new ideology.

The film, on the other hand, begins with a bright pastoral scene,[26] then shifts to a country pub where Jones, a lanky, dead-eyed lush with a ghoulish countenance, is boozing with his cronies. Before retiring for the night, he staggers around the farm's outhouses, distressing the animals. By and large, the animation is painterly, but when the creatures assemble for their meeting, an element of cuteness intrudes. Consider the little duckling, for example, who jumps and flaps its wings as it strives to reach a better vantage point. Gently, Boxer the carthorse picks it up with his mouth and gives it a ringside seat.

Like all the animals, watery-eyed Old Major is voiced by Maurice Den-

ham, who'd made his name playing 60 roles in the forties radio comedy
Much Binding in the Marsh. He sounds suspiciously like incumbent prime
minister Sir Winston Churchill, though Denham maintained 40 years down
the line that it wasn't a straight-up impression.[27] The way John Halas
remembered it, the great man's "authority and pomposity" had been a defi-
nite inspiration, to the extent that Churchill recognized himself and "sent
down a message of displeasure" by way of an undersecretary.[28]

The pig's speech about exploitation, stripped to its essentials, comes
laced with vivid imagery: of Boxer dragging a hay cart uphill; of a human
hand helping itself to hens' eggs; and of a ewe and her lamb, huddled
together and shivering in the snow. Against a blood-red backdrop, we see
a cleaver, a chopping board and headless carcasses on meat-hooks.

The anthem, when it comes, is sung with gusto, though it's not *Beasts
of England* as such—more a tuneful cacophony of bleats, moos, squawks,
oinks and whinnies.[29] Old Major slumps forward, dead,[30] eliciting gasps
from the assembled animals and copious weeping and wailing. From his
bedroom window, Jones breaks up the gathering with a shotgun blast.

*Led by young boars Snowball and Napoleon, with the shifty Squealer
acting as PR man, the pigs disseminate Old Major's ideology. When Jones
staggers home from the pub and dozes off without feeding them, the animals
stage an impromptu revolution.*

*Renaming the property Animal Farm, the pigs paint seven command-
ments on the big barn wall. Stipulating that four-legged creatures are friends
and that bipeds are their enemies ("Four legs good, two legs bad"), they forbid
animals from sleeping in a bed, drinking alcohol, wearing clothes or killing
other animals. The final commandment is: "All animals are equal."*

*At first, the farm runs smoothly on sheer goodwill and enthusiasm. The
pigs, who supervise rather than work, dominate the animals' debates, with
Napoleon and Snowball typically at loggerheads. In what is dubbed the Battle
of the Cowshed, the farm repels a counter-insurgency by Jones, his neighbors
Pilkington and Frederick and their farmhands. Snowball and Boxer are honored for conspicuous bravery.*

The intensity of the revolution, 13 minutes into the film, doesn't dis-
appoint. At Snowball's command, Boxer, two bulls and a billy goat charge
at the padlocked door of the farmhouse. Incensed, Jones enters the doorway
clutching a whip. The beasts circle him *en masse*, eyes reddening with fury,
and send him packing—but in a significant change from the book, he retal-
iates at once, convincing his fellow pubgoers to march on the farm with
rifles and pitchforks. Engulfed in a whirlwind of fangs, hooves and dust,

the men retreat, leaving the animals to build a bonfire of human items. Circling the flames, they sing their anthem in triumph.

Up go the five commandments on the barn—the script combines two of Orwell's and ignores another—and in synchronized formations, the task of harvesting crops and baling hay begins.

Napoleon and Snowball's rivalry grows more fractious as the novelty of the revolution fades. After urinating on the blueprints for Snowball's grand plan—a windmill for generating electricity—Napoleon sets guard dogs on his rival, driving him into exile. From this point on, the imperious pig's despotism intensifies. He abolishes mass meetings in favor of diktats, claims the windmill was his idea, forces the animals to march past Old Major's disinterred skull every Sunday and works them like slaves. Adopting the title of Leader, he flouts the commandments shamelessly, moving into the farmhouse with the other pigs and setting up trade deals with men. When a storm wrecks the half-finished windmill, he angrily announces that "traitor" Snowball has crept back and sabotaged it.

Not content with banishing Leon Trotsky from Russia in 1928, Stalin had him assassinated in Mexico in 1940. In Orwell's novel, we never learn what Snowball's fate is—simply that he's chased off the farm and slandered as a saboteur. Here, though, in what's ostensibly a children's film, hounds chase him though a snowy field and rip him to pieces off camera. He squeals in terror, the camera pans up to a raven (Moses, a minor character from the book) and the dogs slink back to Napoleon, nodding that the deed is done.

It could have been worse. During discussions about the movie's feasibility, a screenwriter in the CIA's pay floated the idea that "a benign looking pig" could visit Snowball in the tropics, unmask itself as a dog and tear open the porker's throat.[31]

Winter falls, the crops fail and everyone except the pigs is famished. The hens defy an ultimatum from Napoleon to hand over their eggs for sale, so he starves them into submission by cutting their rations to zero. For every setback, he blames Snowball. Show trials and public executions follow. Dismayed, the animals consult the seven commandments, but they've been edited by Squealer to give the pigs free rein.

Napoleon, whose personality cult is growing more demented by the day, sells a pile of timber to Frederick in return for banknotes that turn out to be forged. Frederick and his men storm the farm with guns and blow up the windmill with blasting powder. After a bloody skirmish (the Battle of the Windmill) sends the humans packing, the pigs celebrate with a case of whisky.

We've established that this is a uniquely serious cartoon. In fact, with offstage executions, bloodthirsty dogs gratuitously mauling a cat to death, a spot of armed violence as men open fire with shotguns and the bombing (well, dynamiting) of a building, the latter half is despairing. Plus, having Napoleon cower in his bedroom is unfair to Stalin. Honest Orwell, who based the Battle of the Windmill on the Nazis' siege of Russia in 1941, was careful to acknowledge that the dictator had stood his ground in Moscow.

In the years that follow, Boxer, the most loyal and hard-working of the animals, heaves stone to the site of the windmill until old age gets the better of him. Sprawled on the grass, he looks forward to his retirement. A truck arrives, supposedly to take him to an animal hospital. Too late, his friends see a "Horse Slaughterer and Glue Boiler" sign on the rear doors.

Unquestionably, this is the emotional high point of the film. Benjamin the donkey chases after the vehicle with the other beasts, braying in desperation. Boxer, terrified, sticks his head through a hole in the doors, which are painted with a horse's skull and crossbones. The truck roars off, leaving his friends devastated. And though they won't admit it, the pigs are pleased. Their business partner—squat, bald, pinch-faced Mr. Whymper—rewards them with jars of jam in exchange for Boxer's life.

Many years later, the pigs are corpulent, wear clothes and walk on their hind legs. The barn displays a solitary commandment: "All animals are equal, but some animals are more equal than others." Napoleon throws a party for Pilkington, but a row breaks out between them—and as the animals squint through the window, they can't tell pig and man apart.

Yes, it's one of the most celebrated endings in English literature. No, it didn't make the final cut. Shaw contends that Batchelor tried to keep it, fighting Orwell's corner for six months.[32] Leab, while agreeing with his general point, says she'd been open to a happier ending since early in pre-production.[33]

Here, then, is how the movie plays out. By exploiting "lower" animals such as Benjamin, who's now emaciated, Napoleon is in charge of a thriving business empire. With the windmill built, he invites pig delegates from other farms to celebrate. Ferried in chauffeur-driven limos and wearing tuxedos, the guests pass through wire fences and checkpoints that anticipate the Berlin Wall. Infuriated by the "some are more equal" commandment and dismayed at the suffering they've had to endure, the downtrodden species dispatch birds to spread a message of rebellion.

Towards the end of the movie, Benjamin the donkey realizes the full extent of the pigs' betrayal as they adopt all of mankind's worst characteristics (copyright Halas & Batchelor, 1954).

In the farmhouse, Napoleon and his colleagues raise a toast to pig rule. From the point of view of Benjamin, spying through a window, it looks like each of them is morphing into Jones. Out for vengeance, an army of animals marches on the farmhouse and breaks through the walls as Napoleon cowers in fear. If their bitter stares are anything to go by, the tables have suddenly turned.

Pig Brother Is Watching You

The movie premiered at New York's upmarket Paris Theatre on 29 December 1954, with Sonia Orwell as guest of honor. For all their eloquence, writes Leab, the married animators "were overshadowed by her glamour. There is a telling picture of Sonia Orwell splendidly arrayed in a full-length fur coat, wearing a corsage, standing under the marquee of the Paris Theatre advertising 'Orwell's Animal Farm,' alongside a somewhat subdued-looking Halas and Batchelor."[34]

U.S. trade paper the *Motion Picture Herald* called the film "a daring innovation" for the industry, adding: "*Animal Farm* is the first feature cartoon to utilize an adult theme and it does so with intelligence, wit and understanding."[35] Yet *Variety*, while praising its imaginative qualities, technical achievements and "sobering lesson about glib oratorical protestations of equality and brotherhood," had doubts about its box-office potential. In truth, it was "not the kind of film fare which is likely to be 'popular.' A wee mite on the somber side."[36]

The critic had a point, and with New York yielding disappointing box-office receipts, American distributors turned their noses up at the picture.[37] In London, meanwhile, the glamorous Sonia graced a premiere at the Ritz Theatre near Leicester Square on 13 January. Emboldened by the BBC's *Nineteen Eighty-Four* a month earlier, the marketing strap was: "Pig Brother is Watching You."

In the opinion of *Picturegoer*, the movie had "a touch of genius."[38] *Today's Cinema* was sure its comedy elements would "widen the film's appeal beyond the politically well-read."[39] "A major triumph" was the verdict of the *News Chronicle*'s Paul Dehn. "Adults will find much of it frightening; but the children at the press show (were their parents misled by the pastoral title?) laughed their young heads off."[40]

The Times, in a more intellectual review than most, appreciated the film's respect for Orwell, the "pleasantly irresponsible humour" and the animals' depiction as individuals. "*Animal Farm* makes it clear that the cartoon need not spend so much of its time among the frenzied fantasies of the comic 'short' and is capable of the imaginative interpretation of a serious idea," the paper concluded.[41]

The Manchester Guardian's critic, unmoved by the "Disney-turned-serious" style, thought Orwell would have disliked the animation and the ending. "On the other hand, the simple merits of Orwell's satirical story … are such that the film adaptation should still turn out to be a reasonably good one."[42] (A separate story in the same edition reported that journalists at a press screening spontaneously applauded the end titles.[43])

It was, raved CA Lejeune at *The Observer*, "a film for the eye, ear, heart and mind; a film that will outlive a year of Sundays."[44] But the *Daily Mirror*'s Reg Whitley, while impressed, found it hard to imagine the cartoon's political nature would win over the movie-going public.[45] Predictably, the *Daily Worker* was scathing, labeling it "an essay in political distortion and despair" and condemning the "utter emptiness" of Orwell's worldview. "This philosophy of despair is the very heart of the current Orwell boom, in which he is being methodically built up as a major artist and thinker of the Cold War," wrote Thomas Spencer.[46]

In the *Daily Mail*, Fred Majdalany criticized Halas and Batchelor not only for distorting the ending, but for failing to give the animals life and substance. "They are types, not characters; creatures of the head rather than the heart; none of them memorable as Disney's best animals have been."[47] Dick Kisch, London correspondent for *The Sunday Times* of Perth, Australia, said the film was "made in Disney style" but lacked Disney's "ingenuity and wit." Associated British Studios, seeing how indifferent audiences were, was now nervous about making *Nineteen Eighty-Four*, he added.[48]

Harold Conway at the *Daily Sketch* berated British exhibitors for their timidity. "Only since TV's enterprise with 1984 has this brave new film been booked into the West End," he fumed, "and even then at a very small cinema, although it has been on offer for months."[49] His admonishments fell on deaf ears. The Rank, ABC and British Lion cinema chains simply weren't interested.[50]

It can't have helped that John Halas was so honest about the movie in the *Daily Herald*. "It is a horrifying film," he said. "With one exception, there is not a pleasant character in it. I think about 70 per cent of those who see it will love it. The remainder will hate it."[51]

Animal Qualms

A trade union magazine, *The Cine-Technician*,[52] devoted three pages to the cartoon in its May 1955 edition. For his regular column,[53] cinematographer AE Jeakins reported from a branch-sponsored screening[54] in London at which Halas and Batchelor took questions.[55]

At one point, said Halas, they had moved on to a farm and lived practically in the pig sty for several weeks. The hardest section to animate, he added, was the purge. "You can animate a quick-hitting sequence like a fight in your sleep, but when you come to a slow, tedious animation with so many animals in the background, and have to maintain tension and drama right through the sequence, animating every frame of film, that is a real nightmare."

The emotional scene by the windmill with Benjamin and the injured Boxer was a challenge too, said his wife, because there were no actors to convey the emotion of it—only line drawings. "It had to be very carefully handled to avoid slipping over from tragedy to tragi-comedy."

Defending the finale, she said that to end the cartoon in "despair and pessimism" would have been "quite dreadful." A quarter of a century later, Halas made much the same point on the children's TV show *Clapperboard*. Film is a positive medium, he insisted. You cannot send the audience home puzzled.

He denied, however, that they'd added a ray of hope: "We have shown the uprising of the animals, who marched against the betrayal of the system, the pigs—and we implied that this whole condition might repeat itself, stronger than it has been implied in the book itself."[56]

Legacy

Being an out-and-out swine, communist dictator Nicolae Ceausescu never cared for *Animal Farm* and banned all forms of it in Romania. On New Year's Day 1990, a week after his people had risen up and killed him, its TV service screened the cartoon, to the widespread astonishment of viewers. As one young man put it, the story "felt as if it had been written especially for us."[57]

The film's custodian, Vivien Halas, has seen its effect up close, in classrooms in the UK and elsewhere. "Lots of children have written to me and when I do educational screenings, young teenagers are usually very taken with it," she says. "It's not something that they probably are dying to go and see, but once they get there and they see it, I think it has a huge impact on them."

Boxer's last scene always ends in tears. "I think it just gives them an insight into politics, really, and the unfairness of the world. They get very upset by the violent bits, and when you think that what kids see is very violent, this film seems to have an effect that is possibly stronger than seeing crashing and bashing."

Her parents died in the nineties. Did they reminisce about *Animal Farm* in their old age? "Only in that they thought it was good and their most important film. It's their legacy, if you like, because not many people are going to remember *Foo Foo* or *Habatales*. A lot of people say it's Disneyesque because it's 2D animation. If one looks carefully, it isn't at all, it's quite a dark film. As for the design, everybody had a go at it.... It sort of developed, if you like, but my parents were in charge of the overall artistic direction.

"I think the design is still good. I think the pacing is good. The music is very well integrated with the sound. I would say this, because I look after the film, but to my mind, it is a masterpiece."

Animal Farm

Narrator: Gordon Heath	**Producers/directors:** John Halas and
Animals: Maurice Denham	Joy Batchelor
Adapted by: Joy Batchelor	**Music:** Matyas Seiber

4
1984 (1956)

The first big-screen foray into Airstrip One is not, it must be said, well liked. Its chief detractor, Sonia Orwell, held it in such contempt that she forced its withdrawal from circulation in the mid-seventies, relegating it to the status of "unfilm."[1] The general consensus was that British director Michael Anderson's black-and-white movie was inferior to Rudolph Cartier's vastly less expensive TV play, which preceded it by 16 months. But until 2007, when the American edit emerged on DVD in the UK, it was practically impossible to compare the two.

"The BBC TV production caused a lot of fuss, and for its time it was artistically quite an important production, certainly in terms of its shock value," says Tony Shaw, author of *British Cinema and the Cold War*. "A lot of viewers were genuinely scared by it and it was quite a sophisticated production for its time." *Animal Farm* has aged well too, says the history professor, and is a milestone in British animation history. But "the 1956 version of *Nineteen Eighty-Four* was a stinker, I think. It bombed at the box office and was criticized heavily in the press at the time as a badly acted, cheap production."[2]

The blame for this, if one agrees with Shaw's assessment, lies with independent American producer N. Peter Rathvon. The former lawyer,[3] banker and businessman had at one time been a big noise in Hollywood, serving as president of RKO Pictures from 1942[4] to 1948. This ended abruptly when its new owner, billionaire Howard Hughes, unceremoniously fired him.[5] Rathvon, by all accounts, had McCarthyite sympathies, shedding few tears for the "Hollywood Ten"[6] in 1947 when the Senate blacklisted them from the industry for refusing to reveal their politics. Journalist Frances Stonor Saunders, in her book *Who Paid the Piper?*, suggests it was U.S. intelligence officer Howard Hunt who solicited his help with *1984*.[7]

In any event, the film rights passed to Rathvon in 1953, the same year President Eisenhower founded America's public relations arm, the United States Information Agency (USIA). Presented with a chance to veto the

BBC's dramatization, Rathvon shrewdly agreed to let it go ahead and capitalized on the stink it caused. "The smartest option I ever dropped," he told a journalist.[8]

According to Shaw's researches, the USIA granted the movie a $100,000 subsidy and guaranteed worldwide distribution in exchange for control of the screenplay.[9] In September 1954, three months before the BBC controversy, a report in *The New York Times* claimed Rathvon and Lothar Wolff, an associate of Louis de Rochemont, would shoot parallel German and English versions in West Germany, possibly with heart-throb Cornel Wilde.[10]

By Christmas, Orwell-obsessed newspapers in London were running a different story: that Associated British Pictures would produce a movie at Elstree Studios in April with a yet-to-be-finalized British and American cast. To give it a drabber appearance, Rathvon announced, they'd be shooting in monochrome.[11] As assistant producer Ralph Bettinson revealed, the British Board of Film Censors had passed the script without cuts, giving

With its Thought Police riding turbo-charged motorbikes near a beehive-shaped ministry building, this lobby card demonstrates the ambition of *1984*'s production designer, Terence Verity (copyright Columbia Pictures, 1956).

the film a pre-emptive "X" certificate that would bar under-18s from seeing it.[12] This blow to its box-office prospects skewered any chance of casting Peter Cushing and Yvonne Mitchell, who were unknown outside of the UK.

To generate interest Stateside, Rathvon plumped for second-tier American stars—"plumped" being the operative word for Edmond O'Brien, the beefiest "Winston Smith of the Outer Party" we've seen. The 39-year-old New Yorker had just hit a career high, winning the best supporting actor Oscar for his role as a sweaty publicist in Joseph L. Mankiewicz's *The Barefoot Contessa* (1954).

Jan Sterling, a 34-year-old New York blonde, won the role of "Julia of the Outer Party'—though, judging from an interview with Joan Fontaine at the time, she may not have been first choice.[13] The job coincided with her actor husband Paul Douglas filming an Americanized Shakespeare update, *Joe Macbeth*, in Walton-on-Thames.[14]

Lending some British class to the proceedings was Michael Redgrave, playing "O'Connor of the Inner Party"; presumably the new surname was

Winston Smith (Edmond O'Brien) and Julia (Jan Sterling) meet in Victory Square for *1984*'s last scene. Director Michael Anderson shot alternative endings for the U.S. and UK markets (copyright Columbia Pictures, 1956).

to avoid confusion with Edmond O'Brien. For reasons of religious sensitivity, perhaps, screenwriters William P. Templeton and Ralph Bettinson replaced Goldstein with the futuristic-sounding "Kalador" (played by the uncredited Bernard Rebel).

Anderson, at the helm, had made his name with the 1955 war film *The Dam Busters*, in which Redgrave—one of the names on Orwell's list of suspected "fellow travelers" in 1949—portrayed Barnes Wallis, inventor of the bouncing bomb. In fact the 35-year-old director, who had toured with his actor father Lawrence as a child,[15] had witnessed totalitarianism at close hand. Interviewed in 1967 about his Berlin-set spy thriller, *The Quiller Memorandum*, he said: "I was in Germany long before the war, in 1933, at the time of Hitler's ascent to power and was deeply influenced by it."[16]

Anderson, who died in April 2018 at the age of 98, reportedly penned an autobiography in his final years, a project he mentioned to the author of this book in a 2015 email.[17] In 1989, the American sci-fi magazine *Starlog* asked him about the film. "It was done on a shoestring, which is a shame," he said. "But I think it was fairly true to the Orwellian novel."[18]

Oh, Beehive

With so few production staff still around, it's lucky for us that Rathvon and his team at the incongruously named Holiday Film Productions were relaxed about allowing journalists on set. *Picturegoer* magazine ran an especially detailed report from a night shoot in Stepney, East London, where reporter Ernie Player quizzed art director Terence Verity about his distinctive production design.[19] The blue-gray Party uniforms—made to look synthetic and one layer thick—and the Thought Police's turbine-driven motorbikes were in a modernistic style that would, by the time of the film's release, nettle Mrs. Orwell terribly. Verity's main challenge, though, was finding bombed-out locations in a city that was putting the Blitz behind it. "Everything has been cleared up," he said ruefully, as he watched his crew import their own rubble.[20]

At Elstree, Verity rebuilt Trafalgar Square—or rather, Victory Square[21]—installing telescreens in the base of his replica Nelson's Column.[22] The ministry buildings clustered around the Thames (and shot from a great height in some of the establishing scenes) resemble gun-metal beehives, as he reasoned that they "must be bomb-proof and not too noticeable from the air."[23] To viewers now, they're strangely reminiscent of London's Swiss Re building, better known as "the Gherkin."[24]

Speaking to *The New York Times* in the middle of shooting, Rathvon promised to improve on the novel, which he thought was too preoccupied with background. Taking its cues from Templeton's *Studio One* TV script, the film would be about people: "a love story against a background of terror."[25] Speaking to the same paper, Anderson stressed that he was keen to avoid anything that smacked of "the fantastic or science-fiction."[26] Room 101's rats would be suggested rather than shown, he said, as Oceania was more "a tyranny of the mind" than the body.[27]

In a script "freely adapted" from the novel, as the opening credits phrase it, this was by no means the only liberty taken. Julia and Winston meet four minutes in, huddling in a shop doorway as bombs rain down on London; Smith starts his diary on 18 April, two weeks later than the date in Orwell's book; and when he roams the streets at night, searching for a hidden note from Julia, little Selina Parsons demands to know what he's up to.

The prole sector is "the people's area,"[28] *The Times* is now *The Gazette* and Winston's fiery garbage chute, the memory hole, is labeled the VAPOR-ISER. At least Newspeak, so cruelly ignored in Templeton's *Studio One* script, is mentioned in Winston and O'Connor's conversations, albeit sketchily.[29] At every turn, the political message is dumbed down. While Smith is reading from Kalador's book, for example, Julia is going gooey at the sight of a baby outside. "I'd have liked to have had a child," she simpers.

Orwell's ending was mutilated too—for British audiences, at any rate. In fact, Anderson shot two finales: one faithful to the novel, the other with a modicum of hope. To understand why, let's return to Stonor Saunders' research: specifically Rathvon's correspondence with the writer Sol Stein, executive director of the American Committee for Cultural Freedom, an anti-communist body.[30]

Stein's advice as a script doctor was: (i) to make the Big Brother of the posters a human being, rather than a cartoon caricature, which would ground the story in reality; (ii) to replace the Anti-Sex League sashes with armbands, because sashes are rarely seen outside diplomatic ceremonies[31]; and (iii) to avoid trumpets, as they're associated with pageantry.[32] To judge from the finished movie, these suggestions were heeded.

But Stein's gravest misgivings concerned Orwell's ending, which he called "a situation without hope." In its place, he suggested a schmaltzy addendum to Winston and Julia's last meeting, which runs as follows:

• The pair leave the cafe, heading in opposite directions, Winston sees the faces of children, shining with a natural innocence. He quickens his pace, the music swells, and he's "near the secluded spot where he and Julia found refuge."[33]
• Smith notices another loving couple and as he turns to walk away,

the audience hears his heart beating. He peers at his fingers, remembering that two and two make four.

• "We continue to hear his heart beating, and by extension, the human heart beating—louder, as the film ends."[34]

Even for a Hollywood producer, the advice was too sickly to follow.

Dead or Alive

In both of the finales Anderson filmed, the traumatized ex-lovers meet in Victory Square. The more-or-less faithful version ends with Winston joining a mob and chanting: "Long live Big Brother!" in response to good news from the African front. ("This, then, is a story of the future," the narrator declares, in sententious tones and an American accent. "It could be the story of our children if we fail to preserve their heritage of freedom.")

The "happy" ending, missing from the 2007 DVD but available to read in script form if you know where to look,[35] takes an altogether different tack. This time around, Winston defies the crowd by yelling: "Down with Big Brother!"—a phrase he repeats until the Thought Police shoot him dead. Julia runs to join him and is gunned down just as brutally. As her hand reaches for his among the swirling autumn leaves, the camera pans up to Big Brother's poster.

Worried that the first option might be "too morbid" for Americans, Rathvon asked his distributors in the U.S. and UK to put the matter to a vote. Columbia's staff went for depressing, obedient chanting while their British counterparts favored hands-among-the-autumn-leaves mawkishness.[36]

The cheesiness didn't stop there. When London's Warner Theatre hosted the £300,000[37] film's premiere on March 1, 1956, a squad of black-clad Thought Police roared into Leicester Square on motorbikes and escorted Rathvon inside, smiling sweetly.[38] Sonia Orwell boycotted the event, telling the *Daily Mail* that, unlike the BBC's "honest attempt" to do the story justice, the film was a poor reflection of the book. To make matters worse, Rathvon had ignored her pleas to scrap the "happier" ending.[39]

The producer's brazen response was that the rewrite was more logical: "It is the type of ending Orwell might have written if he had not known when he wrote the book that he was dying."[40] This was more than *Sight and Sound*, the most highbrow film journal in Britain, could take. Livid at the movie's insipid, "love conquers all" morality, it accused Rathvon of defending "this cheap and gratuitous piece of bowdlerising in terms almost worthy of Newspeak."[41]

We Are the Deadened

To this viewer at least, the film isn't as bad as it's painted. Once the ominous opening voiceover is out of the way (enhanced by an eerie model shot of the British Isles from space), it settles into a cornily entertaining, shinily oppressive sci-fi groove. Verity's design is an arresting combination of dreary and futuristic; Redgrave makes a convincingly bloodless technocrat; and a handful of Anderson's set pieces impress, whether it's the fast-cut Two Minutes Hate or Winston hiding his diary from the telescreen in his apartment, gracefully kicking it across his floor to the sound of muzak.

Moreover, the images have a scale that the BBC and CBS could never hope to match. Gigantic telescreens, fixed to the sides of buildings, glare down at pedestrians; Thought Police roar through the streets like paramilitary Hell's Angels; trucks with cages attached parade Eurasian prisoners around Victory Square; and for the first time, the countryside looks real.

In 1954, opposite the estimable Peter Cushing, Donald Pleasence oozed star quality as Syme. This time around, as Parsons, he acts Edmond O'Brien off the screen. It's fun, too, to see an uncredited Patrick Troughton of *Doctor Who* fame as a mustachioed telescreen announcer, nine years before he played another sci-fi icon, Winston Smith, on BBC radio.

Unlike *Studio One*, the film dwells on the Party's attitude to sexual relationships. A friend of Julia's, boasting in the cafeteria that the Marriage Committee has arranged her wedding, points out her intended husband: a fat, scowling, bullet-headed older man from the Victory Orations Department who's sitting across the room. At another table, a battleaxe from the Anti-Sex League is talking loudly about smashing the family unit and abolishing love.

The torture scenes, admittedly, are banal, and the image of Edmond O'Brien—looking beery and unshaven, with electrodes attached to his temples—is so silly, you wonder why they used it in the ad campaign (tagline: "A film of tomorrow to SHOCK you today"). Just as Anderson promised, rats are notably absent from the Ministry of Love scenes. There's a darkened Room 101, a cage and some sound effects, yes—but no rodents.[42]

Critics were unforgiving. The book's message, wrote CA Lejeune in *The Observer*, "is pessimistic and negative; its atmosphere cruel and sordid; but the unpleasantness is intellectual. To dress it up as horrid science fiction romance is to miss the point and emphasise its failings."[43]

The *Daily Sketch*'s Harold Conway thought the film reduced Big Brother to "a Little Bore." Heaping praise on Nigel Kneale and Rudolph Cartier's BBC play, he commented: "The film—ten times more costly and spacious— plods through the same episodes without ever capturing Orwell's sardonic,

In the U.S., Columbia marketed *1984* as a standard sci-fi thriller. As well as playing up the romance angle, this poster redesigns the Thought Police uniform and gives one of its spies an Anti-Sex League armband (copyright Columbia Pictures, 1956).

bitter meaning."[44] In the *Daily Worker*, Thomas Spencer agreed that it was "more a dreary bore than a shocker."[45] *Sight and Sound*'s Derek Hill complained that the world shown on screen was "half cheap science-fiction and half studio slum,"[46] while Maryvonne Butcher at *The Tablet* found the whole thing dull—"one of the most resounding disappointments the cinema has yet handed out."[47]

Trade publication *Kinematograph Weekly* wrote off the movie as a "squalid political melodrama" and "the very antithesis of entertainment." The torture would turn stomachs, it warned, adding: "The more realistic the presentation, the more strident and nauseating the hymn of hate becomes."[48] But it was *The Spectator*'s Isabel Quigley who laid into the film most viciously, labeling it "a gloomy giggle" and condemning the ending as a travesty. In the ridiculous torture scenes, she wrote, O'Brien looked sozzled (the actor had a drinking problem in real life). As for Jan Sterling, the "glacial blonde" was "embarrassing beyond critical words."

What sort of audience, Quigley wondered, was this movie hoping to reach? "To anyone who caught even a glimpse of the book's meaning and message, the film must make nonsense; and who would go and see it as a straight, rather coldly acted love story conducted in faintly Martian-looking dress[49]?"

Here and there, critics tempered their misgivings with faint praise. Rather than slate the film for the last few minutes alone, *The Times'* critic, for example, found merit in Anderson's "sombre and sober" approach.[50] The "confined, 'studio' look" was certainly a drawback, noted *The Manchester Guardian*, but overall, the book's force had been diminished, not destroyed.[51]

On 5 March, a BBC show compared the two adaptations, airing Winston and Julia's arrest in its big and small-screen forms. The TV version "had a far more menacing and sinister atmosphere," sniffed Robert Cannell in the *Daily Express*.[52] Kneale, in his 2006 biography, remembered being "hauled" in by TV host Malcolm Muggeridge "to do a live denunciation of it, on the telly. Michael Anderson was there, and Michael and I argued the toss. I said, 'What you've done is, you've turned the story into exactly what Big Brother would have approved of. You've killed it.' Poor Michael looked put out, because he hadn't intended to kill anything. He was the gentlest of people. He'd simply been overridden by the money men."[53]

In fairness, several critics defended the film. These included Edward Goring in the *Daily Mail*, who thought that it was brilliantly directed and should not be missed[54]; Reg Whitley at the *Daily Mirror* ("as a piece of screencraft it is first rate"[55]); and the *Daily Herald's* Anthony Carthew, who found the revised ending "more true to life."[56] *The Daily Film Renter* liked the movie too, informing its readers that "Michael Redgrave as O'Connor gives a brilliant performance; Edmond O'Brien, although physically wrong for the starveling Winston Smith, does give us a sense of the horror of a controlled existence," and "Michael Anderson's direction holds the story in continual suspense."[57]

"Should bring in the customers in droves," concluded another trade paper, *Today's Cinema*.[58] In the event, figures for the Associated British Picture Corporation suggest that *1984* was one of the biggest flops of the fifties, with gross billings of £32,274. Anderson's hit, *The Dam Busters*, took £552,687, while dimly remembered productions such as *Weak and the Wicked*, *Will Any Gentleman*, *For Better for Worse* and *Yield to the Night* all comfortably topped £100,000.[59]

It didn't help that in America, the film was marketed as a standard sci-fi thriller; or that it was released in the fall of 1956 as part of a double bill with B-movie *The Gamma People*[60]—a slice of British, black-and-white hokum in which another burly American (Paul Douglas) curtails a mad scientist's gamma-ray experiments in a minuscule European autocracy.

In common with much of the American press, the reaction to *1984* at *The New York Times* was tepid. The drama, wrote critic AH Weiler, "is fitfully projected and its impact is felt only in a crescendo-like climax. A disturbing fiction that shocked, startled and terrified its readers has been transformed in England into a stark, sober and thoughtful, if not altogether persuasive, film."[61]

By now, Orwell must have seemed like box-office poison. It would be 28 years before another film adaptation made it to the screen.

The Last Laugh

When Sonia finally appeared on camera, it was as part of a documentary on BBC2 in 1965 (see chapter 6). Describing *Nineteen Eighty-Four*, the novel, as "the incredibly subtle working out of an idea," she said that had her husband been in better health, he'd have made a better job of the ending. This wasn't in the sense that Rathvon meant, she maintained. Orwell wouldn't have made it happier, but he would have rewritten it more elegantly.

Agreeing with interviewer Malcolm Muggeridge, who derided the movie's ending as "fatuous," she seized the opportunity to denigrate Rathvon publicly. "The producer said: 'I know it's got an unhappy ending, but I have a belief in human nature.' And I was so cross—I said: 'Well, your belief does you credit, but you've simply missed the point.'"[62]

1984

Winston Smith of the Outer Party: Edmond O'Brien
O'Connor of the Inner Party: Michael Redgrave
Julia of the Outer Party: Jan Sterling
Charrington the junk shop owner: David Kossoff
Jones: Mervyn Johns
Parsons: Donald Pleasence
Selina Parsons: Carol Wolveridge
Outer Party announcer: Ernest Clark
Inner Party official: Patrick Allen
Rutherford: Ronan O'Casey
Outer Party orator: Michael Ripper
Outer party orator: Ewen Solon
Prisoner: Kenneth Griffith
Kalador: Bernard Rebel (uncredited)[63]
Man on telescreen: Patrick Troughton (uncredited)
Big Brother: John Vernon (uncredited)
Telescreen voice: Anthony Jacobs (uncredited)
Screenplay by: William P. Templeton and Ralph Bettinson
Director: Michael Anderson
Producer: N. Peter Rathvon
Art director: Terence Verity
Music: Malcolm Arnold

5

The World of George Orwell: Keep the Aspidistra Flying (1965)

In the years that followed the mid-fifties Orwell craze, it seemed for a time that his most popular works had been well and truly mined out. To Hollywood, this most gloomy of English writers held scant box-office appeal. Yet that bastion of British high culture, the BBC, never quite got over its first *bona fide* screen sensation.

In 1957, theater producer Henry Burke wrote to the corporation's drama department with a view to consulting Nigel Kneale about a *Nineteen Eighty-Four* stage musical, possibly based on his teleplay.[1] (The idea of a musical was mooted well into the seventies, notably by David Bowie.[2])

In the meantime, the BBC's efforts to restage Kneale's play for the millions who hadn't owned a TV in 1954 kept foundering over rights issues. The Orwell estate rejected its overtures three times: in May 1957,[3] July 1959[4] and December 1961.[5] A month after the third attempt, Sonia Orwell decided to play ball, agreeing in January that BBC TV could make another *Nineteen Eighty-Four* in 1962.[6] The year came and went, the rights lapsed again[7] and the odds of a return to Oceania looked remote.

This changed when the BBC launched its minority channel, BBC2, in 1964. Anthology series *Theatre 625*, named after the 625-line UHF system (the high definition of its day, unavailable on older sets), exemplified its experimental nature, adapting literature that sometimes bordered on the obscure. The Sunday-night show set a template when it dramatized three works by early 20th-century novelist Ford Madox Ford in December 1964. When it emerged that Orwell would receive the same treatment, the *Daily Mail* announced: "Big Brother will watch again."[8]

Speaking to *The Stage and Television Today*, producer Cedric Messina said that the idea of an Orwell trilogy "just grewed." Initially, he and Kneale had simply reworked the *Nineteen Eighty-Four* script. "This doesn't mean altering George Orwell's book," he made clear, "but the pertinent points that needed to be made in 1952 (sic) are very different from the pertinent points we want to make in 1965." Once that was out of the way, he and his team had considered Orwell's other novels.[9]

Directing the trilogy was Christopher Morahan, who'd brought to life another of Kneale's scripts—his legendary (and long-lost) science-fiction classic, *The Road*[10]—for BBC1 series *The Wednesday Play* two years earlier.[11]

In the event, *The World of George Orwell* was more of a tetralogy (or quadrilogy, to use a more modern term). Shown in an 8 p.m. time slot, it started on 7 November with *Keep the Aspidistra Flying* and continued with Halas and Batchelor's *Animal Farm*, an acclaimed *Coming Up for Air* and the much-hyped Kneale remake, titled *1984* rather than *Nineteen Eighty-Four*.

Under David Attenborough, "a marvelous controller of BBC2," these were exciting times, says Morahan: "Creative life at the BBC drama department, at the plays department, was all on the same corridor. Everybody's door was open and people were just very interested in each other. Not jealous, but looking for opportunities to do things."[12]

As it was prone to do with archive material, the BBC junked his Orwell plays to save space. That *1984* exists is a tribute to the American Library of Congress, which yielded a treasure trove of missing British shows in 2010.

From Bad to Verse

Published in 1936, Orwell's shamelessly autobiographical *Keep the Aspidistra Flying* is the story of 29-year-old Gordon Comstock, who resigns his copywriting job at London's New Albion agency to pursue his dream of becoming a poet. As far as *The Times Literary Supplement* was concerned, his first volume, *Mice*, had shown exceptional promise. There's a snag, though: sales of the book are dismal.

With the bad grace of a self-pitying whiner, Comstock rails against a society in thrall to "the money god." He's sexually frustrated on top of that, because his girlfriend at the New Albion, Rosemary Waterlow, hangs on tight to her virginity. Women, as he sees it, are born materialists, eager for a life of marriage and respectability with whichever hapless fool they can snare. If he were rich, he thinks, Rosemary would sleep with him. In the meantime, whenever he is short of cash (which is often), he leeches off his sister Julia, a downtrodden waitress and spinster.

Working listlessly in a bookshop in genteel Hampstead by day, then returning to the boarding house of straight-laced curtain-twitcher Mrs.

Wisbeach to write his next masterpiece, *London Pleasures*, it's all Gordon can do to contain his resentful sneers. He has a special disdain for aspidistras, in his eyes the ultimate symbol of middle-class conformity and respectability, and takes sadistic pleasure in scorching the leaves of the plant in his room.

Most of his work is published by Philip Ravelston, a rich friend who runs the magazine *Antichrist*. Ravelston professes to care about poor families in Middlesbrough (a deprived town in North East England) and describes himself as a socialist. His beautiful, languid girlfriend, Hermione, makes the same claim, but talks without irony about how the lower classes smell. She holds Comstock in contempt, thinking him a talentless parasite.

One Thursday afternoon, in response to a party invite, Gordon walks to the townhouse of critic Paul Doring, only to find it empty, save for a maid. Doring has changed the date to Saturday and neglected to tell him. The well-off socialite writes to apologize, but Comstock, stewing in humiliation, writes back: "Go and fuck yourself."

Two-fifths of the way through the book, Rosemary appears in person; previously, she and Gordon have corresponded by post. After tramping the streets and bickering good-naturedly, the pair arrange a Sunday outing to the countryside. On the day itself, they end up in a swanky hotel restaurant, where Comstock spends practically all his cash. Alighting on an isolated alcove of trees and vegetation, the couple lie down to make love, but Gordon's thoughtlessness (he hasn't brought a condom) ruins the moment.

Back in London, a large check arrives from an American magazine to which Comstock has submitted a poem. In jubilation, he treats Rosemary and Ravelston to a slap-up meal in Soho, then, while sozzled, tries to force himself on his beloved. Watching her storm off, Comstock drags a reluctant Ravelston to the pub and, blind drunk, goes hunting for a prostitute.

Passing out in a seedy hotel room, he wakes up next morning in a police cell, charged with being drunk and disorderly. He escapes with a fine, paid by Ravelston, but is expelled from his job and lodging house when the news makes the local paper (a court reporter heard him giving his profession as "poet"). Perversely, he welcomes his descent into abject poverty, renting a room in the slums of Lambeth, South London, and working in a squalid cellar bookshop for Mr. Cheeseman, an amiable philistine who views literature as a mere commodity.

Whereas Mrs. Wisbeach was puritanical, new landlady Mrs. Meakin is relaxed about women staying over. So, on a one-off visit to her pitiful boyfriend's pad, Rosemary spends the night and instantly falls pregnant. Confronted with this fact, Comstock faces up to his responsibilities. He marries Rosemary, follows his natural calling at the New Albion and settles down to a life of domesticity—insisting, as the novel ends, that the Comstocks must have an aspidistra in the house.

A Big Admirer

As script editor of *Theatre 625*, Rosemary Hill needed a talented scribe to do *Keep the Aspidistra Flying* and *Coming Up for Air* justice. The man she picked was Robin Chapman, an actor-turned-writer who'd made his name in London at Joan Littlewood's Theatre Workshop.

"It was there, with the improvisations and the active participation of actors, that one started to think of writing," he says. "Indeed, I worked rather hard with Joan on *The Hostage*—Brendan Behan's [play, which originally featured *Aspidistra*'s lead, Alfred Lynch]—because he was drunk and didn't finish it. Also, I was the third person to read a play called *A Taste of Honey*. Joan had received it from a 16-year-old in Manchester and, as was her custom, she handed it first to the manager, Gerry Raffles, and then to one of her company, and that one happened to be me."[13]

In the space of a year—1963 or thereabouts—a novel, a stage play and a two-part BBC play, commissioned by Hill, changed the course of Chapman's career. In 1965, he says, "Rosemary asked me, would I be interested in doing *Keep the Aspidistra Flying* and *Coming Up for Air*? I wanted to do *Nineteen Eighty-Four* as well, but the Nigel Kneale one was already going to be revived.

"Anyway, I did those, and the reason I did was because as a writer, I adored Orwell's work. I've got a paperback of *The Road to Wigan Pier*, which Gollancz published. I think it's in 1939 it came out, for the Left Book Club.[14] In it there are photographs, and some of the photographs are what working-class housing was like in various parts of the country. One of them is of a Welsh village called Blaina, which was a mining community. My mother was a miner's daughter, and she came from Blaina. The kind of terraced house which her sister, my aunt, lived in and I was occasionally evacuated to during the war was in Blaina. So, when I saw that…

"Also, of course, in *Keep the Aspidistra Flying*, the idea of a man saying, 'Well, how do you keep your integrity and be poor?' knocked me out. *Coming Up for Air*, with its premonitions of war and all the loudspeakers in the streets and everything, pretending that everything was going to be all right, really spoke to me."

Chapman would have liked to adapt *A Clergyman's Daughter*, Orwell's 1935 novel about a woman who loses her memory and falls in with vagrants. "I very much wanted to do that because of the scene in Trafalgar Square.

There's a central episode where, rather like in *Down and Out in Paris and London*, he observes closely and puts into dialogue what happens at night in the square, where tramps and down-and-out poor people huddled together on benches. The police came along and moved them along, so they had to go from bench to bench, clinging to each other.

"But to get back to practicalities about filming in those days, I think Christopher did very well indeed, within the restrictions of what it was to put on a play like that. First of all, he shot a lot in close-up in the studio with studio cameras, but very closely and quickly and cutting. And then, with the little bit of outside broadcasting on 16mm, he was equally clever, and so he managed to create—I wish they still existed, the tapes—something pretty cinematic."

In a full-page preview of *The World of George Orwell* season, the *Radio Times* commended the men for expanding on *Aspidistra*'s "rather slight and novelettish story," so that "it becomes not only a chronicle of Gordon Comstock and his plight but a picture of British life and attitudes in the early 1930s."[15]

"It wasn't as stilted as one might have expected it to be," agrees Chapman. "Christopher did a grand job on both."

Poster Boys

Half a century later, cloudy memories are inevitable. On one matter, though, Morahan and Chapman have sharply different recollections. The director maintains that *Aspidistra* was entirely studio-bound and deliberately non-naturalistic, while the writer is adamant that location filming took place. So, who's right?

It's true that the play was mostly shot on videotape at BBC Television Centre, from 17–19 April.[16] But Chapman is correct: there were indeed film sequences.

In March, Alfred Lynch had been cast on the strength of his stage performance opposite Peter O'Toole in the Royal Court's *Waiting for Godot*. "The part of Gordon, a poverty stricken poet of high ideals will, I suspect, interest you," wrote Morahan.[17] By 29 March, he and co-star Anne Stallybrass were recording scenes in Buckinghamshire.[18] More work followed on 5–6 April, with the second day devoted to filming at Ealing Studios.

Morahan's confusion may have something to do with his reliance on back projection, using his own shots and stock footage. In a contrivance that critics remarked on at the time, actors stepped into and out of these projections, flitting between the media of film (shot outside) and videotape (shot in the studio). If the journalists had a beef, it was that the play was overloaded with gimmicks. Characters break the fourth wall to inform viewers of Gordon's history and family, a talking advertising poster torments him, and fantasy sequences keep the narrative bouncing along in surprising ways.

Chapman's flexing his creative muscles from the off, as Comstock traipses past houses with aspidistras in the windows. Gazing upon a row of advertising hoardings, the poet bastardizes 1 Corinthians 13 from the King James Bible: "Though I speak with the tongues of men and of angels, and have not charity [or 'money,' in the script's case], I am become as sounding brass, or a tinkling cymbal."

The 1997 *Aspidistra* movie, also known as *A Merry War*, lifted much the same joke from Orwell for its opening scene and took a linear approach to chronology, beginning with Comstock's professional suicide. The BBC play, which prefers the back-and-forth structure of the novel, shifts to the Hampstead bookshop almost immediately.

Gordon banters with the browsing customers—the matronly Mrs. Weaver and Mrs. Penn, and a moneyed "nancy boy" who pronounces his Rs as Ws[19]—and draws the young man's attention to *Mice* without revealing he's the author. Just as he's on the verge of a sale, Mrs. Penn gives the game away by calling him "Mr. Comstock."

> YOUNG MAN: I didn't wealise you wote, Mr. Comstock.
> GORDON: Mm? Oh, yes.
> YOUNG MAN: Wather a nerve, weally. To sell oneself, don't you feel?
> (DELICATELY HE PLACES "Mice" ON TOP OF A CAT LOVER'S ANNUAL AND MINCES OUT, GIGGLING. GORDON STARES RIGIDLY AFTER HIM.)

The bitter internal diatribes of the novel—Comstock's rants about money, women, work and so on, which go on for pages at a time—are mirrored on screen by having him talk to himself. Before long, however, Chapman gets around this with a zinger of a concept.

Described by one TV critic as "a sardonic chorus to the story,"[20] the character of Corner Table—a smarmy, bespectacled cartoon clerk who advertises the hot drink "Bovex"—is lifted from the book, where he's the object of Comstock's scorn. On TV, the poster comes alive and gives as good as he gets.

> CORNER TABLE: Buck up, chappie. Why so down in the mouth? Know the trouble with you, old sport? You need a bit of the old rumble tumble, roll me over in the clover. Need a little girlie, you do, old chum. Take my advice, get yourself a proper job, earn yourself a spot of cash, buy a decent suit and then, ah, presto, Rosemary....

How, one wonders, was this effect achieved? When the press in 1965 referred to an "animated" poster, they weren't talking about cartoons. In actuality, Corner Table was a three-foot-high image with movable lips and eyes, drawn by the BBC's visual effects department[21] and given a voice by actor Clive Elliott.

"There was a large canvas—very large, about three feet by four feet—with a picture of the character of Corner Table on it, like a cartoon," says Elliott, who lives in Des Moines, Iowa. "You could operate it from behind—you could make the mouth move and the eyes move. So that was part of my job, doing the voice and operating the picture.

"The mouth was elasticated, so I stood behind this damn thing with a microphone. I don't think I could see what the camera was doing. It wasn't very well arranged and they didn't even support the canvas for me. I had to hold the frame up. Oh, it was wretched."[22]

Morahan was more taken with the idea. "At about that time, I was deeply influenced by the Brecht, shall we say, use of alienation," he says. "You draw attention, in a way, to truth by doing it in a fresh way. To have a talk with a man in a billboard—if you're alone and broke in London, maybe you do find friends there and imagine what it's like for that man to be speaking. 'Has he just said something to me as I was walking down the road?' It's marvelous.

"But it was also very pleasing because, at that time, television was largely naturalistic.... What you were doing was saying, 'This is the real world.' Doing *Aspidistra*, clearly it's not the real world, because posters don't talk to you. You look at it freshly and think about it."

Chapman makes another point. "The thing of big posters was—how shall I say it?—a pre-vision of the posters of Big Brother. They haunt Orwell's work. I did particularly want to do *Nineteen Eighty-Four* but the Nigel Kneale one had been a great success and was reproduced. In the end, I wanted Winston Smith to look up at a poster of Big Brother and it's turned into himself looking at him. By being brainwashed, he had created what had created him. I think it might have been rather a shocking end. Anyway, it didn't happen."

It's a Rich Man's World

If it's any consolation to him, Chapman's words leap off the page. Take the scene at Mrs. Wisbeach's lodgings in Willowbed Road, where Gordon is cursing Rosemary for neglecting to write him a letter. Fellow lodger Flaxman—a lascivious 38-year-old sales rep, who's estranged from his wife—enters flamboyantly, singing *Who's Afraid of the Big Bad Wolf?* Dressed in a grey suit, trilby, yellow shoes and vulgar overcoat, the jolly fat man puts a friendly arm around Comstock and invites him to the Crighton Arms pub, where he intends to pinch the barmaid's bottom. Met with a sulky refusal, he dances airily out of the front door, heart set on some mild slap and tickle.

After trying his best to scorch the aspidistra in his room with matches, Gordon fantasizes that he's in a smart bookshop, autographing copies of *London Pleasures* for Mrs. Penn, Mrs. Weaver and the effeminate young man. All three are fawning over him, watched over by his manager, Ravelston. But as Gordon snaps back to reality, he throws himself on his bed and stretches out despairingly. At the Crighton Arms, Flaxman is having a better time of it: drinking, singing and kissing the barmaid without a care in the world.

Ravelston, Comstock's rich friend, crops up again at the Ascot horse races (a yearly event that gives the wealthy an excuse to show off), breaking the fourth wall to address BBC2's audience directly. As the back projection moves on to the stock exchange, he reels off a multitude of facts about Gordon's poetry, pride, politics, preoccupations and personal life. It's an info-dump, but a classy one.

> (RAVELSTON STANDS IN FRONT OF THE ASPIDISTRA WE SAW AT THE BEGINNING. HE IS A SENSITIVE, CHARMING, FRIENDLY PERSON. HE IS ALSO A RICH MAN WHO WISHES TO BECOME AN HONORARY MEMBER OF THE PROLETARIAT. HE WEARS VERY LOOSE FLANNEL BAGS, A GREY PULLOVER AND MUCH WORN BROWN SHOES. HE HAS A TRICK WHEN EXPLAINING ANYTHING—AND HE IS ALWAYS EXPLAINING—OF RUBBING HIS NOSE WITH THE BACK OF HIS FOREFINGER. HIS TONE IS COMMITTED IRONIC.)
>
> RAVELSTON: Of course, one has to admit this is not a hopeful age to write poetry in. Hardly hopeful at all. Unless one has a private income.
>
> (HE LAUGHS A LITTLE SELF-CONSCIOUSLY.)
>
> > That's why my heart goes out to Gordon Comstock—author of "Mice." My name is Ravelston, by the way. Not that it will mean anything to you but.... I'm a friend of Comstock. Sometimes I feel I must be his only friend. He's rather a lonely person. He's an idealist, of course....

At the end of Ravelston's lengthy monologue, the setting changes. Gordon is sitting alone at the table in his room, head in hands. He stirs, takes a sheet of blank paper and stares at it in despair. Slowly, Rosemary's face appears in the blankness. "I love you," she says.

"You have broken my heart" he scrawls across her face and she fades away, leaving just the words.

Next day, a more chipper Comstock heads over to Doring's house, where the fantasies continue. At first, he imagines mingling with Stephen Spender and Cyril Connolly, the latter referred to in the script as "big male head."[23] So strong is his yearning for sex, however, that when a maid answers the door and says the party's been canceled, he has visions of her taking off her clothes.

> (SLOWLY, IN GORDON'S LASCIVIOUS VISION, THE GIRL TAKES OFF HER CAP. SHE DELIBERATELY UNTIES HER APRON. SHE LETS IT FALL. SHE BEGINS TO UNBUTTON THE BODICE OF HER DRESS. SHE IS SMIL-ING. CUT TO GORDON, HIS FACE SET HARD WITH LUST.)

Ravelston, on exposition duties again, returns in the scene that follows to recount the history of Comstock's family, an uninspiring bunch whose line looks set to end with Gordon and Julia. "They drifted off into little businesses which petered out," he explains, "or boarding houses, or mental homes."

Walking the streets in low spirits, Gordon runs into Corner Table, who challenges him to return to his job at the New Albion.

> CORNER TABLE: Those ads you did for the Queen of Sheba! Boy, oh boy! They were A-1. They stuck. They rankled. A hundred lies in as many words. Snappy, neat. You could be writing copy for me, old chum....
>
> (THE POSTER MAKES A HORRIBLE GURGLING SOUND.)
>
> Excuse me, chappie—don't feel so hot—too much blasted Bovex.... Oh, lor.... Excuse me.... Whoops a daisy....
>
> (CORNER TABLE'S MOUTH SUDDENLY SPEWS OUT A BRIGHT STREAM OF MONEY—HALF CROWNS, FLORINS, SHILLINGS AND SIXPENCES. THEY FALL AT GORDON'S FEET. HE FOLLOWS THEIR FALL AND LOOKS AT THE GROUND AT HIS FEET. NO MONEY, ONLY DRIFTING RUBBISH. GORDON TURNS AND GOES.)

That night, Comstock returns to Mrs. Wisbeach's and finds Rosemary waiting for him outside. She has forgiven him for his last, petulant missive. The two walk the streets to avoid scandalizing his landlady and playfully wage a battle of the sexes, largely with Orwell's dialogue. ("I enjoyed [Gordon's] callowness in pursuing affection with women," says Morahan, "because in a way, I was kind of shy about that as well, and remembered that.")

Urged on by Corner Table, Gordon visits big sister Julia's bedsitter in Earl's Court, lined with photos of the Comstock family looking serious and depressed. With money scrounged from his sibling, he takes Rosemary to an autumnal Burnham Beeches and buys them a meal they can't afford, from a young waiter with a "posh yet foreign accent that hides his native Peckham."[24]

From the failed attempt at outdoor sex to post–Lambeth married life, the remainder of Orwell's plot survives more or less intact. Unlike the nineties movie, though, there are no concessions to modern attitudes or political correctness[25]: no attempt, for instance, to airbrush out the two streetwalkers Gordon hooks up with ("Ooh, you 'ave got a cheek!" they keep exclaiming), or to deny that second-hand bookseller Mr. Cheeseman is—as the script describes him—"short and deformed."[26]

As Comstock calls off his one-man rebellion and drops *London Pleasures* in a trash can,[27] snide Corner Table—alone and talking to himself—welcomes the inspired copywriter back to the human race. The camera zooms in on Gordon and Rosemary's aspidistra.

> CORNER TABLE: At last, at last—something is happening in the Comstock family.
> FADE OUT

Flying High

In the main, critics responded warmly. Peter Black of the *Daily Mail* looked forward to what he hoped would be an "exceptionally interesting" season and judged *Aspidistra* "an auspicious start," despite some misgivings. Its whimsy, especially in the early scenes, was a poor substitute for Orwell's heartfelt anger, he thought. Lynch, in his early scenes, gave Gordon "a touch of humorous exaggeration," *Billy Liar*–like; but when Stallybrass appeared, "with exactly the right shade of hopeful anxiety and niceness," the play began to reflect the book's tone more accurately.[28]

The *Mirror's* Kenneth Eastaugh singled out Chapman for praise, handing him an imaginary bouquet of aspidistras for "a script of supreme craftsmanship" while musing that Morahan's gimmicks "may have been a bit overdone."[29]

At *The Guardian*, Mary Crozier found the play's "technical tricks and affectations" a turn-off at first, but was taken with the story's truthfulness and the charisma of the two leads.[30] In *The Tablet*, she wrote that Comstock's embrace of respectability was "a humane and somehow not entirely a bitter comment on man's predicament."[31] The *Daily Telegraph's* critic, "LL," considered the adaptation "excellent" and wondered what children of the welfare state had made of it[32]; while over at the *Daily Worker*, Stewart Lane liked its "clever use of stills, backdrops and created fantasy" but couldn't resist a dig at his less obviously socialistic follow-ups, *Animal Farm* and *Nineteen Eighty-Four*.[33]

The *Times'* critic admired the play's "raciness" and "geniality," applauding Lynch for his expressiveness and Morahan for his directorial vigor.[34] *Variety* liked Lynch too, but thought Morahan's careful treatment "could not disguise the lack of dramatic horse-power in the story, which was little more than a placid set of incidents in the life of Gordon Comstock."[35] The *Spectator's* Stuart Hood objected to the "novelist's dialogue" and couldn't get over the leading man's sixties accent, observing that "he neither speaks, moves, behaves, nor looks like a young intellectual of the 'thirties."[36] Frederick Laws at *The Listener*, having made a similar point ("No one's speech was quite as class-defined as it should have been"), said the details of life as a young, poor poet in the thirties were "uncomfortably exact."[37]

To Morahan, the play is ancient history, but he retains a fondness for Orwell to this day. "He has so much to offer. He's the most English author I know. Utterly English, with an ability to observe and an instinct to object."

Chapman, for his part, mourns the loss of the archive recording but clings to the memory of Lynch and Stallybrass's chemistry. "One scene was of them going through the autumn woods, kicking up leaves as they danced hand-in-hand," he says.

The World of George Orwell: Keep the Aspidistra Flying

Gordon Comstock: Alfred Lynch
Young man: Charles Hodgson
Mrs. Weaver: Winifred Dennis
Mrs. Penn: Marie Hopps
Tramp: Sydney Bromley
Old woman: Hilda Barry
Voice of Corner Table: Clive Elliott
Rosemary: Anne Stallybrass
Mr. Erskine: Norman Pitt
Mrs. Wisbeach: Margaret Durnell
Mr. Flaxman: Norman Mitchell
Ravelston: Tristram Jellinek
Barmaid: Renee Hill
Hermione: Suzanne Jefferies
Maid: Tanya Trude
Julia: Susan Field

Waiter: Alec Wallis
Bank clerk: Eric Longworth
Tarts: Alicia Catrall, Christine Ozanne
Police sergeant: Arthur Mayne
Police constable: David Locke
Magistrate: Bartlett Mullins
Cheeseman: Sydney Arnold
Mrs. Meakin: Beatrice Greeke
Young girl: Vickery Turner
Librarian: Pauline Winter
Library assistant: Sheila Grant
Dramatized by: Robin Chapman
Director: Christopher Morahan
Producer: Cedric Messina
Designer: Richard Wilmot

6

George Orwell 1903–1950 (1965)

First, let's get the bad news out of the way. Videotape was an expensive and bulky medium in the sixties, which explains in part why the BBC wiped so many of its treasures. Sad to say, the BBC's Orwell trilogy, stored as it was on tape, must have seemed an obvious candidate for destruction.[1]

Now for the good. TV's first documentary to examine the author at length, shot on film in June/July 1965 to complement the *Theatre 625* season, survived the seventies purges and clips of it have been turning up in factual programs since the eighties.

The show was the brainchild of staff producer John Furness, who in April wrote to BBC management about *George Orwell and His Times*, as he called it. The idea was "not only to tell viewers about Orwell, but to place him firmly in relation to his time—socially and politically—thereby adding to the understanding and enjoyment of the plays."[2]

Journalist Malcolm Muggeridge, who'd been friends with Orwell in his later years, agreed to present the show. He would interview three of the great man's confidantes: author Cyril Connolly, a friend from prep school and Eton who'd commissioned essays from Orwell as editor of *Horizon* magazine; Avril Dunn, née Blair, the little sister who'd looked after Orwell on the Scottish island of Jura as he'd drafted *Nineteen Eighty-Four*; and Sonia, the glamorous, tough-as-old-boots widow.

This was the second film to be directed by Jack Bond, then in his 20s. "I was a very impatient young man,"[3] says Bond, whose reputation today rests, for the most part, on *Dali in New York* (a portrait of the artist, filmed over the Christmas of 1965), his *avant-garde* British films, *South Bank Show* arts documentaries and collaborations with the Pet Shop Boys. "I flatly refused to shoot anything I didn't want to shoot, which was dangerous in those days, but I knew I would not stay [at the BBC] long.

"Before that film, I made *The Pity of War*. It was a film about the First World War seen through the eyes of [the poet] Wilfred Owen. Huw Weldon, who I suppose was my promoter, really, was a great director-general, maybe the best ever. Much adored. Those of us that loved him did well and those that didn't get on with him didn't do so well. He was very tough. You had to be tough in return, but he took it. *The Pity of War* was a hit and for your first film ever to be a smash, really sets you on a different path."

Offered the Orwell documentary as a follow-up, Bond insisted on meeting his presenter first. Calling at Malcolm and Kitty Muggeridge's house, "I fell in love with both of them. I don't know what other people say, but I found him a generous-spirited man. Warm to a tee, provided you were fucking bluntly honest about where you stood. He didn't care where you stood, provided you were honest about it. You could not lie to Malcolm. Nobody could. Some people did not like him at all but I adored him."

The same could plainly not be said of the producer. "My unit did not get along with Mr. Furness," says Bond. "He was the wrong guy to put in the game. Didn't fit. I must admit, there was a kind of anarchic friendship between myself, Connolly, Muggeridge and all those around him. This guy just didn't fit in the equation.

"We went up to Scotland. Rather than drag the English guys up there, I hired a Scottish crew and we had a motorboat to get to Jura. Not a big one, but I suppose a 20-foot, open power launch. Furness was really getting up my nose. Anyway, we drew alongside the jetty to moor and somebody went forward with the bow line. Furness had jumped off, but then he tried to come back on board before we'd attached the mooring line with the bow. Of course, he went straight in the drink. Suddenly, you could not see any member of my crew because they were all in the bottom of the boat, crying with laughter.

"I'll tell you an interesting story about Muggeridge and the crew. I like using handheld or, if I'm going to have a tripod, I'll have a Yankee tripod, heavy, with a big, fluid head on it. Heavy kit. The cameraman says to me: 'Christ almighty, the tripod and head are missing.' There was a steep climb up the hill to Orwell's house [Barnhill on Jura], a tiny place. Suddenly I spotted it. There's Muggeridge, halfway up the fucking steep climb, lugging the tripod and head. That was him. He did not believe in letting them do the donkey work. If he was on board, he became a member of the crew. I've never seen that before or since."

Schools of Thought

The 45-minute show aired on BBC2 at 9:15 p.m. on Saturday, 20 November. The opening moments are taken up with images of childhood—of a boy on a bicycle going fishing—and as Muggeridge contemplates the importance of the young Eric Blair's hobby, he reads from *Coming Up for Air* (dramatized the following evening) to illustrate its relevance to George Orwell's writing. A day or two before his death, he visited Orwell in hospital and saw a fishing rod at the foot of his bed, which he planned to use once he'd recuperated. "Towards the end of his life, he increasingly reverted to his origins."

The emphasis then shifts to Connolly, filmed on the Sussex Downs, at Windsor Great Park and at the pavilion near Eastbourne. The two men discuss the all-pervasive snobbery of the years before 1914 and, guided by Muggeridge's questions, their early interest in sex. Blair had almost no homosexual feelings, says Connelly, and all the boys had "a very hard time" avoiding masturbation. The discussion turns to games (both were poor cricketers) and boyhood reading habits (Edgar Allan Poe's *The Masque of the Red Death* and HG Wells, in Blair's case). When asked for a portrait of Orwell the Etonian, Connolly's first instinct is to say that no one could bully him. In one memorable instance, Blair saved him from a gang of bullies.

Much as he enjoys Orwell's writing, Connolly confesses that he doesn't rate him as a novelist. At this juncture, he pulls out a letter from 1916, informing his mother that Blair, the best poet in the school, had honestly critiqued his poem on the death of imperialist Lord Kitchener. "The whole thing is neat, elegant and polished," wrote Eric, whose poem about the same event—considered a national tragedy at the time—made it into the local newspaper. His greatness as a writer, adds Connolly, is that "you feel his presence completely there." The "strange, gentle, critical, cynical personality comes out." Even his pessimism is positive. "It's a bracing pessimism, a feeling that once you admit the worst, everything's a bit more fun all round."

Oh, Brother

In the Jura sequence—which starts on a boat and carries on to Barnhill by road—Avril Dunn takes us through her big brother's adolescence, when his principal fondness was for shooting and fishing. He showed no great literary talent, she says. Instead, she remembers him and his friends gunning down a rare, red squirrel—an act of eco-vandalism that haunted him well into adulthood.

On their father's pension of £400 a year (he returned from India at the age of 50) the family lived quite comfortably, she adds. Richard Blair was a withdrawn, vague man, rather like Eric turned out to be. Their mother, Ida, had a much more vital personality.

At the house, Dunn points out the room where Orwell worked on his last novel. Dismissing the suggestion that he was writing against time, she says he knew he was ill, but never entertained "the death wish."

Muggeridge speaks from experience about Orwell's self-image: the nagging feeling that he was unattractive, even smelly. Dunn replies that it was "obviously untrue" and that he was "a cleanliness maniac." When the two discuss his tubercular problems, Avril brings up his six months' convalescence in Hairmyres Hospital, East Kilbride, in 1947–48 and says that if he'd carried on looking after himself, he'd probably still be alive.

From Me to You

Connolly returns for a segment recorded on the roof of BBC Broadcasting House in London, though this time the emphasis is on Sonia, his former assistant at *Horizon*, making her first[4] (and, it appears, only) appearance on British television. Topics include the ending of *Nineteen Eighty-Four* ("the working out of an idea which must be ineluctable"), his debut novel *Burmese Days* (both touching and absurd, she thinks), his sudden wealth when America's Book of the Month Club published *Animal Farm* (the taxman took 70 percent of his first £10,000) and the affluent young men who identify with characters in *Keep the Aspidistra Flying*.

Muggeridge, alone, pops up on England's south coast next, expounding on Orwell's fascinations. With his essays on subjects such as boys' comics and seaside postcards, the author showed an interest in pop culture that was unusual in its day. Muggeridge asks a kiosk-owner on Brighton Pier, Mrs. Hough, whether children still read *The Gem* and *The Magnet*. No, she says, they want "the American comics and the Beatle books."[5]

The ending—another piece to camera—is a curious mixture of personal reminiscence, history lesson and old-fogey editorializing. Orwell had a passion for firearms, claims Muggeridge, citing the Spanish Civil War and one of his essays on Burma, *Shooting an Elephant*. He loved England but hated the British Empire, which was doomed the minute India gained independence. As for 1984—well, the horror of 1965 is quite different: "an aimless, vacuous one, a pin-table rather than a rock, numbers inanely registering." There's no need for doublethink, says Muggeridge, because no one is thinking any more.

Hidden Tensions

It's clear from the BBC's transcripts, which detail every take, that the documentary could have been markedly different. In one unused sequence, for example, filmed in Salehurst Church, Robertsbridge, East Sussex, Muggeridge gave a detailed description of Orwell's Anglican funeral (which took place in a different chapel altogether). The coffin was long, he remembers, and the congregation sang the hymns lustily.

On his return to the BBC in London, Bond compiled a rough cut that disappointed Humphrey Burton, head of music and arts programs. In a scathing letter to producer Furness, Burton complained that Connolly overbalanced the rest of the contributors, that Orwell's ideas were poorly explored, that the choice of interviewees was arbitrary and that a badly shot Sonia failed to reveal anything about her late husband. The solution was for Bond to prepare another cut, Burton insisted, adding: "I am extremely disappointed that the tensions between you were concealed from me until this stage."[6]

In a preview piece for the *Radio Times*, Muggeridge argued that interviewing a large cross-section of Orwell's acquaintances would have been inappropriate, as he was "altogether too out-of-the-way and angular." The aim, he wrote, "was not to produce an exhaustive critical study of Orwell's work, or a biographical study of him, but just convey an impression of the sort of human being he was as seen through the eyes of the four of us."[7]

The program as broadcast "gave quite a strong feeling of what its subject was really like," wrote *Observer* critic Maurice Richardson,[8] though JDS Haworth in *The Listener* begged to differ, suggesting that Orwell "was only allowed to appear dimly from time to time through Mr. Muggeridge's posturing shadow."[9] In his book *George Orwell: The Politics of Literary Reputation*, Orwell scholar Professor John Rodden calls the documentary "reverential" and "a frank contribution to a cult."[10]

BBC Audience Research estimated that 0.1 percent of the UK's 50 million population—that's 50,000 people—watched the show.[11] A panel of 30 such viewers gave the program a "satisfactory" Reaction Index score of 64. One respondent, a librarian, observed that as well as possessing an intimate understanding of Orwell, all the speakers were interesting in their own right. A third of the sample found the attempts at naturalness—such as Connolly and Muggeridge lying on the grass—"damagingly distracting."[12]

Five decades on, Bond is pleased with the film but full of rancor about Furness, who died in 1996.[13] "I made a decision at the end of it never to have a producer again as long as I lived. And I never have. I do not go near a project unless I'm producer and director. You can't have some wet blanket around. This bastard, he was a sworn enemy, really. The unrelieved joy when he fell in the sea."

George Orwell 1903–1950

Director: Jack Bond
Producer: John Furness

Presenter: Malcolm Muggeridge,
with Cyril Connolly, Avril Blair
and Sonia Orwell

7

The World of George Orwell: Coming Up for Air (1965)

It's a curious book, *Coming Up for Air*, and on first reading, not an obvious candidate for the screen. Published in June 1939, three months before the Second World War broke out, it combines freewheeling reminiscences of a romanticized Edwardian England with premonitions of the Blitz and an underlying suspicion that "progress" isn't all it's cracked up to be.

The protagonist of the novel, written in the first person, is George Bowling, a tubby, 45-year-old salesman for the Flying Salamander insurance company. He lives in the suburbs, in a mortgaged house in Ellesmere Road, West Bletchley, with his nagging, vapid and (rightfully) suspicious wife Hilda and their annoying children Lorna and Billy.

Taking a commuter train into London, Bowling eyes an RAF bomber plane overhead and pictures a grim near-future in which Britain must defend itself from fascism. In the Strand, he imagines the air-raid sirens and the havoc of the German bombing raids. But when a newspaper hoarding about King Zog of Albania catches his eye, it triggers memories of a Sunday 38 years earlier, listening to a sermon in Lower Binfield parish church, Oxfordshire, about Og the king of Bashan. This longing for a gentler, better world that can never be recaptured is really the book's core. Which raises a question: was this lost TV play told in flashback?

A good chunk of the novel—perhaps half—is devoted to George's youth, his army service in the Great War and his early career in civvy street. We read about his father's seed business, which went into a steady decline when a larger store opened up in competition; Elsie, the young woman he "lived in sin" with until he enlisted; and, for a good number of pages, his infatuation with fishing from the ages of eight to 15. One of his strongest memories is of finding an unnoticed pond, alive with colossal carp, in the grounds of Binfield House stately home. For reasons Orwell doesn't really explain, the teenage George vows to return there with a fishing rod but fails to get around to it.

Out on an assignment in his car one afternoon, middle-aged George has a brainwave. With money he's won furtively on the horses, he'll revisit Lower Binfield for a week, telling Hilda he's working on an office reorganization in Birmingham. It's a sobering experience, in the end. The village has been swallowed up by a town; Elsie is a hag who doesn't recognize him; and the pool next to Binfield House (refurbished as a sanatorium for mental patients) has been refashioned as a pond for model yachts. Almost with a sense of relief, George resumes his role as henpecked husband and wage slave.

"I think nowadays you'd call it a mid-life crisis," says Robin Chapman, who adapted the play for the *Theatre 625* slot on BBC2. "He's reached a certain age, he's been traveling, selling insurance, he's come from a rural background and he wants to go back and find out the truth of that. Meanwhile, Orwell himself was deeply concerned about the pressures of industry on the countryside. So there's George Bowling going back and there's the fish doing exactly what he's done. He's trying to refresh himself with another breath of air."[1]

Coming together

Chapman's *Keep the Aspidistra Flying* script begins and ends with a none-too-subtle reminder of the title: an opening shot of Gordon strolling past house plants mounted on windowsills, and a closing shot of the Comstocks' newly acquired potted specimen.

With *Coming Up for Air*, he pulls a similar trick. Pre-titles, a gangling boy in a thick, tweed knickerbocker suit goes fishing. On the soundtrack, his church's congregation sings Psalm 135—the one that mentions Sihon, king of the Amorites, and Og, king of Bashan. The lad peers into the pond and as the singing reaches a crescendo, the camera swims upwards through the water. "It bursts into air," the script specifies. "We see a brilliant hole of light fringed by trees as the voices reach their climax."

The establishing scene that comes next is plucked from the middle of the novel, with George (Colin Blakely) and Hilda (Carmel McSharry) at a meeting of the Left Book Club (the publishing group, founded by Victor Gollancz, that gave Orwell some of his most important breaks). The church hall lecture, by "well-known anti-fascist" A.J. Minter,[2] tips us off that this is the late thirties, and from his voiceover we're party to George's inner thoughts. He's repelled by young Minter's hate-filled rhetoric—the man's itching to smash faces in with a spanner, he concludes—and after the talk, he argues about war with a communist bank clerk. George's jingoism died in 1916, in the trenches.

The couple offer a lift to their friends, Miss Minns and Mrs. Wheeler. As George drives them home, his voiceover continues, only this time it's directed at the viewers: a "here's who I am, here's what I do and this is the state of my life" affair (or "a technique of interior monologue," as the *Radio Times* preview[3] called it). Chapman uses this device frequently, lifting passages wholesale from the novel. It's bellyaching, Bowling-style, from his tirade against building societies to the admission that his marriage is a flop.

Over breakfast, and some mundane domestic strife with the wife and kids, a newspaper headline about King Zog triggers George's memories of Lower Binfield. Once more, we hear the ethereal sound of its congregation.

On the train to work, one of the two commercial travelers in his carriage asks: "Got a match, Tubby?" This paves the way for another of George's inner monologues, about fat men's place in society. With a dash of gallows humor, the three commuters chat about whose house is likely to be flattened in the coming war.

Arriving at the Flying Salamander office, George is tickled pink to learn he's won a £17 share in his colleague Mellors' win on the horses. Mellors gambles using astrological charts. "Praise the Lord, for the Lord is good," sings the unseen, Edwardian congregation.

MELLORS: I'm happy to announce that you have won precisely 17 quidlets on Corsair's Bride.

GEORGE: My ten bob? Good Lord, Venus was in the—something—wasn't she?

MELLORS: Believe in the stars, now, eh? Make a punter of you yet. Yes, she came in like a dream. Three lengths—don't you read the papers?

GEORGE: Here, you put on a lot.

MELLORS: (MOCK POSH) Yes, well, actually I do happen to be one hundred and ten snackerettes better off actually....

GEORGE: Good Lord.

MELLORS: Pleased now you deigned to drop in here from your labors on the road?

GEORGE: I'll say. Seventeen quid.

MELLORS: Would you prefer my personal check with the built-in bounce? Or a few samples of my handmade cash?

GEORGE: Er....

MELLORS: Yes, quite right. Take the cash while it's here.

(HE TAKES OUT HIS WALLET AND COUNTS OUT THREE LARGE FIVERS LOVINGLY AND TWO CRISP POUND NOTES.)

And besides, cash leaves no tell-tale credit slips, does it? For the wife to sniff at. Have yourself an orgy, Georgie Porgie, I dare you.

GEORGE: Maybe I will, after all these years.

MELLORS: Good for the system. Cleans the blood.

Retiring to a milk bar for lunch—and finding, to his consternation, that the frankfurters taste of fish—George emerges into the Strand, where a nightmarish premonition overwhelms him. A loudspeaker blasts out propaganda while bombs fall in the distance and a squad of scrawny soldiers marches by. Lorna appears, howling and begging for bread while she and Hilda huddle in a doorway.... And in an instant we're back at the insurance office, where George, Mellors and Violet the secretary are pondering what to do with £17.

There's another fantasy sequence right after this. George is addressing the church hall, presenting "a memorial lecture with slides" on the subject of his youth in Oxfordshire. We cut to the Bowlings' bedroom, where George drifts off to sleep, dreaming of 12-year-old Katie Simmonds, his babysitter and childhood crush. It's rural England seen through the eyes of a child. Posters on a window announce the outbreak of war, stock footage of soldiers segues into stills of George in uniform—and the memory of an explosion snaps him back to reality.

By now, Chapman's strategy as a scriptwriter is becoming clear. Through stock film and slides, flashbacks shot from George's perspective and regular voiceovers, he's capturing the soul of the book. The next flashback, for instance, has Binfield House caretaker Hodges speaking to George's father in his shop and inviting the young lad to go fishing on the estate. The resultant paean to angling, delivered by Colin Blakely over images of the boy at the carp pool, runs to nearly 350 words. Sure enough, many of those words are Orwell's.

About halfway through the 89-minute play, George concocts his homecoming plan and from here on in, the teleplay follows Orwell's plot in a fairly linear fashion, cribbing his best dialogue as it does so. It's not quite as straightforward as that—his promotion to officer when the army has run out of upper-class gentlemen is told in flashback, as is the time he talks his way into an insurance job with a captain of industry he'd known in uniform—but on the whole, and with all due respect to Robin Chapman, the latter half is essentially a straightforward adaptation.

The first hint that George won't enjoy his holiday comes as he checks into his hotel. He mentions to the receptionist ("She had the most extraordinary squint," remarks director Christopher Morahan[4]) that when the building was a pub, his dad drank there for 30 years. Alas, she's never heard of the Bowlings, and the guest he tries to pass the time of day with is equally uninterested.

A tea shop occupies what used to be the family store. In church, George is shocked to meet the vicar because—back when the cleric was 45 or so—he seemed like an old man. Curiously, Orwell's pivotal scene with Elsie—George's one-time live-in lover, who grew old and fat with another man and sells him cigarettes in a shop without recognizing him—is nowhere to be found.

The search for the carp pond near Binfield House is present and correct, however. George runs into a stereotypical back-to-nature crank—all shorts, sandals and specs—who informs him that a colony has developed there, and the pond drained to make a rubbish tip. "I've been a fool," says George, slinking away dejectedly.

But there's a final twist. Hearing a radio appeal for the husband of Hilda Bowling, George convinces himself that his wife is faking an illness to expose an affair.

Next morning—after a bomber pilot demolishes a house by accident and unleashes panic about the outbreak of war—he bids farewell to Lower Binfield and drives home. At the last minute, it occurs to him (wrongly) that perhaps his wife is seriously ill, but his belated concern cuts no ice with Hilda, who has proof he hasn't been to Birmingham. While George resigns himself to a verbal beating, a camera outside makes for the surface of a pool. It's that symbolic fish again, coming up for air.

Everything in the Garden's Lovely

To this day, director Christopher Morahan cites the production as one of his happiest experiences. "I would love to have shown it to Orwell," he says. "*Coming Up for Air* is one of my absolute favorite things I've ever done. I was very moved by it and enjoyed it immensely."

Hailing the author as "a man who couldn't stand nonsense," he points to Orwell's experiences in the Spanish Civil War, recounted in *Homage to Catalonia*. "The first time he goes out there, there's this heady excitement about belonging to a regiment, which wasn't in fact organized by the communists—he couldn't stand the communists. The killing that went on in Barcelona, organized by the Russian secret police, filled him with appalling horror.

"He loved England and he loved his childhood, his youth. That's one of the reasons why I enjoyed *Coming Up for Air*, because he wrote that one after he came back from Spain. He has that extraordinary picture of [Bowling] standing in the Strand—he'd just been in a milk bar—and imagining what it would be like, the Strand being bombed. The British were ridiculously unprepared for it. In *Coming Up for Air*, what he did was return to the world of his youth, because he'd been brought up quite near Henley-on-Thames. It was a remarkable piece of, not nostalgia, of memory and love of the time.

"He came back from Burma and didn't have anything to do, so he became a kind of practical journalist. There's *The Road to Wigan Pier* and also *Down and Out in Paris and London,* where he threw himself into a world…. As he'd been brought up in a privileged way and had been an officer in Burma, he wanted to see how other people lived. That's something I find fascinating about *Coming Up for Air*—that journey he makes through Oxfordshire. I know Henley quite well because I'd worked [as an actor] in weekly rep[5] there. I'm very fond of it and I can understand entirely him loving the countryside and writing about it, because he felt that that garden view of England—its simplicity and its oddity—was going to disappear.

"He deeply distrusted the left wing and he deeply distrusted the right wing. The right wing were blind and the left wing were blind too, because they all worshiped Stalin. I warm to people who are non-conformist and that's what I found glorious about him."

Prior to making the play, he and Chapman had to deal with Orwell's widow. Neither was exactly enamored of her. "When we were doing *Coming Up for Air*, an arrangement was made for me to meet Sonia Orwell," notes Chapman. "Well, she'd only known Orwell for the last two years of his life or so. Nevertheless, she possessed all his work and copyright and everything, and she was totally snobbish about television. Deeply patronizing. Newspaper reviews of television in the sixties, seventies and eighties were always hugely snobbish. It was a common medium, and vulgar. I was very aware of that at the time. Sometimes one got good reviews but they were always really from what I would call a literary snobbish point of view.

"My impression was she was an awful woman. She did have this kind of contemptuous, 'We need to get the money from the BBC,' I'm sure. But she despised almost everybody who did anything about her husband's work. As though we were all leeches and predators, instead of being admirers and wishing to push it even further."

"She was not at all helpful," Morahan concurs. "She wanted to protect him and she was sure that because we were television, we were going to damage him. She didn't have the grace ever to say how much she'd enjoyed it. Perhaps she didn't."

Road Movie

The pair agree too that Colin Blakely was magnificent as Bowling. "A most marvelous actor," says Chapman. Harking back to his work with Joan Littlewood, he adds: "You didn't act, you *became.* I can tell it at once. Most stars have it, of course, and you'll have observed it many times, but many actors do not have it and they act. We used to have a saying at Theatre Workshop: 'Get on that stage and for heaven's sake, don't act.'"

Morahan recalls standing in a telephone booth just outside the Royal Court Theatre, Sloane Square. "I phoned Colin and said: 'Would you like to do this play based on George Orwell's book?'—he and I had recently done a play in Manchester about a man who worked in an abattoir—and he just jumped at it. He loved it. He was marvelous. He wasn't a Londoner in any way, because he actually came from Belfast, but he had that ordinary personality. Ordinary. He was an ordinary man. He goes into the street in the Strand and imagines the buildings falling down. He goes on a great journey—the same kind of enquiry as Orwell's enquiry into living in [Wigan] when you don't have any money. Or having to wash dishes for a living. Or to lose your memory and then find yourself in a dosshouse. Actual things he wrote about and cared about."

As Bowling, Blakely motored around the countryside in an Austin 7. Morahan looks back fondly on the filming. "It was a matter of traveling—of going to see Oxfordshire and the big trees. Also Berkshire, and finding myself outside a house with the most beautiful pond in the garden. We're talking about the sequence where he goes fishing. The house belonged to a very famous singer…. I can't remember which one."

"It was Richard Tauber," says the production assistant, John Glenister. "Remember Richard Tauber, the tenor?"

Now retired to Wales, with an illustrious career as a director behind him (see chapter 11), Glenister shudders at the pressure he was under in 1965. "In those days, a production assistant was—well, it was like a first assistant director in films now, except he did about ten other jobs. He was first assistant, accounts, floor manager, location finder. It was a multi-tasking job. I'd been a cameraman all my life. I was just making the move across from technical operations to production and this was my halfway house of being a production assistant for a couple of years.

"Chris wasn't the easiest person to work with, I have to say. He was a brilliant director but he could be very difficult to work with. He was very demanding and sometimes not totally reasonable, so, you know, a bit of a tough time. But his results were always sensational so in the end you thought, well, there you go.

"I remember looking for locations for *Coming Up for Air*, which was not easy because it's period stuff in one period and then leaping forward. So you've got to find locations that were like that in the 1930s and like that in the 1950s (sic) … I remember clocking up over 2,000 miles in my little Mini and I never moved more than about 30 miles out of London. Just searching everywhere. God, it was difficult. But it was a good result. Colin Blakely was wonderful, wonderful. Superb."

In advance of a studio session at Television Centre on 8 August, filming in July took in locations as varied as Cassiobury Park in Watford,[6] a sub-post office in Latimer village, Buckinghamshire[7] (representing the shop where George bought sweets as a boy) and Harpsden Woods near Henley-on-Thames, Oxfordshire.[8] In Berkshire, the team filmed at a farm in Binfield and the church and country house at Warfield.[9] It was in Binfield[10] that Glenister found Richard Tauber's house. "I stumbled on that. I suddenly found myself in the back garden by this big pond with goldfish in. I went up to the back door and realized I was trespassing on private land. Anyway, I knocked on the door and I think it was Diana [Napier], his widow. He was dead by then. She was sweet. She invited us in and gave us all tea and sherry."

The scene near the end, at the rubbish heap, was shot at Harrow-on-the-Hill, North West London. "I lived in Harrow at the time," says Glenister. "I did find a place near Wembley called Barnhill which is a little open stretch of green belt. Actually, looking through the trees, you could see the roofs of modern houses and I think that was one of the scenes we managed to shoot. Modern housing was encroaching through the woodland—that was the sort of feeling we were trying to get."[11]

Air Today, Gone Tomorrow

Weeks before *Coming Up for Air* went out, actress Joy Measures, who played Lorna Bowling, wrote to Morahan asking to attend a screening, as her family's TV set didn't receive BBC2.[12] Colin Blakely, concerned he might be abroad with the National Theatre Company when it was broadcast, made a similar request.[13]

Artistically, the play was an unalloyed triumph, eclipsing *Keep the Aspidistra Flying* in the critics' estimation. The *Daily Mirror*'s Kenneth Eastaugh expressed "unbounded admiration," calling Blakely's performance the best he'd seen all year.[14] "LL" at *The Daily Telegraph* argued that Orwell's "evocative, contemplative writing" presented a challenge to television, but said Chapman's adaptation "caught the mood beautifully."[15] Writing in *The Observer*, Maurice Richardson commended the "dead faithful" dramatization, with the caveat that Bowling is too much a projection of Orwell.[16] *The Listener*'s Frederick Laws thought it "powerful in character and claustrophobic atmosphere" and appreciated Blakely as "the solid decent man with dreams."[17]

The sourest note came from *The Sunday Telegraph*'s Philip Purser, who, in a preview of *1984*, wrote that Chapman's "ingenious" adaptations "had me jotting down a word I never expected to use about Orwell: silly."

The poet/copywriter dichotomy of *Keep the Aspidista Flying* "seemed entirely artificial," while the disillusionment of George Bowling was "totally predictable." The saving grace was Morahan's "great style," thought Purser.[18]

In August 1966, the BBC repeated *Keep the Aspidistra Flying*, followed by *Coming Up for Air* in September. Sonia Orwell vetoed a repeat of Morahan's *1984.*[19] Second time around, *Coming Up for Air* attracted as much if not more attention. *The Guardian's* Gerard Fay went into raptures about its compassion, humanity and humor. "Although the theme is tragic Orwell, Chapman made a comedy of it—sometimes almost uproarious, never less than funny and still utterly humane," he wrote. One of his favorite characters was "man in short trousers": "every tedious aspect of the garden suburb Left-wing intellectual (even to the slightly whining tone of voice) was magnificently proclaimed." As for Hilda, the only flaw in McSharry's performance was that "she was too pretty."[20]

Geoffrey Nicholson at the *Daily Mail*, who considered it an almost faultless adaptation, reveled in Blakely's "wonderful irritability."[21] To the unnamed *Times* critic, it was simply "outstanding."[22] Which makes its archival absence all the more galling.

The World of George Orwell:
Coming Up for Air

George Bowling: Colin Blakely
Hilda Bowling: Carmel McSharry
Billy: Robert Bartlett
Lorna: Joy Measures
Mrs. Wheeler: Peggy Aitchison
Miss Minns: Ann Way
A.J. Minter: Frederick Farley
Mr. Witchett: Maitland Moss
Communist clerk: Larry Dann
Mellors: David Pinner
Violet: Judy Stephens
Men in train: Maurice Travers, Richard Merson
Sergeant: Reginald Jessup
Katie: Denise Brown
George as a young man: Roger Bradley
Elsie: Susan Tracey
George's father: Geoffrey Tyrrell
George's mother: Julie May
Hodges: Norman Wynne

Grimmett: Howard Lang
Waitress in milk bar: Faith Curtis
Simpson: Patrick Godfrey
Receptionist: Mimi Whitford
Lady in hotel: Mary Allen
Waitress in the tea shop: Ann King
Barmaid: Isabel Rennie
Yorkshire man: Clifford Cox
Sir Joseph Cheam: Donald Layne-Smith
Vicar: Christopher Banks
Man in the aertex shirt: Richard Caldicot
Shopkeeper: Edward Palmer
Flower sellers: Gabrielle Daye, Harry Shacklock
Dramatized by: Robin Chapman
Director: Christopher Morahan
Producer: Cedric Messina
Designer: Michael Wield

8

The World of George Orwell: 1984 (1965)

Damned with faint praise as a flawed remake and regarded now as one of television history's damp squibs, it's curious to think that *Theatre 625*'s *1984* was a major BBC event in 1965. With the TV rights back in its hands, on condition that all recordings be on videotape,[1] the corporation was convinced it could catch lightning in a bottle a second time.

By the standards of British TV, its investment in the program was remarkable. Typically, a 90-minute *Theatre 625* play merited a budget of £6,150,[2] but on this occasion—anxious that this two-hour "revival of a masterpiece" should not be a poor man's Rudolph Cartier production—producer Cedric Messina asked head of plays Michael Bakewell for £13,390.[3] He was equally bold about man hours, audaciously requesting 2,000 and allocating 500 of those to special effects.[4]

Given its reputation for weighty productions, *Theatre 625* could usually rely on 1,200 man hours, which was 300 more than its less prestigious counterparts.[5] In asking for more, Messina was pushing his luck; indeed, as BBC2 controller David Attenborough pointed out, he wanted nearly a sixth of BBC TV's weekly manpower effort. Agreeing to the hours—as an opera on BBC1 had fallen through—Attenborough went on to authorize a one-off payment of £5,000. To achieve the budget he wanted, Messina would have to cut corners on other plays.[6]

A striking aspect of the new *1984* was its youthful, attractive leads. Jane Merrow, who'd played Lorna Doone in a 1963 BBC serial, was 24, or two years younger than the Julia of the novel. Less expectedly, the role of Winston Smith went to 28-year-old David Buck: "a serious actor, a classical actor," says director Christopher Morahan now.[7] Kim Newman, a film journalist who'd interviewed Nigel Kneale in the nineties, says it was important to the scriptwriter that the two had "only a dim memory of life before 'the Revolution.'"[8] With 1984 just 19 years away, that meant they had to be young.

The play, recorded on 4 June in Television Centre's main studio, TC1,[9] sparked a blaze of publicity as the 28 November air date approached.[10] The *Radio Times* ran a black-and-white photo on its cover, showing Buck with a poster of the trim, bald, clean-shaven Big Brother[11] (the actor Ves Delahunt, uncredited), while a feature inside examined Orwell's motives for writing the novel. Kneale had amended his script, it explained, "to bring the narrative more into line" with the world of 1965.[12]

Morahan, who was 36 at the time and lauded by Messina as "one of the most socially conscious directors we have," reminisced in an *Observer* article about joining the BBC as a floor manager in 1955. The impact of Cartier's play the previous year, he said, showed him how powerful and exciting TV could be. According to script editor Rosemary Hill, technical advances had enabled the team to include more of Orwell's novel than ever before: "You don't need to waste precious seconds tracking in on a telephone while actors move from one set to another. Everything can be so much faster these days, because audiences are so much quicker on the uptake."[13]

BBC2 arts show *Late-Night Line-up* got in on the act too, reliving the uproar of 1954 in its 27 November edition. As well as reading out furious letters and telegrams from the archives,[14] it sought the views of Cartier, Kneale, Peter Cushing, Yvonne Mitchell and Andre Morell. Completing the line-up were Buck, Merrow and Morahan (who felt sure that his *1984* would be the last adaptation to be made[15]).

To some at the BBC, the remake seemed like folly. Irene Shubik, producer of a new science-fiction anthology show, *Out of the Unknown*, had complained to head of plays Michael Bakewell in July that showing two futuristic dramas in the same week, on the same channel, would "be a bit of a bore for the audience."[16] In the event, they weren't—but only because they were so wildly different. A day after *1984*, BBC2 screened *Andover and the Android*: a comedy, adapted from a story by Kate Wilhelm, about the boss of an electronics firm who passes off a robot as his wife.

Back to the Future

The play is a good deal lavisher than Cartier's, flaunting its use of a sandy beach[17] (for the build-up to nuclear war), a nuclear power plant[18] (the Ministry of Truth) and dilapidated terraced housing in London[19] (Victory Mansions). The tone is different, too: for the first 90 minutes, certainly, this is a more naturalistic, less austere piece than Cartier's. The Records Department in 1954 was a shadowy, spartan, oppressive place, staffed by the buttoned-up, nervous Peter Cushing and Donald Pleasence. Here, it's a spacious, well-lit framework of work cubicles, filing cabinets and gantries, where handsome, likable Buck works with the ever-so-slightly shifty Cyril Shaps.

An ostentatious preamble—in which a soldier drives his all-terrain vehicle into a nuclear minefield, prompting military officers across the globe to reach for their hotlines while oscilloscopes bleep in the background—adds little to our understanding of what's going on. A British general approves a nuclear first strike "limited to twenty megadeaths"; Kneale (via a narrator) shoehorns in the book's opening line about clocks striking 13 on an April day; and the setting shifts not to Airstrip One, but to "Pad Three," presumably inspired by Nasa's launchpads.

In London, even the graffiti artists are loyal to the Party: someone has daubed LONG LIVE BB on a corrugated iron fence. Elsewhere, WAR IS PEACE, FREEDOM IS SLAVERY and IGNORANCE IS STRENGTH show up as banners draped across housing developments. Scooting by in a jeep, the Thought Police arrive at a squat, boxy building marked MINISTRY OF TRUTH. It's supposedly in the middle of the city, though viewers who know what nuclear power stations look like won't be fooled.

The establishing scene from 1954, of a telescreen chastising Smith, is present and correct, and Winston's costume has barely changed.[20] Neither have Bernard Wilkie's telescreens—though the actual screen, instead of being circular, is a rectangular TV monitor that broadcasts charcoal sketches of actions going on around it.[21]

Moments lifted from the novel include Goldstein—all wild, silvery hair, jutting goatee and granny specs—talking like a sheep during the Two Minutes Hate ("The revolution has been betra-a-a-a-yed"). Occasionally, it feels as if Kneale is being gratuitously unpleasant because he can: he extends Syme's lunchtime discussion of a hanging, for instance, with Orwell's lines about the prisoners kicking their feet and sticking out their bright blue tongues.[22]

Here and there, the production looks slipshod. Actors stumble over their lines and at one point, the door to Parsons' apartment swings open and stands ajar, revealing an uncomfortable-looking man standing just off set. The performances vary in quality too, ranging from the terrific (Sally Thomsett as Parsons' odious daughter, five years before her role as Jenny Agutter's adorable sister in *The Railway Children*) to the abysmal (John Garrie, playing Charrington like a slavering, snaggle-toothed sex offender).

Kneale isn't shy about the story's emphasis on carnality. "You're only a rebel from the waist downwards," Winston tells Julia at Charrington's place—it's a line from the book, making its screen debut—and in no time, she's showing him her cleavage. Hitting just the right balance of cynicism, seductiveness, recklessness and naivety, Merrow is exceptional as FM-2869 Bowman J (note the new surname). Buck is no slouch either, it has to be said: when Winston fights back tears of shame over what rats did to his little sister, it's one of the play's strongest, most affecting moments.

The spirit of Swinging London, never far from the program's surface, is probably most blatant when O'Brien shows a dignitary around the Ministry of Truth. In Cartier's production, the mass-produced ditty *It Was Only a Hopeless Fancy*—later sung by a prole woman hanging out her washing—was the work of a sentimental crooner. Here, it's a full-blown pop record.[23] In the Ministry of Love as well, real-world permissiveness seeps through, as a surveillance photo shows our heroes naked in bed. By the time he's been beaten by Thought Police in black leather[24] (and interrogated by four nightmarish medics, dressed for the operating theater), Smith is willing to admit to homosexual tendencies and bestiality.

It's a slow-burner, for sure, but the play distinguishes itself in the end. Aided by Tony Abbott's warped designs and a haunting, understated performance by the actor, playwright and novelist Joseph O'Conor—a colorless, terrifying bureaucrat, "a fallen priest," as Kneale was to call the Irishman's O'Brien[25]—the torture scenes are truly squirm-inducing. Encased in a metallic coffin, his skull clenched in a shock device, Smith gradually succumbs to torment. A small, rectangular distorting mirror reflects his fear and despair back at him; and when a cage is strapped to his face, we see his terror from the rats' perspective.

The play ends as its progenitor did, with a broken Winston and Julia meeting in the cafe—and one last shot of Big Brother's portrait. The credits roll, and in the final few seconds, a caption fills the screen:

BIG BROTHER
is watching you

Few people noticed. As Peter Cushing wrote in his 1986 autobiography: "It is a sad reflection upon the times we live in that, when another excellent presentation of this play with a splendid cast was given in 1965, it caused not a ripple, so immune have we become to violence and terrorism."[26]

"It didn't work," Kneale admitted four decades later. "It was a perfectly good production by Chris Morahan, but for the first one the audience had got very upset by all these dreadful images. Ten years later, they were much more sophisticated. It just didn't have anything like the same impact. It came and went."[27]

Instead of throwing up its hands like it had in the days of prime minister Churchill, Fleet Street yawned. The threat of a British police state had faded since Orwell's day, wrote Peter Black of the *Daily Mail*, robbing an "impeccably turned out" drama of its power.[28] *The Sunday Telegraph's* Philip Purser felt the same way, calling such a prospect "cosily remote."[29] *The Daily Telegraph's* "LL" thought the play was "on the lengthy side," with too few sparks until the last 30 minutes[30]; while the *Daily Express*, with a swipe at Buck's "cherubic innocence" and a suggestion that *Doctor Who* might be scarier, pointed out that by 10:10 p.m., the BBC had received only one phone complaint.[31] To *The Observer's* Maurice Richardson, the torture scenes were labored and "the rats underacted."[32] Only Mary Crozier at *The Guardian* could rouse much enthusiasm for the production, calling it "immensely hard and gripping."[33]

The BBC's audience research report, based on the reactions of 76 viewers, suggests that the public enjoyed Morahan's version a great deal more than Cartier's, or at any rate were less divided about it. It scored 75 on the reaction index, compared to 39 for the 1954 play and an average of 58 for TV drama in the third quarter of 1965. Most of the viewers on the panel suggested it had made a profound impression on them, with one from the education sector calling it "absorbing and absolutely horrifying." Though a handful were repelled by its unpleasantness, the sample as a whole found it powerful and disturbing, and the acting "grippingly realistic." Buck was "particularly fine" and his final conflict with the "most impressive" O'Conor was "brilliantly done." Though one or two viewers were critical of Merrow, the performances on the whole were warmly praised.[34]

Still, the master tape was wiped. "At the time," Morahan explains, "the BBC did documentaries on film and studio work for drama with huge television cameras, not at all portable. They were recorded on videotape, probably the size of a motorcycle wheel. When they were finished with, they were piled up in the basement of the BBC and you couldn't get through the basement for them. So they started to wipe them and record again. They just threw the past away."

In 2010, as part of a haul of more than 60 BBC shows screened by New York public TV station WNET,[35] a copy turned up in the U.S. Library of Congress. Regrettably, a seven-minute segment in the middle of the tape was damaged beyond repair. "I'm sad about that," says Morahan. "It's the section where he and the girl go out into the countryside and make love."

Months later, he and Merrow were guests at a British Film Institute screening in London, where he thought the play was "very powerful indeed. As I never saw Rudi Cartier's production, I suspect that the effect [of that version] on an innocent London audience [in 1954] was far greater than the one I made. People had become more sophisticated."

Buck died of cancer in 1989. "I remember him fondly," says Merrow. Their chemistry, she says, was "pretty good—that was really important, because it's sort of the last love story of the 20th century before Big Brother swallowed up society."[36]

The World of George Orwell: 1984

Winston Smith: David Buck
Julia: Jane Merrow
O'Brien: Joseph O'Conor
Syme: Cyril Shaps
Charrington: John Garrie
Scout car driver: Tony Cyrus
Arab colonel: Mohammed Shamsi
Russian marshal: Alexis Chesnakov
French general: Hugo de Vernier
American general: John Brandon
British general: Tom Macauley
Telescreen announcers: Brian Badcoe, Raymond Mason
Goldstein: Vernon Dobtcheff
Prole in canteen: Marjorie Gresley
Parsons: Norman Chappell
Mrs. Parsons: Sally Lahee
Parsons girl: Sally Thomsett
Parsons boy: Frank Summerscales
Pedlar: Henry Kay
Blind man: Eric Francis
Proles: Anthony Blackshaw, Edwin Brown
Old man: Sydney Arnold
Prole youths: John Lyons, David Baxter, Patrick Ellis
Barman: Fred Hugh
Waiter: John Barrett
Jones: John Mincer
Aaronson: Eden Fox
Rutherford: George Wilder
Foster: Peter Bathurst
Singing Prole woman: Julie May

Orator: John Moore
Martin: Paul Phillips
Thin man: William Lyon Brown
Men in white coats: Norman Scace, David Grey, John Abineri, Michael Sheard
Supervisors: Marcia Mansfield, Donald Groves, Joe Tregonino (uncredited)
Technician: Bill Gosling (uncredited)
Woman in cell: Kathleen Heath (uncredited)
Guard in cell: Fred Powell (uncredited)
Withers: John Scripps (uncredited)
Guard: Bernard Egan (uncredited)
Man with bread: Raymond Graham (uncredited)
Outer Party workers: Ann Marzell, Ursula Granville, Renee Roberts, David J. Grahame, Leon Broder, Patrick Gorman, Bill Howes, Peter Whittaker, Maxwell Foster, Derek Chaffer, Philip Moore, Anthony Gilby, Robin Burns, Fred Davies, Ricky Lansing, Bill Beasley, Sylvia Lane, Laura Deane, Jill Marlow (uncredited)
Adapted by: Nigel Kneale
Directed by: Christopher Morahan
Producer: Cedric Messina
Designer: Tony Abbott
Music composed by: Wilfred Josephs
Visual effects: Bernard Wilkie

9

The Road to the Left (1971)

It's the early seventies and British politics is going through a rough patch. Edward Heath is prime minister after the Conservative Party's surprise victory in the general election of 1970. But the trades union movement and Marxist ideas are still a force to be reckoned with, as Heath will learn in the course of his four-year premiership. With industrial relations at a low ebb, the miners' strikes of 1972 and 1974 will ultimately finish off his government.

Looking back on these turbulent times, it seems fitting that the two substantive Orwell documentaries of the decade should hinge on *The Road to Wigan Pier*, his seminal non-fiction work, written in the Depression era for Victor Gollancz's Left Book Club. It's easy to imagine this sociological study of conditions in the industrial North of England—tied together with socialist polemics, though there are jibes about bourgeois, sanctimonious left-wingers—acting as a rallying cry for Heath's ideological opponents.

In late 1973, director Frank Cvitanovich devoted a whole Thames Television film to Orwell's Wigan odyssey, as this book's next chapter will illustrate. Nearly three years earlier, however, the BBC's Melvyn Bragg had taken a more wide-ranging approach, looking at 1936 in its entirety. The springboard, according to Bragg, was a thesis that "had begun to obsess me"—that a personal landmark year reshaped Orwell's character and paved the way for his most culturally significant works.[1]

The 57-minute documentary, made in color for BBC1's arts series *Omnibus*, went out at 10 p.m. on Sunday, 10 January 1971. Billed as "an essay on George Orwell by Melvyn Bragg," it's a warts-and-all biography in which friends, relatives and acquaintances paint the late author as a lonely, physically awkward, ill-at-ease, sometimes insensitive man. "I'm sick to death of these saint artists on television," Bragg told the *Radio Times*. "Though Orwell, as it happens, is nearer a saint than most."[2]

To the accompaniment of doleful brass band music, the film sets the scene with its opening black-and-white slide of a cobbled path. But as the titles fade, we begin in a London office, where left-wing politician Michael Foot—once Orwell's editor at *Tribune* magazine, though this is never mentioned—is rattling off phrases (and catchphrases) from *Nineteen Eighty-Four* and *Animal Farm*. Orwell—"the authentic voice of English radicalism," says the man who'd be leader of Britain's Labour Party a decade later—gave us the language with which to discuss totalitarianism. Were he alive, says Foot, he'd consider this possibly his greatest accomplishment.

Orwell's National Union of Journalists card appears briefly in Melvyn Bragg's BBC documentary.

Writer-director Bragg, whose doesn't appear on camera, weighs in with a brief biography next, sketching out the events of Orwell's first few decades, and says that the film is a portrait of the author based on the year he discovered his political purpose. Every interview is in close-up—a technique borrowed from another of Bragg's idols, the Swedish film director Ingmar Bergman.[3]

For a while, the documentary relies on those closest to Orwell—that is, his own well-to-do social class. Mabel Fierz, a friend of the Blair family, remembers him as a lonely middle child, living with his mother and two sisters. He felt less unhappy at Eton, among boys, she says, but worried when his classmates teased their half-blind French language teacher, Aldous Huxley.[4] He was a misfit in the Burmese police force too, and his decision to leave it gravely disappointed his father.

Humphrey Dakin, widower of Orwell's elder sister Marjorie, saw his brother-in-law as "curiously aloof," with a contempt for his fellow human beings—especially the poorer ones. "I think he had many of the characteristics of an aristocrat who's seen better days." A runny-nosed, stubbly Sir Richard Rees (*Adelphi*'s editor, who died shortly after filming in 1970, as did Dakin) thought of Orwell as dependable and reliable, but certainly not wildly exciting or original. *Horizon*'s Cyril Connolly, meanwhile, is lukewarm about his school chum's pre–1936 output.

Another friend, the anthropologist Geoffrey Gorer, is terribly honest about the anguished bachelor he knew. "He was fairly well convinced that nobody would like him, which made him prickly," says Gorer. As a gangling man, well over six foot and liable to knock things off tables, it seemed to Orwell that even the inanimate world had it in for him. The reaction to his third novel, *Keep the Aspidistra Flying*—finished in early 1936, while he was working as a bookshop assistant—did little to alleviate his persecution complex. But Bragg finds a fan in author Norman Mailer.[5] Labeling *Aspidistra* "a dry, small, sour, sad little book," the effusive American says one of its central themes has stayed with him: that when the poor experience good fortune, "they have to blow it, they have to ruin it." It's an insight that has given him more compassion, he says.

If There Is Hope, It Lies in the Proles

Eighteen minutes in—at a point in Orwell's life where a £500 commission from Gollancz gives him the wherewithal to marry his civil servant girlfriend, Eileen O'Shaughnessy—the documentary's tone changes, as relatively privileged southerners make way for salt-of-the-earth northerners.

It still horrifies Bragg to think that Gorer could compare Orwell's time among Wiganers (and vagrants before that) to anthropological surveys of the Congo.[6] But to be fair to Gorer, watching the program from a 21st-century vantage point is like looking at a vanished tribe. It's a culture shock, seeing these proud, articulate, self-educated trade unionists, dressed in their Sunday best with a bookcase full of hardbacks in the living room. When was the last time someone like that appeared on television?

Take Joe "Jerry" Kennan, a five-foot-tall Wigan electrician who took lanky, cosseted Orwell down a coal mine. In dry, laconic tones worthy of a stand-up comedian, he recalls the author knocking on his door one Saturday afternoon, letter of introduction in hand, while "we were just having tea."[7] Orwell, he notes more in sorrow than in anger, never thanked him for the free meals and snacks.

Rigged out in a helmet and lamp, the writer entered a section of pit where the girders were buckled. Having walked no more than 300 yards, says Kennan, he banged his head and fell to the floor, out cold. Once revived, he carried on, stooping more and more as the roof got lower and lower. For about three-quarters of a mile, Orwell was bent double, says Kennan—another participant who died shortly after filming—until the pair reached the working coalface, measuring just 26 inches, in utter exhaustion. Lying on the coal, Kennan turned to the Old Etonian and joked that if his bosses knew what they were up to that day, they'd more than likely trigger a cave-in.

Another contact, Mary Deiner, takes up the story. After two days' recuperation in Wigan, Orwell took a train to Liverpool, turning up on her doorstep one frosty February morning. He was a strange, shivering figure, she says—"no overcoat, no hat, no bag"—and when he collapsed, more or less, and refused to see a doctor, she and her husband put him to bed and plied him with hot lemon.

In Wigan's public library, says Bragg, Orwell gathered facts and statistics that would bolster his case. But the book is by no means a dry read, as an oft-quoted passage from it proves. Orwell writes of sitting on a train, passing a row of slums, and of catching the eye of a woman in her 20s as she tries to unblock a drainpipe. Kneeling on cold cobbles, she looks about 40, and as she glances up at the carriage, clutching a stick, a look of sheer hopelessness crosses her face. She's not a dumb animal, this woman. She knows how appalling her fate is. This "elementary sympathy," says Bragg, put the Old Etonian in a class of his own.

In March, Orwell witnessed Oswald Mosley, leader of the fascist blackshirt movement, addressing a meeting in Barnsley. A protester at the time, ex-miner Tom Degnan, is convinced that Orwell barely understood the working class and is scathing about the details he missed that evening. A late-night ruckus between the two groups passed him by completely: perhaps he went back to his digs as soon as the event finished, says Degnan.

It's left to Ellis Firth, a jolly old fellow who was on welfare in 1936, to lighten the mood considerably. Clutching a silvery horse-head walking cane and squinting through Mr. Magoo glasses, he remembers the writer as a detective of sorts, "trying to find that missing link," and wishes he could have gone on tour with him.

Apart from a couple of book-related vox pops—with trade unionists at a factory gate and teenagers from a school near Barnsley—that's the last we'll hear of the proletariat. Like Orwell in 1936, the documentary is ready to move on.

Creating History

Back among the intelligentsia, *The Road to the Left* dutifully completes Bragg's thesis. Critic Ian Hamilton reads snooty reviews of *Keep the Aspidistra Flying*, friends speak approvingly of Eileen—the marriage, says Rees, caused a smoldering fire in Orwell to burst into flame—and the couple's involvement in the Spanish Civil War is skilfully explained. Arriving in Barcelona, Orwell is thrilled to find the working class in the driving seat, but after serving with an anarchist militia, ends up running from a communist purge.

Noam Chomsky, the American philosopher and critic of the Vietnam War, admires how his hero cut through ideological constraints and focused on "the ordinary, decent, common man." But it's Orwell's own essential decency that takes up the closing minutes of the film, as novelist Angus Wilson describes his honesty as "a guiding light"; the poet W.H. Auden, who met him in Spain, calls *Homage to Catalonia* "the most extraordinary, brave work"; publisher Fred Warburg recalls the sensation *Nineteen Eighty-Four* caused across Europe; and Mailer marvels at the novel's prophetic, Vietnam-style proxy wars.

As a piece of oral history, the film is hugely important, but in 1971 the reviews were mixed. "Toughly written and most tenderly directed," wrote *The Observer*'s critic, Mary Holland. By limiting himself to a single year, she added, Bragg had simplified Orwell's politics, relying on Angus Wilson to touch briefly on "the conflicts which beset his thinking" during and after the war with Germany. That said, Bragg "did not shirk the difficulties of Orwell's personality—his lack of grace, the fact that he always seemed to have to steel himself to meet his fellow men."[8]

Michael Ratcliffe in *The Times* thought "too much was made of Orwell's misunderstanding or otherwise of the working class." He was painfully aware of "all the false social shades and attitudes" and "made far less of a fool of himself than many who went slumming after him."[9] The *Financial Times'* Kenneth Adam, positing the idea that Bragg was a little too much in awe of his subject, thought the program was a pedestrian effort from a gifted documentary-maker. "I knew Orwell and found him to be an agreeable and gregarious man. Too much was made here of his solitude and his pain."[10]

Bragg—now Lord Bragg, a Labour peer—doubts that such an austere film could be made today. But it gave him a glimpse of Orwell the human being, and led him to conclude that, more than anything else, meeting tough, intelligent working men had changed the author forever. "He was stunned at their political knowledge and commitment, and I think chastened by it."[11]

Omnibus Presents the Road to the Left: An Essay on George Orwell by Melvyn Bragg

Written and directed by: Melvyn Bragg, with Mary Deiner, Tom Degnan, Ellis Firth, G.D. Kennan, Cyril Connolly, Humphrey Dakin, Mabel Fierz, Geoffrey Gorer, Sir Richard Rees, W.H. Auden, Noam Chomsky, Michael Foot MP, Ian Hamilton, Norman Mailer, Fred Warburg, Angus Wilson, Alan Collins, Fred Johnson, Jim Murray and children from Kirk Balk School near Barnsley

10

The Road to Wigan Pier (A Musical Documentary) (1973)

Since its founding in 1955 as a commercial rival to the BBC, the independent television network has had to cope with the sneers of Britain's army of cultural snobs. To its detractors, the bulk of ITV's programming is little more than bubblegum for the mind—a sad parade of tawdry soap operas, vulgar gameshows and sub-par sitcoms made for profit, not love. There's an element of truth in this, particularly since the Conservatives deregulated broadcasting in the nineties. But to dismiss the channel out of hand is to overlook its gems: *Coronation Street, The World at War, The Avengers, Brideshead Revisited* ... not to mention *The Prisoner*, an audaciously Orwellian slice of pop art masquerading as a late-sixties "spy-fi" adventure show.

The evening of Tuesday, 16 October 1973 had a more political flavor than most. At 7:15 p.m., ITV screened *Never Let Me Go*, a 20-year-old film, made in Britain, that starred Clark Gable as an American reporter and Gene Tierney as the Soviet ballerina he marries and helps to defect. Thames Television's *The Road to Wigan Pier (A Musical Documentary)* followed at 9 p.m. Conceived, produced and directed by Frank Cvitanovich, a 46-year-old Canadian, it's an unusual, heartfelt film that echoes Orwell's calls for a fair, just, socialist society. Five-and-a-half years later, voters would deliver a body blow to the political left by propelling Margaret Thatcher into Downing Street.

Cvitanovich, the son of a Croat who'd founded a Vancouver fishing fleet, had by all accounts been something of a drifter in his youth, working at various times as a poker player, film runner, theater hand and footballer. Eventually he talked his way into a directing job on "singing cowboy" Gene Autrey's TV show and by 1957, he was in London.[1]

Under the patronage of Thames TV's director of programs, Jeremy Isaacs, he made a profoundly moving, Emmy Award-winning documentary in 1972. *Bunny* followed Cvitanovich and his wife, the film-maker Midge Mackenzie, to an unorthodox clinic in Philadelphia, where therapy held out the promise of a better life for their severely brain-damaged son.

His next project, by contrast, drew on Orwell's peerless prose—throwing archive footage, staged reconstructions, folk music, still photographs and a Welsh male voice choir into the mix. Speaking to ITV's listings magazine, the *TV Times*, he was unashamedly effusive. "The man had incredible honesty," he said. "Unlike many people with a social conscience, Orwell's opinions rose out of the facts, not the other way round."

The kind of issues that preoccupied Orwell—career satisfaction, job security and the quality of life—were still pertinent in 1973, he added. "Incredibly, he also describes how a large portion of the middle class had lost their nerve. How they couldn't see themselves as healthy, happy, useful or anything else—just like today."[2]

Pier Show

Using Orwell's words and nothing more, actor Michael Jayston narrates the 55-minute film in a crisp, compassionate, sometimes sardonic manner. The passage about the wretched young woman and the drainpipe, quoted in Melvyn Bragg's *The Road to the Left*, is used early on as a hook, only this time recreated with an actress. Kneeling in a cobbled back street, she looks up from her filthy task, the camera dwelling on her blank-faced despair[3]— and then, somewhat surprisingly, a man starts singing.

It's the Tyneside-born folk singer Bob Davenport, wearing the suit and cloth cap of a working man. Framed by an industrial urban landscape and miming to his own politically charged recordings, he kicks off with *The Song of the Lower Classes*, written by the Chartist Ernest Jones in 1852.

> Down, down we go, we are so low,
> To the hell of the deep sunk mine
> But we gather the proudest gems that glow
> When the crown of the despot shines[4]

From this point on, the documentary leans heavily on black-and-white archive footage, flitting occasionally from old film to new and turning up the color to reveal its trickery. These flickering excerpts—of miners at the coalface, wives at the scene of a pit disaster, a brick factory in operation, the coronation of George VI—possess a startling power and urgency. And when Jayston (as Orwell) reminds us of society's debt to coal miners, Davenport pops up with another traditional song, *William Brown*.

> A bright young lad was William Brown
> He worked for a wage in a Northern town
> He turned a wheel from left to right
> From eight in the morning till six at night
>
> And keep that wheel a-turnin'
> Keep that wheel a-turnin'
> Keep that wheel a-turnin'
> And do a little more each day

This, then, is the program's *modus operandi*: archive film plus prose, punctuated by songs. A diatribe about inadequate safety measures sets the scene for *One Day While in the North Country*, about the widow of a miner who's been killed in an accident[5]; and after Jayston sets down the facts about slum housing, Davenport performs *Moving Day*, an American tune from the Great Depression about being evicted for failing to pay the rent.

Time and again, Cvitanovich and researcher Barbara Sussman take Orwell's haunting words—the slag-heap scavengers pushing bicycles weighed down with coal; the proud men gone to seed, forced into years of idleness by economic forces beyond their control—and find novel ways to bring them to life visually. There's room for wry amusement too: when Orwell skewers bourgeois socialists, who fawn over "the workers" at cross-cultural summer schools but secretly despise them for slurping soup, we see men in shorts and T-shirts doing star jumps.

The cure that Orwell prescribes for the world's ills—globally applied socialism—is, he concedes in the book, inherently distasteful to the disadvantaged people who ought to support it. Provocatively, Cvitanovich cuts to Davenport indoors, sitting in front of revolutionary posters and singing the melody to *Battle Hymn of the Republic*:

> We'll turn Buckingham Palace into a public lavatory
> We'll turn Buckingham Palace into a public lavatory
> We'll turn Buckingham Palace into a public lavatory
> When the red revolution comes along
>
> Solidarity forever
> Solidarity forever
> Solidarity forever
> When the red revolution comes along

Towards the end, the film ditches the Orwell readings to push Cvitanovich's own political manifesto. The first sign of this comes as Davenport watches a chimneystack being demolished and turns to the audience at home. "Well, Mr. Orwell, whatever happened to your dream of socialism?" he asks.

In the blink of an eye, the flat-capped scamp finds himself in a gleaming white control room where monitors spew out British politicians' old speeches and a satirical, pre–YouTube mash-up shows them hurling non-sensical soundbites at each other.[6] The bickering continues into 1973, with Conservative prime minister Edward Heath, Labour leader Harold Wilson and their Liberal Party counterpart, Jeremy Thorpe. Then, as the scene takes on the trappings of a science-fiction nightmare, Davenport attempts to escape, hurtling down corridors while reels of magnetic computer tape spin and whir menacingly.

Whichever way he turns, a woman's voice—like a telescreen's—blares from the nearest speaker. Her message, essentially, is that he's living in a godforsaken nation.[7] The number of new houses in 1972 was equal to that of 1937, she says. In 35 years, the national average wage has risen a mere 45 percent. Annually, doctors prescribe amphetamines, barbiturates, tranquil-izers and antidepressants in their millions. And every five days, on average, a miner dies in a pit accident.

For socialists, at least, the finale is a rousing one. Coal miners, their faces blackened like they've just come off a shift, stride over the brow of a Welsh hillside, singing all ten verses of *The Red Flag*. In actual fact, they're the Morriston Orpheus Choir from Swansea, play-acting. But on a channel that was maligning the USSR an hour earlier, this cheerleading for collec-tivism must have seemed extraordinary.

Peer to Pier

Cvitanovich, who died in 1995, was honored by the British Film Insti-tute in 2016 when it screened several of his Thames documentaries at its BFI Southbank venue in London. One of its guests on the night of *The Road to Wigan Pier*'s screening was Bob Davenport, still going strong in his eight-ies and something of a legend on the British folk scene.

Born in the North East town of Gateshead in 1932, Davenport had moved south in the fifties as part of his National Service—a stint in the military then compulsory for young British men. At weekends he would leave his Hampshire barracks for the intellectual maelstrom of London, which, as he remembers it, had become Europeanized after the war. In time, he says, American culture came to dominate, but when he was in his 20s, the capital was a very different place.

As a free spirit and a lifelong anarcho-syndicalist, the singer feels an affinity for Orwell, whose influence was growing in the years that followed his death. *Down and Out in Paris and London*, together with W.H. Davies' *The Autobiography of a Super-Tramp*,[8] inspired him to hitch-hike around

Europe in the mid-fifties. Politically too, in the anarchist bookshops and left-wing circles of London, Orwell helped to mold his ideas. "He was trained as a district officer to report back from the colonies and he was trained in a particular, very precise English," says Davenport. "We had great arguments with the communists about whether *Homage to Catalonia* was an accurate book."[9]

It was in this fifties milieu that Davenport became friends with Midge Mackenzie, who as a teenager used to hang around the same radical book-shops. By the early seventies she'd married Cvitanovich, who insisted on using Davenport in his documentary after hearing one of his LP records. Joined by his regular backing band, the Rakes, and the Boldon Banjos from what at that time was his native County Durham,[10] Davenport recorded the songs—which he'd chosen personally—at a studio in Wembley, London.

That, as far as he knew, was that. "The next thing was that Frank phoned me and gave me the locations for the film," the singer recalls. "I said: 'Well, that doesn't apply to me.' He said: 'Yes it does, you're the everyman. You're in it.'"

One of Davenport's more vivid memories is of filming the *Moving Day* sequence. "That's from a 1930s 78 of Charlie Pool and his North Carolina Ramblers and I just adapted it. When we were up in Bolton in Lancashire, we were filming in a back lane. The sound was produced through an amplifier, I was mouthing to it, and all the back doors opened. The women came out to see what the noise was.... Afterwards, they were saying: 'We know that song.' It could have been a British music hall number."

Another day's filming, with the reel-to-reel computers, took place in London. "It was the machine taking over, which Orwell warned about, really. I knew that the police used to listen to you on the phone, steam open your letters and that kind of stuff. The technology was changing and workers were being replaced by machines."

At Brynlliw Colliery near Swansea, Davenport attended the filming of *The Red Flag*, in which the choir crossed the brow of a hill in a triangular formation. Tenors Ben Edwards and Cyril McCrane sang the first two lines.[11] "We were in the pit canteen," says the folk singer, "and the women who worked there asked the choir if they would sing *Myfanwy*, the Welsh love song. They just sat there and sang it, no conductor, and everybody was in tears."

Powerful though it was, the final scene sat badly with Cvitanovich's boss, Jeremy Isaacs, who wasn't allowed to see the film until it was finished. "I never wanted to hear another verse of *The Red Flag* again," says Isaacs (or Sir Jeremy, as he is now). "He found about ten different versions of it. It went on and on and on and on. I thought that film, in retrospect, was a bit heavy-handed.

"When he said he wanted to make a film called *The Road to Wigan Pier*, some of us had read the book and thought we knew what he was going to do. What shook me when I went and saw it in the dubbing theater, by which time it was far too late to do anything about it, even if I'd wanted to, was the stuff at the end of the film, which appeared to be about Gaitskell versus Wilson and so on and so forth. And I thought, 'Frank, I didn't really think you were going to do this.' But if you believe in employing people who are good film-makers, and whom you honor and trust, you let them get on with it and that's what we did. It's a film that, miraculously almost, works. It hangs together."[12]

Pier Review

Critics were much more enthusiastic. Calling it "television at its very best," *The Observer* wrote that it slashed away "at class humbug, squashy socialism, intellectual postures, and the abiding mythology that if you abolish slums you abolish poverty."[13] At *The Times*, Leonard Buckley called it "brilliant" and "studded with arresting images," though bringing Davenport and the choir into a film about the thirties was a little too contrived for his liking.[14]

The Guardian's Peter Fiddick considered it not so much a documentary as "a polemic, a personal column" by Cvitanovich. "He built his thesis that in forty-odd years nothing has fundamentally changed: that conventional politics brings us no more than the promises it has always brought us, that socialism is no nearer being achieved, but that the road lies ahead."[15]

At the right-wing *Daily Telegraph*, Richard Last applauded Cvitanovich for adding force to Orwell's messages and praised *The Red Flag* sequence as "a tour de force."[16] James Thomas at the *Daily Express* thought the program was spoiled "by the regular interruptions of Bob Davenport, singing some of the folk songs of an era which had little to sing about," but was amused by scenes of bourgeois socialists "trying to embrace the proletariat."[17]

To *The Tablet*'s Mary Crozier, the film was vivid, moving, dramatic and admirable—until, that is, the "unfortunate change" with the politicians and the "superfluous" reciting of statistics. *The Red Flag*, too, was "a touch of showbiz utterly out of keeping with the grim fidelity of the Orwell part."[18]

The most unexpected comments came from Clive Gammon in the conservative *Spectator* magazine, who remembered his mother and her friends weeping tears of joy when a Labour government swept to power in 1945. *Wigan Pier* had been a fixture in the family home, its covers curled by repeated reading. Gammon was impressed by the film's archival finds: "grimly," he wrote, "there was much film quite new to me, some of it from private sources, of strikers and marchers rioting, of police baton charges, of the hungry tramping their way to demonstrate in Leeds or Trafalgar Square." Orwell, he felt, would have relished both "the comic cuts of our leaders" and the choral ending.[19]

Perhaps the final word should go not to a journalist, but to Winifred Smith of Corringham, Essex. In a letter to the *TV Times*, Mrs. Smith shared what it was like to be married to a jobless man in the Depression years. The "gaunt Labour Exchanges" with "no smoking" signs when cigarettes were a luxury; "the dreaded means test"; the "pitiful, limbless ex-Servicemen in the gutters, the enforced idleness"; the jibes of the better off; the question "Where did you look for work yesterday and the *day before*?"

"To the present generation, those bitter years are of little interest outside academic research," she concluded. "But fate plays ironic tricks.... That which has happened once may happen again."[20]

The Road to Wigan Pier
(A Musical Documentary)

Director/producer: Frank Cvitanovich
Executive producer: Ian Martin
Researcher: Barbara Sussman
Photography: Frank Hodge, Bill Brandt

Music: Bob Davenport
With: Michael Jayston, Bob Davenport, Morriston Orpheus Choir of Wales

11

The Crystal Spirit: Orwell on Jura (1983)

One day in Barcelona's Lenin Barracks, Orwell briefly swapped pleasantries with an Italian militiaman. The memory of their instant camaraderie stayed with him for the rest of his life and in 1939 he wrote a poem, *The Italian Soldier Shook My Hand,*[1] that paid tribute to the young man's "crystal spirit."

Forty-four years later, another eloquent left-winger, Alan Plater, borrowed the phrase for a plaintive BBC drama, steeped in his characteristic dry wit. The ex-architect from Hull, East Yorkshire,[2] who'd made his name on gritty cop show *Z-Cars* in the sixties, was forging a reputation in the Britain of Margaret Thatcher as one of the most talented jobbing screenwriters in television. His play—billed in the *Radio Times* simply as *Orwell on Jura*—revisits his hero's twilight years in an isolated farmhouse in the Inner Hebrides, writing *Nineteen Eighty-Four* in his bedroom and battling the sickness that would cut short his life.

"He loved Orwell," says his widow, Shirley Rubinstein. "He was on the committee for the Orwell Prize for journalism [in later years]. He called himself an old-fashioned socialist. He admired Orwell enormously."[3]

Shown during the Christmas 1983 festivities, to the bemusement of its writer, director and star, *The Crystal Spirit: Orwell on Jura* was a premature reminder of a year that seemed grim before it had even started. But critically and artistically, it is one of the most accomplished works in this book, securing a Bafta nomination for best single drama in a vintage year for television. It holds a special place, too, in the hearts of those who made it.

"Music and arts producers are grave robbers,"[4] says retired BBC Scotland producer Norman McCandlish, detailing how the project came about. "They find out anniversaries that are coming up and try and get an idea in before anybody else, and of course 1984 was coming up. I knew about it and loved Orwell but I hadn't got any ideas. I was having a drink with Iain

Cuthbertson, the actor, and he said: 'You remember that Orwell wrote *Nineteen Eighty-Four* on Jura?' and I said: 'Oh yes, that's a good idea.' He said: 'I am very keen on sailing. Why don't we do a program on Jura and on sailing and do a bit about Orwell with quotations as well?' Everybody thought it was a great idea and then Iain Cuthbertson took a heavy stroke. He couldn't speak. I didn't know what to do and I suddenly thought, 'OK, let's turn it into a drama.'"

Scriptwriter Alan Plater, a trained architect, added a drawing of Barnhill to his script for *The Crystal Spirit* (photograph by David Ryan, courtesy estate of Alan Plater).

McCandlish knew vaguely of Plater's work, "and someone put me on to his agent, Peggy, who was a formidable character. I phoned her up to say: 'We'd like to see if Alan would be interested in doing a piece on Orwell writing *Nineteen Eighty-Four* on Jura.' The first thing she said to me was: 'You're very lucky that Sonia's dead, because she was so protective, I don't think you'd get away with it. Do you think you'll get away with it?' I said: 'Yes, I do! If we have a decent enough script, the estate's not going to worry too much.'"

Plater was sufficiently intrigued to go up to Glasgow, north from there to the west coast town of Crinan, and then on to Jura, a ruggedly beautiful wilderness with a population of just 200.[5]

"He went over there, I think with Norman, and he stayed on the island for about a week," says John Glenister, who directed the play. "He kept this extraordinary diary of what he'd experienced and just his general feeling of the whole place. Being a trained architect, he was a very good draftsman, so he did lots of accompanying pictures in his diary. It's a wonderful read."[6]

"Before Alan started writing it, we'd got to know Susan Watson, who was the nurse," says Rubinstein. As a young woman, Watson had looked after Orwell's son Richard, first as a live-in housekeeper in Canonbury (a neighborhood in Islington, North London), and then for a time on Jura. "She was living near us in the Kings Cross area. When we first came down to London, we got a flat at the back of Kings Cross and she was living near there and we got to know her quite well. Alan would go and listen to her for hours, talking about the Jura adventure and the life with Orwell. She talked about the things Alan [went on to] put in the play. What life was like on Jura. What Orwell was like to work for. A difficult man, and what was happening in his private life. She saw herself very much at the center of the story." Chatting with Susan, adds Rubinstein, "you had to sort out what was real and what was fantasy."

Plater widened his research to include others who'd known Orwell.[7] In his early production notes, he wrote: "I've dug around the geographical/ family/friends landscape of the subject, and it's pretty clear that we can't and mustn't play the traditional game of demonstrating how day-to-day contacts and incidents influenced the form and content of the book. It would be a grotesque cheat. According to [biographer Bernard] Crick's account,[8] the heart of the book was set before Orwell arrived on the island. The real battle was to get the bloody thing written, against various odds— though with some things working in his favour too, notably [his sister] Avril.

"Our film has to be about a man writing a book. This is a dull event to a camera. It will only come alive if we reveal some of the mystery of the man and that *can* be done by a careful examination of his behaviour in family situations—a parallel examination—rather like those arty documentaries where we cut between an interview and extracts from the Work In Question. In our case it won't be an interview, though with luck it will be even more revelatory."

The style of the film, he added, "should exactly reflect the style of Orwell's prose: clean-edged, precise, lucid, cool and ironic. Supercool. Maybe we should invite Chabrol to direct it!"[9]

The Authorial Voice

With Glenister at the helm, it was time to cast the lead. "We didn't actually approach him," says McCandlish, "but one of the suggestions was John Cleese as Orwell, purely because he was tall and slightly saturnine, avuncular and eccentric. Eventually I said: 'No, I don't want that. John only has to do one or two moves and it'll spoil the whole atmosphere.' So they said: 'What about Ronnie Pickup?' They auditioned Ronnie Pickup and I said: 'I'm not even sure about that.' [Plater and Glenister] leant on me very heavily, till I said: 'OK, fine. If you're both so certain, we'll go with Ronnie,' and boy, were they right."

Few who've seen the play would dispute that 43-year-old Ronald Pickup was an inspired choice. Even today, the actor remembers opening the envelope from his agent. "A script by Alan Plater called *The Crystal Spirit* about somebody called Eric Blair, which didn't mean anything to me because I was ignorant. I suddenly twigged that this was about a man who'd withdrawn. And it was riveting. It's one of those rare things that happen, particularly with a new script. I just knew I wanted to play this part.[10]

"For someone with his working-class roots, Alan had this extraordinary capacity to actually get into the skin of the upper class, the nobs, the toffs, which of course Orwell famously was, despite his Marxism and all of that. Two years later I did a part called Prince Iachimov in *Fortunes of War*—a strange character, but very posh, and Alan again was able to catch the rhythm, the sound, the tone of these sort of people. There are just some parts, you know how you're going to play it without thinking about it, and you knew everything, somehow, about the man. He'd compressed it into an hour and a half.... The compression of a life into that one short period was just extraordinary."

With time on his hands to research, Pickup read a selection of Orwell's prose and the 1980 biography by Bernard Crick. Along the way, his thoughts turned to Orwell's speaking voice. "I thought, is there a recording of him?

And that's where we found out that famously, no. There's no recordings of him. So I thought, who knew him? And someone said, 'You know Michael Meyer?' The translator and adapter of Ibsen and Strindberg, who I knew quite well because I'd done quite a few of his adaptations at that point. He was a lovely man. Loved talking and being helpful. So I rang him.

"I said: 'Michael, can you tell me any little anecdotes that I can't really find in the biography? The script is wonderful, it catches something very laconic about this man.'

"He said: 'Oh, yes, yes, yes, he was. He was.'

"I said: 'Did you talk to him a lot?'

"He said: 'Well, none of us talked to him a lot. I belonged to a club...' I think it was called the Pen and Ink Club, some literary club. He was very young then, Michael. They used to meet in London, perhaps once every month or two months. A bunch of writers. People like Kingsley Amis and so on."

Pickup asked Meyer how Orwell sounded. "And he said: 'Ah, well, yes, he didn't really want to talk. You have to remember, he had this wound in the throat from the Spanish Civil War and he had TB by then—incipient, but it was there. He didn't like to talk because it hurt him. He made a scraping sound.'

"I said: 'Do you mind? I know you're not an actor but do you mind doing it for me over the phone?' And he adopted this funny, sort of scratchy voice, sort of throwaway, almost incomprehensible. And I blessed him. That for me was as much a peg, like it is for any actor, where there is one particular thing, however small or big it can be, that just triggers things off for you."

To cap it all, Pickup was a heavy smoker like Orwell (and Plater). Time after time, the script places him in his bedroom, typing through the night and puffing on a roll-up. Writing for *The Observer Magazine* in 1983, Plater shared some of his contacts' recollections: that Orwell often seemed amused beneath his stern exterior, for instance, and used to stop in mid-sentence to roll a cigarette, carrying on once he'd lit it. This, he wrote, was "food and drink" to Pickup.[11]

"Ronnie was amazing. I mean, producing the damaged voice," says Rubinstein. "When they were casting it, Alan insisted, and John agreed, they had to have an actor who smoked. If the actor was a non-smoker it would show, no matter how good they were."

Sun, Sea and a Brush with Death

In Glasgow, meanwhile, McCandlish had to figure out how to make a TV movie on a music and arts budget. Grudgingly, he says, BBC Scotland's drama department loaned him several members of staff, including the talented production designer Campbell Gordon.

"We then had the problems of logistics," he says. "Jura's a small island with a very small population, and Kinuachdrachd, where Orwell stayed, is right up at the north end, at the end of a single-track road. There is no accommodation until you get about halfway down, where there is the Astors' house, the big estate house.[12] When you go down to the bottom end of the island, which faces on to Islay, the other island, there is a township, but it's a very small population and not much in the way of hotels or other stuff.

"I did a deal with the Astors where we would rent the estate house, which was a smallish, castle-type house, and that the wardrobe, make-up and cast would stay there, and the cameramen and all the principals [sound, lighting crew and so on] would be over on the mainland. No mobile phones, remember, at that time. They stayed at Crinan, which is on the mainland, and they had to arrange with a boat-owner—he owned the Crinan Hotel and was quite glad of the business—that the crew would be brought over every morning to shoot at the north end of the island and we would drive up. We had to hire Land Rovers instead of normal cars."

The island's tiny population was well aware of what was going on. Most of them had been around in Orwell's time, says Glenister, "so they were aware of the island's importance in that particular respect. I think they had a pride and of course, they have a very good distillery over there, so that adds to their fame. Margaret Fletcher, the laird's wife of the island, was still alive and she knew Orwell well because he used to stop off at her house on the way, cycling into the village. Her memories were obviously important to Alan and she lived in this crumbling Edwardian manor house with about ten bedrooms and an old downstairs kitchen with a huge Aga and God knows what in this lovely, lovely dining room. She moved out to stay with her daughter and handed the whole house over to us."

The bulk of the drama takes place at Barnhill, the stone farmhouse Orwell rented from Fletcher. A challenge for Gordon, the designer, was recreating the garden he planted to reflect different stages of growth throughout the year. "The weather was sometimes almost too good," adds Pickup. "It started on the first of June and we had day after day after day of beautiful sunshine, and the long evenings, and we'd go back to this wonderful old [estate] house and it was so civilized. We did it for virtually no money. It was one of those things you'd have done for even a token amount. We all got on terribly well. I keep going back to the script—nobody's having to worry or have big discussions about how we're going to change this or modify that or whatever. Even if the weather had been perpetually dreadful, it would still have been a joyous experience."

Except, that is, when McCandlish and two young women almost drowned.

On a boating trip in 1947, Orwell misread the tide table and was capsized with his son, nephew and niece, almost perishing in the currents of the Corryvreckan whirlpool.[13] "We filmed the scene," says McCandlish, "and I, being a cheapskate, said: 'I'm not paying for stuntmen to come over. I will row the boat in costume and we'll get a couple of make-up girls.' This was for the very long shot." A fishing boat was on standby, just in case. "There were walkie-talkies: one on the boat and one with John way up on the hill. John said: 'Action.' I rowed away and he said: 'Cut.' I shook the oars and signaled to the rescue boat to come in."

The boat came in "far too fast" and threw down a rope with a buoy on the end. This ran so swiftly along the floor of McCandlish's boat, "I knew that if I'd kept my hand there, it would have taken my hand off. [Before we knew it], the boat had disappeared and we were left bobbing about on the fringes of the Corryvreckan. Fortunately the hotel owner Nick Ryan had come over for the day because he was also doing the catering. He was in a small, outboard rib of his own and he pulled alongside and got us very gently back to shore."

Glenister calls it a "very hairy" incident. "It was touch and go. I thought for a minute we were going to be on BBC News that night."

Spirit of the Forties

So, what of the play itself? Set across three summers, from 1946 to 1948, it stands as one of Plater's most perceptive, compassionate works. For one thing, it's a remarkably assured, measured piece, free of the hamhandedness that often mars biopics in general. Where others would shoehorn in the details of his life and times, Plater gives us a rounded Orwell— a kind, rude, doleful, weary, frightened, stubborn, loyal, awkward, boyishly enthusiastic, difficult genius—and supporting characters to match. As the story unfolds and the dialogue sparkles, it's clear that he's at the top of his game—as is everyone on the production. Plater himself called it "the gentlest, most low-key piece I've ever been involved in."[14]

"Like looking through a windowpane," are Orwell's first words. He's quoting (or misquoting) his own work—the well-known line about good prose in the essay *Why I Write*—but in this instance, he really is looking out of a window at Barnhill as landlady Mrs. Fletcher introduces him to his new summer home.[15] In the weeks that follow, he shares "a wee dram" (and his reasons for leaving London) with new neighbor Donald Darroch;

describes his impressions of the island in a letter to his little sister, Avril; and shoots and skins a rabbit, just as she's arriving on his doorstep to take care of him.

When toddler Richard Blair and his nurse, Susan, join the household, the two women's arguments over Richard's welfare prompt Orwell, somewhat embarrassedly, to lay Susan off with four weeks' wages. Her place is soon filled by Orwell's friend and one-time benefactor Richard Rees, who turns up effectively unannounced, his letter and telegram lying uncollected in the general store and post office at the south end of the island. Over late-night drinks, the men chat about *Animal Farm*'s financial success and the theme of Orwell's work in progress. It's about two and two making four, he says. Or five, as the case may be.

It's the summer of 1947. New neighbor Bill Dunn, an invalid soldier, is playing the bagpipes for Avril, Darroch and the two Richards. Orwell, trying to write, comes down from his room warily and into the garden. "If the sound of my typewriter disturbs anyone," he says dryly, "please let me know."

From coughing fits, it's apparent that his health is worsening. After almost drowning in the Gulf of Corryvreckan, he's admitted to a TB unit in East Kilbride for six months, where a gift from one of his friends—an early ballpoint pen, capable of writing upside-down—fills him with delight. "Specially designed for tubercular novelists," he grins.

Finally, it's 1948. The novel, its name changed from *The Last Man in Europe*, is nearly finished. Orwell confides in Rees that the book isn't what he'd hoped—that he's "ballsed it up." And with no typist available, he has to finish the manuscript himself, even though the effort is killing him.

The play ends with Orwell, Richard, Avril and her new fiancé, Bill, driving away from Barnhill for the last time. During a torrent of rain, the car gets stuck in the mud, forcing Bill and Avril to go for help. Orwell turns to his son, sitting next to him on the back seat, and tests his arithmetic. What do two and two make? "Four," says Richard. Yes, agrees dad, but governments may try to tell you it's five. Be a farmer, not a writer, he advises his son as the child nods off. And as Eric Blair ponders the rewards of fatherhood, we, the viewers, hear a 1950 news report on the death of George Orwell.

Doubleplusgood

When Plater, Glenister and Pickup learned that *The Crystal Spirit* was scheduled for 20 December (at 9:25 p.m.), the three of them shot off a letter to the controller of BBC1, Alan Hart. "We are deeply concerned that the film will be lost in the Christmas rush," they wrote. What, they asked respectfully, were the reasons?

"ITV had made a similar sort of thing, not nearly as good, with James Fox playing Orwell," says Glenister. "That was due for schedule in the New Year so the BBC wanted to get ahead of that, which they did. As it happens, Nancy Banks-Smith in *The Guardian*, when she reviewed our film, said: 'Don't bother to watch anything else about George Orwell. This is the one. There's nothing going to beat this, ever.' Which was very sweet of her. Something like that, anyway."

Banks-Smith did indeed say something like that, adding: "If BBC Scotland will pass on my congratulations to everyone concerned, it will save me a fortune in stamps."[16] In *The Times*, Dennis Hackett lauded Pickup's "virtuoso performance" and said Plater had "made a brilliant job" of the script, "the dialogue spare, mordant, intuitive and sadly humorous."[17] The *Daily Mail*'s Elizabeth Cowley thought Plater had captured Orwell's speech, humor and crusty temperament exactly, while Pickup resembled every photo of the great man ever. "An award-worthy delight in every way," she wrote.[18] And she was right.

"We did win the two top prizes at the Celtic Film Festival that year," says Glenister. "Dilys Powell—who was film critic of *The Sunday Times*, the doyenne of film critics in a way—was one of the judges and gave a lovely speech saying what a wonderful film it was."

At the 1984 Bafta Awards, *Orwell on Jura*, as it was billed, was shortlisted for best single television drama alongside Stephen Frears' *Saigon—Year of the Cat*, Desmond Davis's *The Country Girls* and Colin Gregg's *To the Lighthouse*. The winner was John Schlesinger's *An Englishman Abroad*, a play by Alan Bennett about the exiled Cambridge spy Guy Burgess. In the best actor category, Pickup lost out to Alan Bates, who'd played Burgess.

Much to everyone's annoyance, *The Crystal Spirit* has never been released commercially or screened again. Such was his frustration, Glenister wrote to a BBC executive in 2003. "I said please, can we just, in tribute to the man himself, on his bloody centenary, show the film? The BBC always come up with this rubbish about, 'Well, we're not sure who owns the rights any more,' and all that bollocks. I get so cross. Never been repeated."

McCandlish, too, admits to being intensely annoyed. "I suspect that it's because it came out of left field and it was made in Scotland by the music and arts department rather than the mainstream drama department. I don't even have a decent copy of it."

For Pickup, the real genius lies in Plater's screenplay. "It's one of the most remarkable distillations of a very complex man and what it's like being a writer, what it's like being creative. He made this very private, very shielded man come to life and it was vivid because he had him doing things all the time: skinning rabbits, digging the garden, smoking, riding his bike. Always active, despite the thing that was killing him. All that came over in the script, but not completely. One only realized the joy of the script even more when we were actually doing it, like all good scripts. Alan was a great film writer and he knew how it needed this activity—this physical activity of a dying man. The tension between the two made it thrilling to play."

To Glenister, the play is "perhaps the most rewarding piece of work I ever had the privilege to do." He says: "The very last scene in the car, when he's talking to his son and the car's broken down. That was sensational. I think Alan's writing there, when he's talking to the boy about two and two making four, and people will tell you it makes five, I think that's an extraordinary speech. I said to my wife: 'I want that read by Ronnie Pickup at my funeral.' Unless he goes first, in which case I shall read it at his. It says everything about politics and politicians and, well, the whole of Orwell's philosophy contained in that one speech, almost. They were almost spiritual twins, Orwell and Alan, because Alan was a very strong human socialist, as indeed Orwell was, and I think he saw so much in common with Orwell's thinking that that's why he homed in so precisely on the man himself."

"One of the happiest experiences of my life,"[19] says Pickup—who in a letter to the author of this book, explains why: "I do not ignore the great privilege I have had over the years working with the great directors and actors on great texts. However, all the elements do not always gel, come together! Here they did—a beautiful cast, including two old friends, Fiona Walker and David Swift—director John, producer Norman, Scotland, weather—but supremely the great Alan Plater's evocation of this craggy, laconic, rude (often), honest, awkwardly tender and pure creature—'a crystal spirit.' I just loved playing him, wishing to be like him."[20]

The Crystal Spirit: Orwell on Jura

George Orwell: Ronald Pickup
Avril Blair: Fiona Walker
Richard Rees: David Swift
Bill Dunn: Kit Thacker
Margaret Fletcher: Lucinda Gane
Donald Darroch: Bill Riddoch
Shopkeeper: Eileen McCallum
Susan Watson: Melanie Parr
Richard Blair (age 2): Graeme Rozga

Richard Blair (age 3): Ross Rozga
Henry Dakin: Robin Davies
Jane Dakin: Wendy Marsh
Lucy Dakin: Sally Kinghorn
Doctor: Edward Gray
Written by: Alan Plater
Director: John Glenister
Producer: Norman McCandlish
Designer: Campbell Gordon

12

Arena: George Orwell (1983–84)

In the dying days of 1983, a fierce, mustachioed face stared out from Britain's magazine racks. To mark the New Year, and for the first time since 1965, the front cover of the *Radio Times* was largely given over to a "Big Brother is watching you" poster. But in this instance, a specially commissioned color illustration showed the poster peeling back, revealing eighties-style electronics in the wall. "You know the book," ran the cover line. "Now watch the year arrive."[1]

In a three-page feature, science-fiction novelist Christopher Priest reflected on the prescience or otherwise of scribes like himself, barely touching on Orwell's significance. More usefully, however, at the foot of the page, the magazine listed that week's Orwellian programming on BBC television and radio.[2] On the pop music station Radio 1, for example, *Saturday Live* was devoting its New Year's Eve afternoon show to the author, with singer Ian Dury reading extracts from *Nineteen Eighty-Four*. More sober-minded listeners could tune into Radio 4, where the actor Kenneth Haigh was reading a serialized version for *A Book at Bedtime*.

At the same time, BBC2 was going to town. On 1 and 2 January, it broadcast *Beyond 1984*, an exercise in futurism that took "a cool look at the prospects for the UK in the next 25 years."[3] After that came *1984—Voices in a City*, a documentary about social conditions shown on 5 January as part of its *Forty Minutes* series.[4]

A five-part documentary on Orwell, which began in December, was also on the list. "It was the early days of [arts strand] *Arena*," says Nigel Williams, its director. "The BBC in those days was a massive program-making organization, all of which was finished really by [nineties director-general] John Birt and Margaret Thatcher, not necessarily in that order. In those days you would just suggest an idea and make it. As it developed, the films got longer and longer and longer and we ended up doing five, because you could do that in those days. Originally it was one film."[5]

Such, Such Were the Joys (29 December 1983)

The programs, each lasting about 50 minutes, were shown in a teatime slot on consecutive weekday evenings. The first relies to a large extent on Orwell's official biographer, Bernard Crick, who provides a running commentary on Eric Blair's early life while speaking to contemporaries such as the poet Jacintha Buddicom, a friend, neighbor and childhood crush of Blair's. Once, the smitten young man gave her a copy of *Dracula* with a cross and a clove of garlic enclosed. She never took his infatuation seriously, but did hang on to the crucifix, which she wears in the film.

Sir John Grotrian, a classmate from St. Cyprian's prep school, remembers Blair as a much-bullied recluse, "dull, uninteresting [and] unattractive." Historian Sir Steven Runciman is kinder about their time at Eton, where Eric was satirical and very good company; while Mabel Fierz, in footage from *The Road to the Left*, expresses his concern for Aldous Huxley, the myopic French master who was the butt of his pupils' jokes.

Dennis Collings, son of the Blairs' family doctor, shares his bafflement—and that of Eric's father Richard, who'd hoped his son would join the Indian civil service—as to why his friend took a grim policing job in Burma. Collings suggests his much-vaunted anti-imperialism wasn't as cut-and-dried as he made out: "I think he thought we ought not to be there, but he was pro what we'd done for the country."

In the genteel Suffolk beach resort of Southwold, where Richard retired with his family, two sweet old ladies sum up the Eric they knew. He was a shy, quiet, well-mannered young fellow, too wrapped up in his thoughts to mix with his peers, says a Miss Fox (her first name isn't mentioned). Joan Mullock thought him "just that little bit above ordinary people like myself" and says he was fond of taking walks beside the River Orwell.

As the story moves to Paris and Orwell's deliberate descent into poverty, Williams brings on Southwold tailor Jack Denny, who used to make flannel trousers for Blair costing almost a working man's weekly wage. He was, says Denny, "a good payer."

In a hostel or "common lodging house" in Tooley Street, London, used by Orwell in his tramping days, the director speaks to supervisor Paul D'Acosta. Have conditions changed since the 1920s? "No," he says. There are more down-and-outs than ever, and they're fighting for fewer resources.

The Road to Wigan Pier (30 December 1983)

Part two devotes itself almost entirely to Orwell's polemic of 1937, but finds time in the first ten minutes to deal with *Keep the Aspidistra Flying*.

Mabel Fierz, filmed this time in 1982, tells of how his bookshop job sprang from him visiting her in London; and Kay Ekevall, a customer who "went around" with him, describes their social life, taking long walks on Hampstead Heath and meeting "friends who were also interested in books."

One of them, writer Jon Kimche, condemns *Aspidistra* as a "sordid, depressing" distortion of what the shop was like and accuses Orwell of "thinking in stereotypes" when he makes fun of the customers. He suggests Orwell wronged not only the owners (who welcomed Blair into their home) but also the "most charming and unaffected and helpful and rich" Sir Richard Rees, lampooned in the book as Comstock's patron, Ravelston.

Ekevall—whose precise relationship with the author is left vague—talks about his budding romance with Eileen O'Shaughnessy and the wedding plans that led to him accepting the *Wigan Pier* commission. She and Orwell had agreed that, should either of them meet someone else, they would go their separate ways—so when Eileen came along, they did.

For the rest of the film, Williams is lucky to have Bragg's 1970 interviews. Those shot in 1983—with the grown-up children of Orwell's contacts, modern-day trade unionists and welfare officials—reflect Wigan's ambivalent attitudes to the book. Again, Orwell comes across as less than saintly: a nice man, prone to thoughtless, insensitive behavior. According to Gerry Kennan, whose dad stole the show in *The Road to the Left*, the author broke his promise to send the family a copy of the book.

"I thought it was really a terrible book," says old flame Ekevall. "I thought it denigrated all socialists and it put the working class in a terrible, sordid light."

Homage to Catalonia (2 January 1984)

The third installment starts with Eric and Eileen's wedding and their attempts to run a village shop in Wallington, Hertsfordshire. Before long the focus moves to Spain, where Londoner Stafford Cottman, who was 18 when he knew Orwell, offers a tour of the trenches and buildings in which they served. When his comrade Francisco Ramirez, who joined the civil war at 16, admits he's never read *Homage to Catalonia*, Cottman isn't fazed. He may not have read it, says the Englishman, "but he's certainly the subject" of it.

In Barcelona, Williams talks to Spaniards about the communist purges of May 1937, when authorities targeted the anarchist POUM militia to which Orwell belonged. Shot in the throat, he nearly died on trench duty and was lucky to escape to France—but before he did, he made a dreadful impression on his Spanish roommate in hospital, who found him boring company and "a frightened and bitter man."

Back in Britain, the director confronts Frank Frankford—an elderly communist and sometime writer for the *Daily Worker*—with the consequences of his actions in 1937. Frankford, who was manning the same trench when Orwell was shot, already disliked him for *The Road to Wigan Pier*. As the turmoil mounted in Barcelona, an article bearing his name alleged the POUM had hidden weapons to bolster the fascist cause. Looking sweaty and uncomfortable, Frankford responds to the allegations with "I never said anything like that" and "Certain tactics are legitimate when you're fighting a battle like this."[6]

The Lion and the Unicorn (3 January 1984)

Orwell's emergence as an English patriot and political sage, selling the war against Hitler to leftists with reservations about it, forms the basis of part four. With a wealth of newsreel footage and slightly younger contributors than before, it tells with some assurance of his time at the BBC, producing literary programs for India; his reasons for joining the socialist magazine *Tribune* as literary editor; publishers' qualms about *Animal Farm*'s demolition of wartime ally Stalin; and his transformation, late in life, into a family man.

Interviewees include radio producer Douglas Cleverdon, who reckons EM Forster's show on Proust was Orwell's greatest scoop; Cleverdon's wife Nest ("He was a big, shambling man, rather hollow-chested, very white, very odd eyes, very pale blue eyes"); Lettice Cooper, a friend of Eileen's at the Ministry of Food's PR department; and *Tribune* colleague Tosco Fyvel, who remembers how Orwell, out of shyness, would break the ice with a firm, positive statement on entering a room. His essays start in much the same way, Fyvel observes.

While literary figures offer dispassionate appraisals of Orwell the writer— Malcolm Muggeridge and Julian Symons disparage his skills as a novelist, even though they were friends of his—it's Cooper who gives the program its heart, portraying him as a kind, polite klutz with no idea how to look after himself. When baby Richard came along, Eileen was "a bit uneasy for fear she couldn't love it enough," but she did, "and it was all right."

1984 (4 January 1984)

Starting with Eileen's demise on an operating table and ending with Orwell's death from a ruptured blood vessel in his lung, the last film is shot through with melancholia. It takes for granted that the London of *Nineteen Eighty-Four* is a distorted reflection of bankrupt Britain in 1948: Julian Symons says as much, citing shortages, clothing coupons and broken lifts.

Housekeeper Susan Watson visits Orwell's old apartment in Canonbury, Islington—one of London's seedier areas in the war, says Crick, but gentrified now—and remembers him as a nice, interesting man with a rigid domestic routine. Symons recalls how he would almost revel in discomfort, tucking zestfully into the practically inedible "Victory pie" at lunchtime. Orwell could see the appeal of totalitarianism, his friend believes, because he was suppressing a sadistic streak in his own nature.

His landlady on Jura, Margaret Nelson, and a grown-up Richard Blair relive the time Richard fell and split his forehead badly, on an island where the doctor might be hours away. Avril Blair and Sonia Orwell appear thanks to Jack Bond's 1965 film, and Muggeridge speaks of his friend's "enormous thrill" when "buxom, blooming" Sonia agreed to marry him. Muggeridge, who describes Orwell's church funeral touchingly, reflects on his lifelong unhappiness and agrees that right-wingers probably gained the most from his work. "The great success of George has been that he has leftish credentials and takes a rightist's view," he says.

As the film becomes more openly reverential, his close friend David Astor, who secured him his burial spot in a country churchyard in Oxfordshire, says: "I loved him."

Richard, batting aside a question about his adoptive status, states: "George Orwell was my father and that's that." In the end, he emerges from his suburban house, gets into his car and drives off—into a Britain that, for all its shortcomings, is not the police state his dad warned about.

"All you want is this guy's address book"

The way Williams tells it, the story of the *Arena* films is of trying to sideline Bernard Crick, the authorized biographer whose *George Orwell: A Life* came out in 1980. In the beginning, Crick had been a crucial component.

"One of the early interviews we did was with David Astor, who was really a friend of Orwell—a very, very good friend of his—and he lived in St. John's Wood, next to Paul McCartney, actually," says Williams. "We went round and did the interview and Crick asked these questions, which lasted about half an hour, that were mainly full of him talking about himself and his views of George Orwell.

"I was quite a young guy. I didn't say anything. So I went back, and in the office next morning they said: 'David Astor's on the line.' Oh fuck, am

I in trouble? He was a very distinguished guy and I really admired him and liked him. David Astor came on the line and he said: 'It was very nice to meet you, Nigel. I wonder whether you'd like to come round and sort of do the interview again?'

"I said: 'What's the problem?'"

"He said: 'He just spent his time telling me about this bloke who was a dear friend of mine.'"

"I said: 'Well, that's sort of what I thought.' So then I came round and I did another interview with him. Crick just wanted to tell people things, so more and more it was just kind of, 'lose him from the film,' really. It got to be an absolute nightmare. It got to the point where the crew couldn't stand him. I don't want to be horrible. He's dead, good luck to him, but this is the truth about what happened. We're talking about George Orwell, so let's tell the truth."

According to Williams, the sound recordist grew so tired of Crick's voice that as interviews dragged on, he would stop putting tape in the machine. Midway through the film's production, another colleague summarized his position like this: "Nige, all you want is this guy's address book."

"Gradually it became more about the witnesses and less and less about him, so he was absolutely furious with me. The film got really good reviews on the whole but he wrote the one bad one, in [the literary magazine] *Granta*, where he had friends, which he sent to me with all his most negative comments underlined, which I thought was hilarious."

"What you saw was what you got"

As it turned out, Orwell's friends and acquaintances were very keen to talk about him. "I think he was a very much-loved guy," says Williams. "There was a woman called Mabel Fierz who was in the movie, who was really sweet. She was quite hard to track down. Various people were hard to track down but I think the real coup we had was Stafford Cottman, who I don't think has been in many other films. He's dead now. He became a really good friend. He's the most wonderful, wonderful man and it was an honor. Having fought in the Spanish Civil War, he became a rear gunner on a Lancaster. What an amazing guy.

"He was more or less our discovery. I can't quite think how we tracked him down. It was a mixture of original people leading you to people, contacts who'd been in Crick's book and … it was hard to track down [Orwell's] son, I remember. As you got to know one person, they would suggest another person and so it went.

"There was a bloke in the film [Sir John Grotrian] who was at prep school with him who is absolutely hilarious. He said, 'Yeah, I remember him well. He was not very good at games.' He just happened to be alive and took a dim view of Orwell. I can't remember how we found him, but I remember thinking, 'Bloody hell.' We even at one point found his tailor in Suffolk. It was rather an interesting interview, I thought, because it showed what a toff Orwell was really. He had his clothes tailor-made. He went to fucking Eton, you know, so we're not talking about a working-class lad at all, and I thought that was rather revealing."

The interview with Frank Frankford is probably the most toe-curling part. "An old communist, yeah. I gave him quite a hard time. He was not happy. I'd been in the Communist Party so I knew what these people were like. The thing about those dyed-in-the-wool communists is that they still think you can't make an omelet without breaking eggs. That's their attitude. It's extraordinary. I think he's in Crick's book. From my memory of it, Crick said: 'You won't get him to talk,' and then we did get him to talk. And then of course when you do an interview, they can usually tell from the angle of the questions, but that's how it goes. You might as well tell the truth as you see it."

The Wigan shoot was particularly interesting. "We filmed outside the social[7] and then we just asked people on the street and some old bloke remembered him. I think he's in the film. He says: 'Oh, we thought he were from the government. When he came along, talking about the working class and so on, we thought he were stopping scroungers.' Because of course, he had a very posh voice.

"Malcolm Muggeridge was brilliant in it. He was an amazingly nice man, Muggeridge. We did the interview and he said a wonderful thing. He said: 'Then he said to me, "Well, Malcolm, I don't think you can die if you've still got a book in you." But I'm afraid he did die.' I wish we'd kept the off-cuts.

"He came out after the interview and he said: 'I remember he was having an affair with a woman.' [Orwell] wasn't very happily married to his first wife towards the end of the relationship. This may be in subsequent biographies, I don't know. But he said: 'He was having sex with her in the park, because you know he was a very, very tall fellow. And he remembered it being very, very difficult to get out of the headlights.' An incredible George Orwell story. And he couldn't think who the woman was. We finished the interview, we were packing up the car and he said: 'Oh, I remember, it was [the poet] Stevie Smith.' How about that? George Orwell and Stevie Smith. That didn't get in the film, but it's quite an image, isn't it? Two characters. Two very tall, quite mournful people."

Williams agrees with Cyril Connolly that Orwell is like DH Lawrence—
that his personality shines out of everything he wrote. "I think what you
saw was what you got, and I think he was a guy who couldn't help but say
what he thought about things. I think he was quite an awkward person,
awkward with people, and quite shy and quite damaged by his experiences.
But if you look at the amazing forward-thinkingness of those early essays,
his attitude to Burma, his attitude to the Communist Party, he was the most
incredibly honest and direct person and I think that's what came through.
The world he came from was unbelievably antediluvian, but he had his fin-
ger on the pulse of politics in a way that I can't think of any other writer.
The film confirmed all my hero-worshiping instincts. It was a pure pleasure
to do."

A Lost Voice

At the end of the series' run, Stewart Lane of the *Morning Star* (formerly the *Daily Worker*) was thoroughly fed up. "Viewers must surely have
had more than enough of the media's deification of George Orwell, during
which nothing has been too trivial to recall," he wrote waspishly.[8] But his
colleagues on British newspapers begged to differ. "Sober without being
staid" was the verdict of Lucy Hughes-Hallett in *The Standard*.[9] *The
Observer*'s Julian Barnes, now an award-winning novelist himself, admired
how the series highlighted "all the writer's old, irreducible virtues of clear
vision and clear expression."[10]

In a lengthy review for *The Times Literary Supplement*, Peter Kemp
praised the series for shining a light on those (such as Frankford) less committed to truth than Orwell was, and showcasing a range of views that often
revealed more about the interviewees than Orwell.[11] Just one thing struck
him as unconvincing: the voice of the man reading Orwell's prose. "A mystery bordering on a disaster," agreed Christopher Dunkley in the *Financial
Times*.[12] The "strong home-counties lisp" irritated Hugo Williams in the
New Statesman too.[13] It was "weird," thought the *Sunday Telegraph*'s Philip
Purser, to use such a "flat, thoroughly modern, undistinguished voice."[14]

"That was me," says Williams.

"In those days Alan Yentob[15] was a very hands-on producer. He was
really good, but he was hysterically involved and he was an amazing worrier.
In order to dub films in those days, they didn't have what they call rock 'n'
roll, so if you made a mistake in the dub, you had to go back to the beginning and dub the whole thing through again. So you can imagine what a
business that was.

"Anyway, we were at the dub and we were halfway through. I had hired to do Orwell's voice Alan Rickman, who in those days was not a very well-known actor. Alan did the voiceover and as we played in the voice, both Alan [Yentob] and I said: 'It's too middle class.' We got into a state where we decided Alan's voice was wrong for George Orwell and that I'd do it. I really don't know … egomania, arrogance, sheer ignorance. So we got rid of Alan.

"Alan was absolutely sweet about it. I was really embarrassed. He said: 'Look, if you'd hired another actor, I would have been annoyed.' I think what we were after, with the idea that this was particularly the journalism, was to get the non-actor voice sort of thing. We couldn't find a recording of Orwell's voice, and then years later, because it had always haunted me, we found the only recording that there was. This is ages ago. It was in the old gram library of the BBC.

"We found this disk, but it wasn't classified under 'Orwell' because of course the producer was Eric Blair. It was broadcast for the Burmese service during the war. We put the recording on the record player and he sounded exactly like fucking Alan Rickman. We went back to look for it again about 15, 20 years later. Couldn't find the record…. So that's how George Orwell disappeared."

Arena: George Orwell

Director: Nigel Williams
Producer: Alan Yentob
Program consultant: Professor Bernard Crick
Research: Diana Mansfield, Melda Gillespie

13

The Road to 1984 (1984)

Like *The Crystal Spirit*, which aired a month earlier and met with more acclaim, commercial TV's *The Road to 1984* can boast location filming on Jura and a respected leading man. Apart from that, the two have little in common. Rather than present a wistful snapshot of Orwell's final years, as the BBC chose to do, Granada Television's biopic looks at his life in a broader context, from his service to the British Empire in Burma to his solitary, blood-soaked demise at University College Hospital, London.

On balance, writer Willis Hall and director David Wheatley have served up a useful primer on Orwell, cramming in most of the life-changing experiences you'd expect from such a venture. Granted, they stumble on occasion—piling flashback upon flashback in the opening 15 minutes and lumbering the actors with more exposition than is credible—but in many ways, their ambition does them credit.

After an attention-grabbing Two Minutes Hate ahead of the titles, the TV movie begins towards the end of his life, in 1949. His young fiancée, Sonia Brownell, is with the hospital chaplain, finalizing the paperwork for their wedding. Looking at the groom's birth certificate, the cleric is surprised to see the name Blair. Isn't he George something-or-other, the chap who wrote *Nineteen Eighty-Four*? "He writes under the name of Orwell," says Sonia. "His real name's Eric Arthur Blair." Orwell, played by James Fox, remains in bed for the ceremony, wearing a red smoking jacket that Sonia's bought him. A radio bulletin announces their marriage to the nation, with a precis of the novelist's entire life to date.

As he sleeps restlessly later in the day, a nurse enters his private room and hangs his jacket in a wardrobe. He splutters and turns, and while she's leaning over him, has a fever dream about Maurice, an Old Etonian homosexual he'd met as he lay in a flophouse one night. Keeping their dormitory awake with a rendition of the *Eton Boating Song*, Maurice offends Orwell by assuming he's fallen on hard times. "I'm a writer," says Orwell peevishly, his mind drifting between the two settings.

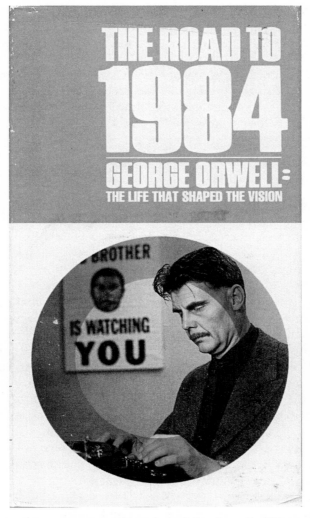

In 1984, Simon and Schuster Video released the Granada TV movie, starring James Fox, on VHS for an American audience (copyright Granada TV).

Before long, we're into another flashback. Blair's on a beach in 1920s Southwold, spelling out his literary ambitions to stuffy parents Richard and Ida. Dressed in a white linen suit and drawing insouciantly on a cigarette, he announces out of the blue that he's resigned his police job in Burma to become a writer. Horrified, like her husband, at the thought of Eric chasing a pipe dream, his mother berates him. "No one can do just as they please," she says— a nod, perhaps, to Orwell's *As I Please* column in *Tribune* in the forties.

Flashback number three dramatizes *A Hanging*, his 1931 essay about the sordid business of executing a Burmese prisoner. "Oh Ram, oh Ram," chants the man on the gallows, a noose around his neck and a bag over his head. Strangely enough, this isn't the last we'll see of him.

A steam train chugs by, transporting Orwell to Wigan in the thirties. His trip down a mine—presumably too expensive to film—barely gets a look-in, so instead we see boys scrabbling for coal on slag heaps and a dejected, beaten-down woman poking a stick up a pipe. It's an almost horizontal waste pipe, not a drainpipe, by the way—a discrepancy the script acknowledges by slyly rewriting Orwell's prose.

Come on Eileen

Following a commercial break, part two covers Orwell's first marriage and more. The film is finding its feet by now, eschewing the overdone flashbacks and clumsy infodumps that characterized part one. With credible reconstructions of Spain's battlefields, it makes a decent job of dramatizing *Homage to Catalonia*—although when Orwell is shot, the condemned man from *A Hanging* returns, flashing before his eyes like an angel of death. "Oh Ram, oh Ram," says the poor soul.

Much better handled are the internecine conflicts of Barcelona in 1937. In a hotel lobby decorated with a mural of Stalin, a recovering Eric learns from his beloved Eileen that their anarchist allegiances have made them targets for the Soviet-backed authorities. While Orwell surveys a ruined church and prepares to take a pew for the night, the secret police turn his wife's hotel room upside-down in search of evidence. Alone in the darkened chapel, he takes a match to his identification papers and, in voiceover, declares that every serious line he's written since has been against totalitarianism and for democratic socialism.

Back in London, where the left-wing press isn't interested in communist atrocities, Orwell takes out his anger on a generic editor figure. "Do you know their latest bit of doublethink?" he rages. "The five-year plan in four years. The Russians are telling their own people that two plus two makes five!" Working at the BBC, he loses his temper again, complaining to his boss that producing poetry for a handful of Asian radio owners is a waste of time.

On a trip to the movies one night, he and Eileen see a newsreel promoting Churchill and Stalin's friendship in the war against Hitler. This sets in motion his next project, *Animal Farm*, which he reads to his wife in bed every evening. In parallel, Wheatley's film brings the animals' rebellion, the seven commandments, pigs sleeping in beds and "some animals are more equal than others" to life, with real livestock.

The Blairs adopt a baby, Richard, and while Orwell is reporting from what's left of Germany, Eileen dies unexpectedly in surgery. As he stares in shock at the suitcase on her hospital bed, a matron tells him she was a wonderful person. Yes, he replies stiffly, "She was a good old stick." In Islington, he hires Susan Watson as a live-in housekeeper and children's nurse, asking: "You will let him play with his thingummy, won't you?" as she's bathing Richard.[1] But to her alarm, Orwell wakes in the middle of the night, coughing up blood. "Oh Ram, oh Ram," says the Burmese man.

Visiting the offices of *Horizon* magazine, Blair, who has taken to calling himself George Orwell in everyday life, tells editor Cyril Connolly about his plans to write a novel on Jura. Subsequently, over tea at his flat, he lunges like an adolescent at the assistant editor, Sonia. Kissing her on the mouth, he invites her to join him in the Hebrides, adding a marriage proposal for good measure.

As Clear as Crystal

Part three, set mostly on Jura, differs markedly from *The Crystal Spirit*, finding different points of interest in Bernard Crick's biography. Here, for instance, there's room for David Holbrook, an ex-army officer and communist who locked horns with Orwell during his stay at Barnhill as Susan's guest.[2]

Scenes alternate between Jura and the fictional Oceania, where Fox plays a bespectacled, clean-shaven Winston Smith, Julia looks like Sonia with an eighties hairstyle, and the Stalin mural from Barcelona provides the template of sorts for "Big Brother is watching you." Admiring a framed photo of Sonia on his bedroom mantelpiece, Orwell imagines her naked in the room above Charrington's shop, in an arrest scene that prefigures Michael Radford's unashamedly sexual *Nineteen Eighty-Four* movie. It's jarring and gratuitous, to put it mildly.

In a more intelligent juxtaposition, Donald McKillop doubles as O'Brien and the doctor who treats Orwell's tubercular condition. One minute he's pushing a long, metal implement down the writer's throat in a Scottish hospital; the next, he's interrogating Winston about how many fingers he's holding up. Back in the operating room, the kindly medic finishes up. "Sorry I had to put you through that torture," he says.

Finally, in Orwell's London hospital room, he and his new wife plan a sojourn in a Swiss sanitarium. The socialist author, who's now wealthy, gripes about American critics mistaking *Nineteen Eighty-Four* for an attack on the Soviet Union alone. Once Sonia has left, the "oh Ram" flashback returns. A trapdoor in Burma opens, the prisoner drops through it ... and in London, a nurse finds Orwell dead, his chin and pajamas red with blood.

A BBC news report from 1950 (also remounted for the end of *The Crystal Spirit*) and an extract from one of Orwell's letters about totalitarianism—"don't let it happen," essentially[3]—bring the TV movie to a natural end. Except that after the credits have rolled, there's a coda set in Blair's down-and-out days.

As he and a gray-haired tramp sit around a brazier, the old man points at Aldebaran. It must be difficult, says Blair, to take an interest in astronomy when you're living rough. Not at all, says the man, tapping his forehead and insisting that his mind is still free. Blair, lost in thought, nods. The seed of his *magnum opus* has been planted.

Inner Feelings

Having cut his teeth on arts documentaries at the BBC (he directed *Arena*'s title shot of a bottle floating on water, still in use more than 40 years later[4]), the late David Wheatley, then aged 33,[5] pitched *The Road to 1984* as a project he could write, direct and produce. When this proved too demanding—he'd only recently turned to drama, after all—Granada suggested that playwright Willis Hall, best known for the 1963 movie *Billy Liar*,[6] help with the scripting chores in return for the writer's credit.[7] Steve Morrison, Granada's head of features, would produce.[8]

In an interview with *The Stage and Television Today* six weeks before the film aired, Wheatley discussed the merits of the drama-documentary format, which he felt offered far more scope than traditional factual programs. Used with imagination, he said, it could convey inner feelings and show how earlier events had influenced a person's behavior.[9] In *Broadcast* magazine, he went further: "To make a profile of a person, the secret is to find out what made them what they were. You research the facts so you know every detail, revisit their life and then, and only then, can you try to get inside that person."[10]

"My goodness, the detail with which David went into everything," says Julia Goodman, who played Sonia. "We had to do all the history, the politics, everything. We had a lot of rehearsal and it was very much about mining the whole of the Orwell back story. This is a very interesting thing for an actor."[11]

For Janet Dale, assuming the role of Eileen held a more personal significance. "I was a great fan of Orwell's," she says. "I lived in a rented place in Hampstead and I used to do a little mini-pilgrimage to Parliament Hill, where he lodged for a time. I did a lot of research even before I went to the interview. But of course, there was a set script, as you know."[12]

Goodman remembers Wheatley with affection and a few reservations. "He had such extraordinary energy but at the same time you felt, how authentic and how good are you actually? I was never quite sure. He was unlike any director I've ever worked with. He seemed to know a lot about film but I felt he was a bit of a fake. He was quite pretentious. I think his approach was very intense but I kind of wondered how much he really knew. How good he actually was. I didn't feel entirely safe in his hands and when I see the film, I think, 'Yeah, I was right. You weren't as good as I thought. Or you weren't what I thought you should have been.'"

Filming commenced on 8 August 1983, with five weeks' location work in Manchester, North Wales, Cheshire and the Severn Valley.[13] "The point of the piece," explained producer Morrison, "is to show that *Nineteen Eighty-Four* was not a leap into the future but came out of the things which had happened to Orwell and which he saw in the 1930s and forties."[14]

James Fox, playing his first major TV role in a decade, had only recently resumed his acting career. Having shot to fame opposite Mick Jagger in 1970's *Performance*, he'd been an evangelist for Christian group the Navigators all through the seventies.[15] "I took the role because I admire Orwell," the 44-year-old explained, shooting the Southwold beach scenes in the Welsh town of Anglesey. "I can identify with anyone who has gone off in a totally different direction to find a new spiritual dimension."[16]

Unlike smoker Ronald Pickup, Fox insisted on herbal cigarettes while in character. Shaken by his father's death from lung cancer, the one-time 40-a-day man had given up tobacco for good.[17] "Sometimes there's one knock too many in life for even the most resilient," he said. "I think, in fact, that we're all immensely frail. Orwell wrote terribly frankly about his life at the end. He just wanted someone to look after him and love him."[18]

The Naked Truth

Three decades on, Goodman's principal memory is of going topless with next to no warning. "We were, very often as you are, in one of these tiny little rooms with an entire film crew in there. David came up and said: 'Now, dear, I want you to do this naked.' I thought, 'Oh, yes?'

"I said: 'You never said this. I wasn't warned about it.' I'm actually quite tough on things like that. I've gone on strike in theaters and all sorts of things if people aren't treated properly. So I said: 'No, you didn't warn me of this. I'm not going to do that. Why should I do that? It's ridiculous.' He said: 'You did it in *Equus*.' I said: 'Yes, because that had been part of the play and it was all upfront and I'd agreed to do it. You don't just spring it on somebody just as you're going to film, with an entire film crew with you.'

"I went up to James and I said: 'James, I've got this problem. What do you think I should do?' I was thinking, 'I will actually get some support. He's the lead actor on it.' And he said: 'I don't know.'" She laughs. "Oh, great. He said: 'You'll have to make your own mind up.' Anyway, needless to say I did do it, with all the camera crew and everything else. So, that was a bit of a naughty one."

The wedding scene, filmed in a disused hospital in Manchester, also affected her. "By then we'd really got into the characters and it was very moving to think that she was marrying him on his deathbed. It was sad. And I just really found it very interesting, getting to know a little bit about George and the magazine [*Horizon*]. You always get these enclaves of highly *avant-garde* and interesting intellectual ideas coming together. They were fairly communist-minded, I suppose."

Bouquets and Brickbats

The film, which runs for 86 minutes without its commercial breaks, aired on Thursday, 19 January—two days before the anniversary of Orwell's death—at 9:30 p.m. on Channel Four.[19] Christopher Dunkley of the *Financial Times* called it "superb," adding: "If you had to choose just one Orwell programme for a time capsule this would surely be it." Fox seemed "absolutely right as the complex, idealistic, paternalistic, anxious intellectual," while Hall and Wheatley had "managed the difficult trick of depicting not just the writer but the writing."[20]

Judith Simons in the *Daily Express* thought its fine prose, idealism and drama made it "a treat," while the *Daily Mirror*'s Hilary Kingsley labeled it "a disturbing drama only a fool could switch off."[21] To *Sight & Sound*'s Jill Forbes, however, the film was too uneven, with Orwell "woodenly written" and Hall taking "too many short cuts for his account to be convincing."[22]

At *The Times*, Dennis Hackett found Fox "robust-looking" and "very effective," but on balance preferred the "snapshot" approach of *The Crystal Spirit*. "This biography, with its dramatised sketches of the major incidents in Orwell's life, did not give the cast a lot of scope—though, within its constraints, it was excellently acted—and lacked a sense of continuing drama."[23]

As Janet Dale remembers it, the film was overlooked "because it was

1984 itself and 'would it all come true' and so forth—after all that work and really, I thought, a good script, and James Fox was terrific. He was ever so sweet, a lovely person to work with, and he did a lot of research. We thoroughly, thoroughly got into making that. Sometimes now you do things and they're done so quickly, there's no chance to get deeply involved and care about it very much.

"It was a very significant thing for me, because I really love [Orwell's] work, but I don't think I'd been quite as aware before I did it that he wasn't a desperately nice man. I'm not saying he was horrible, but he wasn't the nicest and I didn't feel he was a good husband to Eileen. He probably would admit it himself. These great men often aren't good at that sort of thing, are they? I don't think it came out in the film, but recently they've realized she was quite an academic in her own right."

Watching her dusty VHS recording in 2015, Julia Goodman was disappointed in the film, "because I thought David was a better director than that film seemed to show. I didn't know his work before and I didn't know much about him, but I got the sense that he had a real vision for this, and it was episodic. They dumped bits of information, trying to get it all in."

Nonetheless, she was left with a certain regard for Sonia. "I think she was ambitious, I think she was a bit of an opportunist and I never quite knew whether she genuinely loved him. I think she felt sorry for him, and the kind of man that he was then—you know, women go for power and he had a huge intellectual reputation and he was quite famous, and I think that's always a hugely attractive quality. But he wanted her to just go off into the country and there's no way Sonia was going to do that. She wasn't that kind of woman. And the first Mrs. Orwell, played by Janet—they had such a loving relationship. You couldn't quite see what he saw in Sonia, to be honest."

In Goodman's estimation, Sonia "was flying a bit on the tails of a famous man, which was common practice, in a way, but also highly ambitious for herself—and, I suspect, like a lot of women, frustrated that their intelligence and ability was repressed a great deal of the time." At the same time, "she was passionately protective of what she felt Orwell meant and what he would have wanted. It's quite an interesting dynamic, isn't it?

"Looking at it from a feminist perspective and what I've gone through in my own life, having to make my own way and start up my own business, having originally started off as an actor—that fight as a woman is pretty tough…. We have moved on a lot, but not as much as people really think. It just makes me put Sonia into a perspective that, boy, did she have to fight."

There's one last twist to the story, however. In June 2017, Dale was visiting Sutton Courtenay churchyard when members of the Orwell Society paid their yearly visit to the author's grave.[24] Among them was the society's patron, Richard Blair. "I ended up telling him I'd played his adoptive mum," says the former Eileen. "In the film there was a baby, and that was Richard … and there he was, in the flesh."

The Road to 1984

George Orwell: James Fox
Eileen Blair: Janet Dale
Sonia Brownell: Julia Goodman
Avril Blair: Amanda Murray
Susan Watson: Judy Holt
O'Brien/Doctor: Donald McKillop
Goldstein: David Hirsch
Richard Blair (Snr): Hugh Cross
Ida Blair: Pauline Jefferson
David Holbrook: Mark Jax
Cyril Connolly: Michael Wynne
Bozo: Jack Walters
Refined tramp (Maurice): Bryan Coleman
Hospital chaplain: Stuart Richman
POUM soldier: Derek Harman
Magazine editor: David Webb
Department head (BBC): Brian Spink
Matron: Olive Pendleton

Indian actor (BBC): Madhav Sharma
Spanish police officer: Robin Hayter
Condemned prisoner: Jimmy Fung
Shop manager: Bernard Atha
Superintendent: Geoffrey Annis
Missionary: Carl Sheppard
Working class woman: Brigid Mackay
1st nurse: Lesley E. Bennett
2nd nurse: Delia Corrie
3rd nurse: Christine Lohr
Spaniard: Jose Miguel Mendoza
1st tramp: Leslie Clark
Written by: Willis Hall in association with David Wheatley
Director: David Wheatley
Producer: Steve Morrison
Production designer: Stephen Fineren
Music: Bill Connor

14

Nineteen Eighty-Four (1984)

Chicago corporate lawyer Marvin Rosenblum had a problem in the early eighties. No one, as far as he could tell, was interested in making a movie of *Nineteen Eighty-Four*. Some time earlier, the frustrated screenwriter[1] had spotted the book in a library and theorized that with 1984 looming, someone could make a killing by buying the screen rights.[2] All that stood in his way was Sonia Orwell's legendary antipathy to the 1956 film. So, before he met her in England, he painstakingly studied Orwell's work, to the extent of speed-reading the essays as his plane touched down at Heathrow.[3] In their meetings, he "spouted Orwell like a fountain"[4] until at last, after falling ill and being admitted to hospital, Sonia succumbed to his schmoozing. They signed a contract on 1 December 1980. Nine days later, she was dead.[5]

Over the next three years or so, directors Francis Coppola, Milos Forman and Hal Ashby spurned Rosenblum's approaches, just as Hollywood executives were telling him his project was "not life-affirming."[6] A Brit called Hugh Hudson got in touch, offering to show him his forthcoming athletics movie, *Chariots of Fire*, but the Chicagoan was reluctant to work with an unknown.[7]

"I don't know how he found us, really," says producer Simon Perry, who ultimately made the film, "but he found [the agent] Linda Seifert, who he knew looked after a director called Michael Radford. She didn't really look after me, but I was connected with Mike. Somehow he'd heard that we'd made a promising first film called *Another Time, Another Place*[8] and he was just calling to see whether we might be interested. He was saying: 'I can't get any action on this in Hollywood and so I'm thinking about coming to Europe with it.'"[9]

Once he'd discussed the idea with Radford, Perry called Rosenblum back. "In that phone call, it was kind of done, in a way, because I said: 'Look, I think you should come over to London and we should sit down with Mike and talk about doing this together. Putting the rights into a British company, which you and I will own. Mike will write the script, and I think we can find the money for this even before we have a script because of the strength of the concept.'"

At the time, Perry was working on a project for Richard Branson's Virgin Films. "I thought, the Virgin people are the most likely people to go for something like this, in this sort of impulsive way." Days later, when Rosenblum turned up in London, "I said: 'We can do this, because Mike can write the script in three weeks and I'm going to go for the money tomorrow morning. We'd already worked out that if we started pre-production on kind of the second of January, then we could deliver the film in time for an October release, in other words in the year of the title.

"We were lucky, because I went to see the people I was working with at Virgin and they said yes. They were quite happy with the script—Mike did indeed deliver it three weeks later—and by mid–November, we knew that we were going to do the film. We were crewing up and so on. Mike made only one condition, actually. He said: 'I can't do this film unless John Hurt can play Winston Smith.' We went off to John and he said yes immediately, without reading the script, on the basis of the book and Mike Radford's reputation."

When he agreed to write and direct *Nineteen Eighty-Four,* Michael Radford insisted that John Hurt should play Winston Smith. As a fan of the book, Hurt agreed instantly (copyright Virgin Films).

Breaking All the Rules

Setting to work on the screenplay, 38-year-old Radford reached the conclusion that *Nineteen Eighty-Four* was a great book, but not necessarily a great novel.[10] "Actually, it's an essay," he told an Orwell Prize event in Oxford in 2009. "It's an essay couched in dramatic language but with very archetypal characters who inevitably I'm trying to bring to life.[11] The thing about cinema is that it instantly, instantly exposes any narrative weakness in anything. People get it so fast … [*Nineteen Eighty-Four*], of course, breaks all the Aristotelian rules of narrative. The hero gets beaten and beaten and beaten to a pulp and finally, he's wiped out at the end. In a sense, what I tried to do with it was to give it some psychological truth and to try to create a sort of a poem, if you like."

As others have noted *ad nauseam*, characterization is hardly Orwell's strong point. "Julia is a real problem, because Orwell was an unreconstructed male chauvinist with a sort of public school undeveloped sense of what women actually are: the under-assistant matron who he fantasized was going to have sex with him as many times as he could possibly imagine." To counter this, Radford gave the character "a sense that she simply didn't care about anything, that she had a kind of strength of her own." When Winston visits O'Brien,[12] for instance, she doesn't join him, as she does in the novel. "Why would she, except to trail along behind him? She doesn't say anything in those scenes. She just is there. This is a girl who knows that they're doomed. She knows it from the beginning and she's a free spirit, so she wouldn't go. He would go because he's tormented and tortured and trying to think it all out."

Another problem, as Radford sees it, "is that actually, in the worst possible situations, it's not as bad as that. There are always people who are saying, you know, 'Eff you.' There are always people who are fighting. Even in the depths of depravity, in the worst of the totalitarian regimes, whether right or left, there was always some sort of resistance movement, even if it was internal resistance. My first wife had been a Young Pioneer and grown up in Czechoslovakia and to be honest, she said that by the time they'd reached the age of 15, nobody, but nobody, believed in the system at all. This is a great hope, I think. But nevertheless, that wasn't Orwell's point. Orwell was trying to make a structural and essay point, a point of philosophy and a very powerful one in mythological terms. You might say why make it a film, in that case. Why bother? The answer is there is something immensely vivid about it. Even though it is very depressing, there is something vivid about Orwell's imagination."

Sober Environment

Radford's memory of casting the film goes like this: "There were three people I had to get—well, four really. Winston, O'Brien, Julia and Big Brother. Casting John Hurt, I remember I actually went up to him at a party. I said: 'John, if you don't do this, I'm not going to do it.' He said: 'Fair enough, I'll do it.'"

"This is early, mid-eighties," says producer Perry, "and John was not really a big star. He was a star. He was drinking an awful lot and it was worrying to employ him, in a way, but I don't know, we were very relaxed about that and we said to John, 'Look, if you do this, it's going to be about 15 weeks and we can't do it if you're going to drink.' And he said: 'I won't.' And he was absolutely good to his word."

Former child actress Suzanna Hamilton, cast as Julia, was 24 at the time of shooting. An alumnus of the Anna Scher Theatre School in Islington, London, she'd made her movie debut in 1973's *Swallows and Amazons* and had recently played a catatonic young woman opposite Sting in writer Dennis Potter's *Brimstone and Treacle* (1982). Radford, who thought of casting Jamie Lee Curtis but was told she wasn't available, saw a freshness, an innocence, a slightness and a ferocity in Hamilton. As far as he was concerned, Julia was the genuine rebel, "the one with real balls"—more so than Winston the dreamer, at any rate.[13]

Before granting Hamilton a screen test, Radford—who'd used her to film make-up tests—had interviewed 70 other women and seriously considered another 50, according to *Film Review* magazine. "I rather like the way Julia cuts through all the political stuff," said the actress. "I admire her ability to live on a cliff edge."[14] All the same, she wasn't quite the heroine Orwell had imagined. "Julia has been updated somewhat," Hamilton agreed. "Many people have said she's a complete fantasy figure, and obviously we've had to cut that out. She's still a very vital character, but it's slightly more modernized. If I played it exactly as it is in the book, it would be a bit like out of an old 1940s movie."[15]

During production, Perry said that he and Radford wanted its Big Brother to be "benevolent, stern, handsome, commanding and reassuring" without being a blatant Stalin clone.[16] Radford, speaking 25 years later about Bob Flag, the person they settled on, described the selection process as "a fantastic escapade. We ran a competition in *The Guardian* for anybody who thought they looked like Big Brother and we got 100,000 photographs. Eventually I chose a man who was actually a small, part-time clown-comedian who'd just come back from the Falklands, where he'd been entertaining the troops. He just had this way of staring. Bulging eyes, I don't know what it was. The most amazing thing about it was that he was a *Guardian* reader."

Trickier still was persuading an actor of international stature to assume the role O'Brien—a process Radford remembers as "a catalog of disasters" that would never be allowed to happen today. "We didn't actually cast O'Brien finally until we were six weeks into shooting. If you can imagine, the financiers didn't know who was playing one of the major roles in the film. I remember my producer coming to me and saying: 'If nobody else plays it, I will.'

"What happened was that we offered it first to Sean Connery. Sean Connery then hummed and hawed and hummed and hawed and then actually, terrified, walked away from it. He literally kept us on the go for about six or seven weeks and then realized that just those long speeches, torturing him and everything—he wasn't going to cope with it. So he left." The next choice, Paul Scofield, broke his leg.[17] "So then we offered it to Rod Steiger, who'd just had a facelift. I received this telegram, which I have to this day, which said: 'My dear Mr. Radford, this is Rod Steiger's assistant speaking. I'm afraid Mr. Steiger will not be able to play the role of O'Brien in *Nineteen Eighty-Four* because his facelift has just fallen.'

"Then we offered it to Marlon Brando. We didn't have a lot of money—we had $80,000 to pay for the main character, which seems like a lot of money but it wasn't to those kind of guys, particularly as Marlon Brando's agent said: 'Do you realize that Mr. Brando does not get out of bed for less than a million dollars a day?' To which Simon Perry, bless his heart, my producer, said: 'Oh, he's given up serious acting, then?' So that was the end of Marlon Brando. Then we finally, finally, in desperation, thought of offering it to Richard Burton. This wasn't because he wasn't a good actor, it's because he was a notorious drunk. Nobody would trust him, nobody would insure him, nobody would do anything and anyway, he lived in Haiti. Later he claimed he lived there because it was the only place where nobody would recognize him. Whatever he said, you had to take with a pinch of salt.

"Only one plane a week went to Haiti, so we flew him in the script and waited a week and he came back with his answer. And he arrived, and he was absolutely charming. He gave up drinking throughout the entire shoot. He had this friend called Williams who was a fellow drunk who used to bring him an open can of Diet Pepsi and hand it to him. Richard would then hand it to me and say: 'Would you have a drop?' I would drink it, taste it, make sure there was no vodka in it and then I would hand it back to him. He behaved himself amazingly."

Young and Restless

In the fifties, Penguin Books' paperback of *Nineteen Eighty-Four* cap-tivated John Vincent Hurt, a clergyman's son in Lincolnshire who identified strongly with its main protagonist. "Yes, the parallels between myself and Winston Smith are very, *very* distinct," he told *Photoplay* magazine. "I read *Nineteen Eighty-Four* in 1956 when I was 16. And at *that* time and living in Grimsby, I suppose it would have been easy for me just to have rolled along and accepted things the way they were in those days. But *that*, for me, was the totalitarianism I just had to escape from. I *had* to get away from there in order to breathe."[18]

During a 1985 tour of Australia to publicize the movie, Hurt's sister in Sydney handed the exact same copy back to him. Speaking days later to Fiona Kieni—a 16-year-old from Melbourne, interviewing him for the Aus-tralian Teachers of Media magazine *Metro*—the actor recalled how "immensely pleased" he was when Radford collared him at London's Eve-ning Standard Drama Awards in November 1983.

In general, Hurt said, he didn't approve of turning novels into movies. But he'd read most of Orwell's work and wished he was young enough to play Gordon Comstock in *Keep the Aspidistra Flying*—"a sensational book." *Down and Out in Paris and London* would make a tremendous film as well, he thought.

So, why the attachment to *Nineteen Eighty-Four*? "I think every think-ing person perceives something of themselves in it," said Hurt. "What it does, by creating that extraordinary but simple imagery and breaking down the complications of life … is to create a somewhat different context in which to look at ourselves objectively." Orwell, he explained, had simplified society by breaking it down into four categories—Big Brother, the Inner Party, the Outer Party and the Proletariat. By setting the story in a post–Christian era, he'd also sidestepped the notion of one side being good and the other being bad.

Working on the film meant scrutinizing the text to a much greater extent than simply reading the book, Hurt added. "As Richard Burton said: 'You know, this really is frightening because I'm seriously beginning to believe that what I'm saying is correct.'"[19]

Speaking in 1984 to French freelance journalist Dominique Joyeux, Hurt described the story as "a brilliant modern tragedy, without any ques-tion. Winston is a singled-out man from the beginning, as in *Lear*, as in *Hamlet*. It is pure tragedy and the fall of Winston must happen. But I do not find it depressing for the reason that there are many things to be learned from the story of *Nineteen Eighty-Four*."[20]

At Last the 1948 Show

As the debacle of 1956 was a sore point with Sonia, her contract with Rosenblum specified that "the purchaser will make good faith efforts not to make the picture in the *Star Wars* or *2001: A Space Odyssey* genre of science-fiction."[21] Fortunately, this tallied with Radford's vision of "a 1948 vision of 1984"—a parallel world, in effect, that's gone off at a tangent since Orwell's time.[22] Production designer Allan Cameron, who at that time was making the transition from television to movies, had the job of building Orwell and Radford's dystopia. His police-state paraphernalia—be that a book of matches or a giant telescreen—makes use of a series of visual cues, such as a victory V and the image of a handshake; though as Radford pointed out, "one of the hands is a black glove and the other is a woman's hand being crushed."[23]

Principal photography took place in spring and early summer, mostly in and around London—"the exact time and setting imagined by the author," the credits boast. "With the money we had, we could plan a very long shoot," says Perry. "It was a 13-week main shoot preceded by two weeks shooting stuff for the telescreens." Since the movie had to be finished by the fall, pre-production continued during shooting.[24]

"The telescreen is a very good example of some of the technical problems of translating the book into a film," says Radford. "Orwell grew up in a world where propaganda was basically radio, public speaking and posters. Those were the big elements of the time and he uses those a lot, and we used them a lot in the film. He also invented the telescreen but he had absolutely no idea about the power of television. He had no conception of it. I discovered this while I was actually making the film, that the telescreens just took over. The posters just become a backdrop and the other stuff was just sort of a backdrop. As I realised they were taking over—and by the way, I won an award for special effects on this movie but there are actually no special effects at all, everything is done live, in camera—the telescreens are actually happening, although I shot a lot of material, pre-shot it—but that telescreen stuff starts to have a visual impact that you have to adjust to, which is what we did."

Dissecting totalitarian imagery became second nature to Radford. "We needed a salute, a flag, a leader and some propaganda films. We got a salute [wrists crossed and held above the head] that nobody had done before and it was a sort of doublethink salute. It's V for victory but it's also manacled, your hands are manacled.... I remember thinking of this one evening in the studios, in my office. 'Yes, that's it!'

"I saw a lot of propaganda films and the one I made is based on a propaganda film written and made by Dylan Thomas, who worked for the Ministry of Information during the war. Basically, what happens in a propaganda film is always the same, wherever you go. A Nazi one, a communist one, a British one, it's always the same. Here are we, a peaceable lot, going about our business in our own way and here is the black threat that's coming to destroy. And you always have pictures of people happily mowing meadows, doing things, baking bread, and then you have a horrible dark threat and it works all the time."

The national anthem, too, was very important "and here I discovered another thing. All left-wing totalitarian national anthems are written in the minor key and all the right-wing ones are written in the major key. This is a golden rule and it kind of dribbles into the idea that left-wing oppression is about guilt—guilt happens in the minor key—and right-wing oppression is about violence. Inner violence against outer violence, mostly."

On the Strip

Finding suitable locations presented a further challenge, as a behind-the-scenes documentary on BBC2 made clear at the time of the film's release. While devoting the best part of 25 minutes to Cameron's talents, *1984: Designing a Nightmare* spoke to Perry on a night shoot at north London's Alexandra Palace. Surrounded by proles and Party members—500 of each—the producer explained how difficult it had been to find a suitably shabby Victory Square. In what he called "a very nice sideways step,"[25] it occurred to the locations team that the much-loved "Ally Pally," gutted by a fire in 1980 and now a vast, empty, roofless space, would be the perfect substitute. At night, its four large interior walls would look like the exteriors of buildings.[26]

Daytime scenes were shot in the Docklands of East London, near the disused Beckton gasworks. In the midst of what was literally an urban wasteland, Radford's team transformed the old Co-operative Wholesale Society (CWS) building into the Ministry of Truth records hall where Winston works. "There's 200 booths stretching off in perspective into the distance," said Cameron.[27]

At several points in the picture, we're privy to Winston's dream of a "Golden Country." A long, dark corridor leads him to O'Brien and the door to Room 101, which opens out on to a pastoral idyll. In reality, it's a picturesque hill in Wiltshire. "Down the A303, just past Stonehenge," says Radford. "You look up on the right and you suddenly see it."[28] Surprisingly, perhaps, there's no back projection in these sequences. "We constructed a corridor up there, a 60-foot-long corridor, which looked like a gigantic articulated truck sitting on the hillside…. We just built a door with 101 on it and we launched John Hurt up to the edge of it."

Winston's dream of a "Golden Country" was realized in Wiltshire, on a pictur-esque hill near Stonehenge. A 60-foot corridor led Hurt and his co-star Richard Burton, as O'Brien, to Room 101 (copyright Virgin Films).

Nearby, the hangar shed where Barnes Wallis built the *The Dam Busters'* bouncing bombs became a venue for the Two Minutes Hate. "Two thousand people in there, all from Wiltshire, with strong Wiltshire accents," says Radford, "and if you listen very carefully, they're not saying: 'B, B, B,' they're saying: 'Bey, bey, bey.' Very sane, comfortable country folk, all dressed up. OK, now, here's the interesting thing. We've got the leader, we've got the national anthem, we've got the salute and we've got [the Two Minutes Hate]. I asked them to do it about nine times in all, for various different camera angles and so on and so forth. Every take, an average of about 16 people had passed out in hysteria and had to be ambulanced out. I swear to God. It was quite extraordinary. It's just the mass hysteria. Even though they knew it was a movie, even though there was nothing about it which wasn't fake, it became true. It's frightening."[29]

Interior Monologue

Most of the shoot took place at Twickenham Studios on the outskirts of London, where production designer Cameron gave the BBC a guided tour of his torture chamber set. After pointing out its "slightly medieval" rack, on which Winston is stretched, and its hosepipe wrapped around a tap for reasons we can only guess at, he turned his attention to a shower unit with a broken glass panel. The room is littered with hints of everyday ghastliness[30]—there's a suggestive quality to it, as Cameron pointed out in the program. Elsewhere, he turned to ration books, matchbooks and bottles of Victory Gin for examples of graphic design. Each carries a "heroes of the revolution" theme, "so whenever one of the proles or the Party are drinking gin, they're looking at propaganda."

For props, Cameron sought the help of Keir and Louise Lusby, a husband-and-wife team with a workshop at Shepperton Studios, Surrey. Their principal task was to mass-produce speakwrite machines, resembling early Bakelite televisions, for the Ministry of Truth scenes. "The other large prop that we made," says Keir, "was the big screen for O'Brien's office, which has the V for victory symbol on it, and has the on-and-off switch."

An additional job, handled by Louise, involved Julia's initial love note to Winston. Her arm in a sling, Julia pretends to stumble as she approaches him in a concrete underpass, then passes him an "ink-pencil" with a coiled

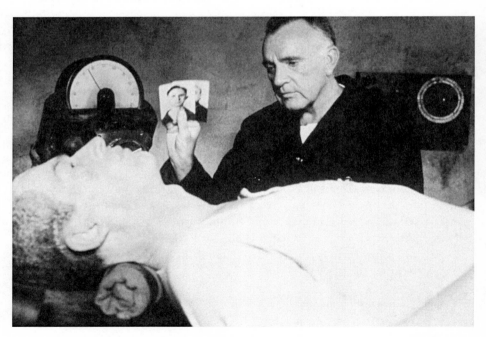

Given his reputation as a drunk, Richard Burton (shown here torturing John Hurt's Winston Smith) was a last, desperate choice for the role of O'Brien. Having turned in one of his finest performances, he died within weeks of filming (copyright Virgin Films).

strip of paper hidden inside. The prop that Louise created was a graphite stick in a cardboard tampon tube.

Winston's paperweight, from Charrington's antiques shop, was another contribution of the Lusbys. In fact, they still own an early version of it—a piece of red coral suspended in a clear resin—because the film-makers, who'd devised a shot that involved looking through the resin, thought the coral was too big. "When you put something like that into a sphere, solid, it magnifies it," says Keir. After a good deal of trial and error, they "ended up with a piece of coral probably no bigger than your little fingernail."[31]

Everyone, it seems, was under pressure, as a TV report from the news service ITN starkly demonstrated. At a launch party at the BFI in April, the actors seemed buoyant, but as the shoot drew to a close in a disused underground passageway near Wembley Stadium, their weariness was unmistakable. "It's been absolutely exhausting," said Suzanna Hamilton when the love note scene was in the can. "Much more exhausting than any other work I've ever done."[32] Spare a thought, too, for John Hurt, who suffered for his art when a rat cage was strapped to his face. As the studio lights came on, the frightened rodents—who'd been smeared with glycerin to make their fur look dirty and spiky[33]—turned around and farted in his face.[34]

Behind the camera, Radford and Perry were laughing it up. "Because the whole world of Ingsoc is so mad—it's all so satirical and funny—we just giggled our way through the whole creation of the logos, and the choice of colors, and the stupid food they had to eat," says Perry. "As a matter of fact, if I have one slight regret about that film, it's that I think it could have been a little less solemn. I think if the film itself reflected a little bit more the fun that we had making it, and the comedy that's running through that satire, then it might have been even slightly more popular. I don't know. I think if we were doing it again, we'd probably make it sharper and more satirical."

Burton

In June 1984, the *Daily Mail* published an interview with Richard Burton and Sally, the former continuity girl he'd married the previous year. At 58, the Welshman considered himself semi-retired and, he claimed, usually sent scripts back unread. *Nineteen Eighty-Four*, though, was "dazzling." "To play O'Brien as a total villain would be a piece of cake, but the director believes he feels a kind of love for Winston," he told journalist Lynda Lee-Potter. "When I get back to the hotel at night, I have a bath and dress entirely in white to try to get rid of O'Brien.[35] He obsesses me."[36]

Heavily made up to look pallid, and with his hair cropped short like a military man, the former idol was giving his last performance. Weeks after filming wrapped, and hours after playing host to John Hurt at his villa in Switzerland, he would die of a brain hemorrhage on 5 August. His last role, wrote Melvyn Bragg in the biography *Rich*, "was right for him." He "played it quietly, even casually. This torturer and pillar of the state is simply doing his job and with plenty of time to spare; even able to sympathize a little, certainly to understand, quite interested in the victim but in the beginning and in the end utterly immune to any trace of feeling which might take him away from his task: to break the opposition. It is a very fine performance and was reviewed as such."[37]

"The big problem," Burton told theater critic Michael Billington during filming, "is how to play a villain, especially one as bland as O'Brien. The most important thing Mike Radford said was that O'Brien must believe in what he is saying. You have to wipe out atavism and play as if you have no memory of background, of the past, of anything that has happened to you before. I change my eyes to marbles and negate the Burton voice so that O'Brien is stonily impassive."[38]

David Cann, playing a non-speaking role as O'Brien's manservant Martin, watched the two leading actors at close quarters over a three-day period. It's hinted in the book that Martin is Chinese, but since no experienced East Asian actors were available on those filming days, he was cast for what he calls his "slightly Oriental-looking" eyebrows. "It was quite an interesting experience," says Cann. "Richard Burton was very friendly and chatty and very sociable. John Hurt was much more reserved and slightly unfriendly, but he was playing a very distressed character, I think. Actors tend to adopt the persona of the character they're playing and he was a little less relaxed than Richard Burton was." Burton's Rolls-Royce was parked in the yard, he remembers. "The effects of years of alcoholism had taken their toll, but was quite talkative. He was physically somewhat frail but he was very chatty and very animated, although not so much physically animated, if you know what I mean. He was all there mentally. He was good company."[39]

As Perry remembers it, Hurt and Burton made filming a joy. "Because John was amazing. To see his dedication—he was behaving himself totally. And the other massive pleasure was Richard Burton, who was such a delight. I can see him now, standing.... He had to stand most of the time because he was in such bad physical condition. Couldn't lift a wine glass. When he lifts a wine glass in the film, it was an assistant director pushing his arm up under a desk. His back was just rotted away. But he would stand up in this caravan in the car park at Twickenham Studios, endlessly telling stories about Elizabeth Taylor in front of his current wife, who was wonderful. He was just such a pleasure to work with. For Mike, he was delightful. And he was so funny, too. Mike would say: 'Fine, that's OK. Now I want you to take the famous voice out of it.'

"'Oh, yes, that's right,' said Richard. 'Of course, you didn't hire the voice, did you? I know you're not paying me much. That's probably because you didn't hire the voice. I'll get rid of it, then.' As Mike said, he was like an oven. You just put something in and it comes out perfectly cooked. It was great."

The BBC documentary shows Radford and Burton on the torture chamber set, as the actor speculates that perhaps O'Brien is Big Brother himself. "There's always a slight hint," says Burton.[40]

"His legendary memory was completely gone. Gone," says the director. "So we had to have cue cards everywhere, [lines] written on John Hurt's forehead and stuff like that. Seriously. I'm not kidding. He was a sick man…. But he was a towering figure and he was the most charismatic person. While I was making the film, three women arrived at the gates of Pinewood Studios claiming to be Elizabeth Taylor.

"Anyway, I took on the job of directing him, basically, and I knew that guys like that for a long time had not been directed. People were terrified of them and the one thing you mustn't be is terrified of them because they're actors, they need directing. So, we're doing the torture scenes and stuff. We're doing the shots where he's looking at John Hurt and inevitably you have to move John Hurt out of the way. You put a little yellow cross on the camera and he looks at that. He wasn't doing it very convincingly. In fact, he was doing it very unconvincingly. I kept saying: 'We'll do it again.' Suddenly, he said: 'Stop!' And he said: 'You don't like the way I look, do you?'

"I said: 'No, it's not that, Richard, it's just that—.' He said: 'You don't like the way I look.' And he marched off the set.

"Frozen. Everybody's frozen in silence. Disappeared. Disappeared for about half an hour…. Finally he walked back on to the set again, carrying a little box, and he said: 'Go on, open it. It's for you.' So, right in front of all the crew, I opened this box and in the box there was a prize. It was a crystal ball on a sort of plinth. 'Go on,' he said, 'read the inscription.' And the inscription read: 'To Richard Burton, the 1983 award for the world's most beautiful eyes, from the American Ophthalmic Association.' He said: 'You can have that.[41]'"

Radford remembers him as "an old, wounded lion" and treasures a photo of the two of them, given to him by Burton at the end of filming. "Of the 72 film directors I've worked with, only eight have given me a new dimension and you're one of them," wrote the star.[42] *Nineteen Eighty-Four* is dedicated to him "with love and admiration."

Cash Flow Problems

Away from all this horseplay, a real-life drama was playing out with Virgin. This was only Perry's third film and, he admits now, much bigger than anything he'd handled before. "I made some mistakes," he says, "in terms of putting the crew together and so on." Getting the film off the ground had been a piece of cake. "I'd never, ever had or heard of a process that was as easy as this. In a way it was sort of deceptive. There are two reasons for that. One was the project, the concept, the timing. We could say, 'Look, we have the rights to this book. It's called *Nineteen Eighty-Four*. We can make the film and release it next year.' That was very, very attractive but we also relied completely on finding a company, a person, who would respond to that and was able to say yes to the whole deal, the whole thing: Richard Branson. This is very much Richard's way of working.

"It was all much more complicated later on because, as I say, we were not very experienced. It was a very big film. The design side of the film, building this whole world at Twickenham Studios and then finding locations which were scattered across the old Docklands—it's all gone now, the Beckton gasworks has been built over—that was a very much more costly operation than I had anticipated." In the initial conversations with Virgin, "I had had to say what it was going to cost and I made a mistake. I underestimated it and I said it would cost £2.5m. That was the money that Richard committed. Unfortunately it was not enough and we discovered in the course of late pre-production, early shooting, that we were going to need more money, which is a measure of my inexperience.

"It was OK. It was very, very difficult to explain to Richard. We said it would cost $4.5m and it ended up costing $6m, which is a very big overcost. But when you say, 'This film was made for $6m,' and you look at the film, it's not bad. It was very good value for money even after we'd gone through the shock of discovering that we were going to spend more. As soon as we did discover, I went straight to see Richard at his houseboat with a new accountant who I'd brought in and a new production supervisor I'd pulled off another film. I had much more experienced people with me by then and we went in and we said: 'Look, it's not going to be this, Richard, it's going to be that.' To give him his due, he rode it out very well. He was determined that the film should still be, as he put it, 'the film Mike wants to make,' which was very supportive."

Another Brick in the Wall

The ad line for the movie was: "George Orwell's terrifying vision comes to the screen." It was, said Virgin's press book, "a story of impossible love and tragic betrayal set in a twisted, horrific world." This time, though, the hyperbole was fully justified. Yes, it's a grim production, but it's faithful to Orwell in ways that, for budgetary or censorship reasons, its forerunners in the fifties and sixties were not.

Taking its cue from the 1949 text, in which "there seemed to be no color in anything, except the posters that were plastered everywhere," the film looks purposely drab. Using a new processing technique, Key Laboratories desaturated the color[43] from each print and brought black-and-white tonal resonances to Roger Deakins' remarkable cinematography.[44] The effect—a kind of halfway house between black-and-white and color—was arresting in itself, though not everyone cared for it. "Every image is bluish-grey, the color of murk," moaned *The Wall Street Journal*.[45]

Regardless, Radford and company's world-building is astonishing. From *Oceania, 'Tis for Thee*, the operatic anthem[46] played over the opening credits, to the jaw-dropping production design and pitch-perfect performances, there isn't a false note in its 105-minute running time (except for the Eurythmics' score, perhaps). Here, for the first time on screen, are the malevolent black helicopters of the Thought Police, hovering outside Winston's window; his dreams of the Golden Country; the telescreen aerobics instructor, berating him for struggling to touch his toes; and the Victory Square rally in which Eurasian soldiers, paraded in open trucks, are gunned down in front of cheering crowds.

The Party's plan to abolish the orgasm and introduce wholesale artificial insemination (so that it may wipe out self-reflection and thought-crime) receives an entire scene of its own. There's even room for Comrade Ogilvy, the war hero that Winston invents and immortalizes during a flight of fancy at the Records Department; though, in a twist devised by Radford, he haunts Winston on his own telescreen. An undercurrent of horror and violence is never far from the surface: witness the Parsons children watching televised hangings, or Winston's visions of his mother lying dead in a field while rats swarm over her torso.

But it's the frank depiction of sex that's probably most startling. Winston's encounter with an over-the-hill prostitute in the prole quarter ends with her lifting her skirt to reveal her pubic hair; and during his countryside liaison with Julia, the girl from the Fiction Department strips in slow motion and strides towards him in her birthday suit. The full-frontal nudity continues at Charrington's place, although the most we see of Hurt is his backside; and once they've been arrested, O'Brien tells Winston dispassionately that photos of them copulating "will be recycled for proletarian use."

Months after the movie's release, the American writer Danny Peary argued in his book *Guide for the Film Fanatic* that this matter-of-fact attitude to carnality was pure Orwell. Whereas the 1956 film "was about whether love can endure—a trite theme," this adaptation examined Julia and Winston's "need for physical contact and sexual release,"[47] as the author intended.[48] "Orwell's tale is cautionary," wrote Peary, "in that it warns us never to allow such a totalitarian state to develop, because at that point there would be no chance for the individual to buck the system."[49]

If anything, the violence in this movie is even more explicit than the sex. Orwell writes of Winston "being wrenched out of shape," his joints "being slowly torn apart." In Radford's dramatization, his scrawny, bald-headed body is stretched on a motorized rack, leaving him so weak and damaged that O'Brien can rip out a front tooth with his fingers.

Where, then, does the film take liberties? Julia's absence from the meeting at O'Brien's apartment means that the lovers are never quizzed on the lengths they would go to for the resistance. On his way to meet Julia, Winston stands on a decaying railway platform where a gay man tries to pick him up. And on the train itself—a steam locomotive with the Ingsoc "V" on its side (it's never mentioned that Ingsoc is English socialism)—Youth Spies on an outing sing a half-sweet, half-sinister patriotic tune.

Instead of an alcove, Winston's diary is hidden behind a loose brick, next to his wall-mounted telescreen. The resulting visual—of him crouched to one side of it while it churns out spurious statistics—is certainly a powerful one, but at no point does he write: "Down with Big Brother." In fact, his entries are less frequent and more eloquent than readers of the novel might expect.

The infamous "Big Brother is watching you" posters are, for the most part, hidden away in the background. And the Party slogans?

WAR IS PEACE

FREEDOM IS SLAVERY

IGNORANCE IS STRENGTH

Lines spoken in a telescreen broadcast, once.

Film of the year

Struggling to meet its deadlines, in late July Virgin pulled *Nineteen Eighty-Four* from the Venice Film Festival, due to start on 27 August. It also put back the UK premiere, planned for 21 September, to mid–October so it could devote an extra week to editing the print.[50] The film finally premiered at the Leicester Square Theatre in London on Sunday, 7 October, with a galaxy of pop stars present. Phil Collins and Boy George were there, as were Sting and his wife Trudie Styler; Tony Hadley, Gary Kemp and Martin Kemp from the band Spandau Ballet; Duran Duran's Nick Rhodes; and singers Steve Strange and Marilyn. The likes of Tracey Ullman, Hayley Mills, Billy Connolly and Zandra Rhodes added to the buzz.[51]

Five days later, a stone's throw away, the film opened to the public at the Odeon Haymarket, where it was an instant sensation. The critics liked it, too, so much so that Virgin put out the following double-page ad in UK trade magazine *Screen International*[52]:

Virgin Films proudly presents 1984, "The film of the year"

"Gripping, frightening and expressive."—THE GUARDIAN

"'1984' is a wonder."—THE STANDARD

"A film of power and integrity."—THE OBSERVER

"A remarkable achievement."—THE DAILY TELEGRAPH

"A twisted, brilliant, horrific nightmare…. John Hurt's performance surely deserves an Oscar."—THE SUN

"Richard Burton—one of the best performances of his later career."—THE TIMES

"One of the rare films that is considerably better than the book that spawned it … a remarkable film…. Richard Burton at last found the one serious role for which he searched all his life."—TIME OUT

"The pic's poetic intensity will guarantee box office performance … a standout performance by Richard Burton."—VARIETY

"A brilliant piece of film-making."—DAILY STAR

"It's got to be the film of the year—and deservedly … a horrific masterpiece."—SUNDAY PEOPLE

"John Hurt confirms that he is the best British actor now working."—CITY LIMITS

"Richard Burton's performance must surely rank as one of his best appearances on film."—NEW STATESMAN

Not included, of course, were journalists who'd been turned off by the film, such as the *Daily Mail*'s Quentin Falk, who called it "unrelievedly grim,"[53] and the *Mirror*'s Arthur Thirkell, who complained that "total despair is stamped into every scene."[54] Amusingly, in an otherwise positive review, Nigel Andrew of the *Financial Times* poked fun at the main actor. "It's suffering time again with John Hurt," he wrote. "Hurt the name, hurt the game, his Equity dossier must say, or 'Have nerve ends, will unravel.'"[55]

Radford expected an audience of over–35s: "People who knew who Orwell was, admired his work, wanted to go and see a literary adaptation."

In the event, "the audience was almost 95 percent 16 to 25. It was hugely popular. Hugely popular among young people who tend to have at that age a very nihilistic view of things. That sort of nihilistic vision of the world, if you like, became immensely popular. The film was a huge hit."

But trouble was brewing. Serious trouble.

Out of Tune

Radford takes up the story. "There was a huge scandal at the time. It made me famous, which was terrific.... It was a big argument I had with Richard Branson, which goes something like this. Virgin financed the film and they didn't have any completion bond, which is a cinematic term for insurance, and we went overbudget because we were making the film very fast.... And so they demanded that we had a major artist [provide the music] so they could sell records on the back of the film.

"The person who loved *Nineteen Eighty-Four* more than anybody was David Bowie, so he came along and we had this big meeting on Richard Branson's boat, where David Bowie announced that he was going to do 'organic music' for this film. Nobody knew what organic music meant and I could see all the Virgin executives looking kind of...."

(Eyes darting anxiously from side to side.)

"'What's organic music?' We never did find out what organic music was because they decided that organic music wasn't going to sell, whatever it was, and so David Bowie got shoved off. And then I heard nothing. I heard nothing at all from Branson or anybody else and I'd hired Dominic Muldowney, a very well known theater guy, a musician, to compose the anthems and stuff. I was getting close to the release date of the film and I still didn't have a composer, so I said to Dominic, 'Look, can you do me a track?' And he did one—he did a really nice one.

"We were sitting mixing the final, final version of the movie and in the dubbing theater, putting the music on to the film, and the dialogue and all the rest of it, and the phone rings on the mixing desk. I pick up the phone and it's Annie Lennox, who I'd never spoken to in my life, phoning from Bermuda, saying: 'Why aren't you here? We're doing the music for your film.' And that was the first I'd heard of it. So I said: 'You can't, because we've got music here. We've got music, we're mixing the film.' There was a terrible silence at the other end and she said: 'Oh.' Not only that, they'd got a copy of the film which wasn't the final one, so they were doing all this music, and because they'd never done [film] music before, they were putting effects into the music—putting explosions in—because before a film is finalized, you don't have all the explosions, you just have the dialogue, basically. And they thought that this film didn't have enough effects in it.

"I said to Richard: 'Look, you can't do this to me, you can't. You absolutely can't.' And he said: 'I'm trying to sign them up and we've got to produce a record.' I said: 'Well, how much do you need on the movie?' And he said: 'Legally, to say that they've done the music…. I'll have to check it out.' It turned out it was ten seconds. So I put ten seconds of their music on and forgot about it. The movie went out and then the next thing I heard was that every single copy of the film … a thousand copies were withdrawn and the Eurythmics' music was put back on and it went back out again. So when the Evening Standard Awards happened and I knew that I'd won, I came, and I stood up on television—it was live—and I said: 'I know I'm supposed to thank my mother for giving birth to me and my father for helping her, but I've got a much more serious thing to say, which is that the film you're giving me this prize for is not the film that's out in the cinemas today.'"[56]

To make matters worse, Branson was in the audience.[57] "Can you imagine, all the drunken journalists at the British Film Awards, somebody doesn't stand up and thank his agent and, you know, everybody else, just makes this speech. Everybody woke up. The next day, it was on the front pages as opposed to the back pages and the upshot was the following. The movie shot to number one. I was offered a huge, gigantic picture by Dino De Laurentiis, who called me up from Italy, saying: 'I want you to do my next picture.' And I said: 'Erm, yeah, Dino, but have you ever seen any of my work?' He said: 'No.' He said: 'I saw you on television. You're a good guy.' The really interesting thing was that I got thousands and thousands and thousands of letters from people around the country who knew that I'd stood up for something but didn't know what, because it was too technical for them.

"It ended up with the Eurythmics on it and I was very upset at the time. Years later I had a look at it and thought: 'Oh, actually the music's really quite good.' You know, because you're so fixated on what you're doing, you have to make choices and decisions and decisions and choices. Anything that throws you like that is very hard to deal with. I've made friends with Annie Lennox, so all is fine. I flew to New York on Virgin Airlines about ten years ago[58] and it was four hours late. Richard came personally on to the plane to apologize to absolutely everybody personally. Finally, he sat down next to me and said: 'I really apologize that the plane was late and I also apologize for the row we had.'"[59]

Interviewed in 2017, and addressing his remarks to Branson (should he be watching), a regretful Radford apologized "for making such a fuss."[60]

Big Bother

Perry's experience was rather different. "I got it right in the neck from Richard and his executives," he says, exempting co-producer Al Clark, who remains a friend to this day. "Other people in the Virgin organization gave me a very hard time, whereas Mike was cosseted and allowed to know nothing about what was going on. Then the whole blow-up of the music made Mike very angry. I'd been through a libel suit Richard brought against me because of something I'd said in the *Daily Express*, and various other little horrors, but when the film came out, and it was really a considerable success, we went through a big painful moment and were very angry with Richard and all the rest of it. And he very angry with us, and me in particular. But damn it, you grow up and out of it. Looking at the film now with the Eurythmics' music on it, it's not destroyed by the music. The original score is still much better but nobody knows about it, and we're not upset about it. We're still very proud of the film."

Virgin released the Eurythmics' single *Sexcrime (1984)* on 22 October, followed by a soundtrack album, *1984 (For the Love of Big Brother)* on 12 November.[61] Later that month in *Screen International*, Virgin Vision and the Directors' Guild of Great Britain quarreled about the music in an exchange of open letters.[62]

The same issue carried an ad from Key Laboratories, congratulating everyone who'd made the movie "a record-breaking success."

First five weeks at the Odeon Haymarket (600 seats).

£199,232 gross and 50,635 admissions (all-time records for any film at this theatre).

Evening Standard best film of the year and John Hurt best actor.

Thirty Years Later

Perry, who moved into film funding and now works in Sweden, has for years helped to organize a French event, the Festival of British Cinema, in Dinard, Brittany. To mark the film's impending 30th anniversary, he suggested a screening in 2014. "I went to the festival as I always do and with Mike, watched the film," he says. "I hadn't actually watched it for I think 25 years, so it was a fairly edifying experience. I didn't feel it was so solemn. At the time, I had felt it was. It looked so much more like a film made then than I expected it to. The sound is mono and there's no visual effects at all. The telescreen stuff was all projected on to the set at the time.

"It also has this color process which we invented for the film, in fact, whereby some of the silver was left in the emulsion on the celluloid, which takes out most of the yellow, so the red becomes very dark and there's a sort of blue-gray-silver cast to the whole film. I think it's quite lovely, actually. My wife, who watched it with me, didn't known the film at all and she was very, very taken with it. She didn't find it tough. She found it very serious—a rather studious work, I would say, which I think it is—but she found it beautifully done.

"I enjoyed it. I find it so strange with films that you've made, you find you remember every single frame and when you watch them again, you know exactly what's coming. I do feel good about the film, actually. And I do also feel, for all the tribulations with Virgin and the tough time they gave us and we gave them, I do really take my hat off to Richard for having done that. For having so totally and impulsively said yes to it."

The Trump Effect

In an extraordinary turn of events, the movie has enjoyed a new lease of life since the U.S. presidential election of November 2016. The idea of Donald Trump as Big Brother is, of course, highly debatable—but it did gain currency the following January when, during a row on NBC's *Meet the Press* about crowd numbers at his inauguration, his aide Kellyanne Conway used the term "alternative facts."

Sales of the 1949 novel went through the roof[63] in an instant and by May of 2017, a well-tested stage version from London had opened on Broadway. Radford's movie was revived too, for a so-called National Screening Day on 4 April[64] dedicated to Hurt, who'd died on 25 January. Nearly 200 arthouses in 187 U.S. cities took part, as did five in Canada. The UK, the Netherlands, Sweden, Croatia and New Zealand contributed one venue each.

Dylan Skolnick, co-director of the Cinema Arts Centre on Long Island, New York, and Adam Birnbaum, director of film programming at the Avon Theatre Film Center in Stamford, Connecticut, came up with the idea. "No one is suggesting that we're living in Orwell's world," Skolnick told Al Jazeera. "But the road to that world is people just becoming disengaged and allowing their government to do whatever it wants."[65]

As the organizers' website put it: "Orwell's portrait of a government that manufactures their own facts, demands total obedience and demonizes foreign enemies has never been timelier. The endeavor encourages theaters to make a stand for our most basic values: freedom of speech, respect for our fellow human beings, and the simple truth that there are no such things as 'alternative facts.'"[66]

While making a movie in Rome, Italy, Radford recorded a three-minute introduction. "Everything that is happening in that film and in that book is happening today," he said ominously, citing surveillance, fake news and the fraudulent threat of external "dark forces." The aim, he told audiences, was for those in power to exercise control for the sake of it.[67]

In an hour-long interview about the making of the film, cut to 15 minutes and shown at the end of the night, he added: "We're in a very, very strange moment where political systems are breaking up and people are afraid of what's coming next. I hope it isn't 1984, that's all I can say."[68]

In the words of *The Hollywood Reporter*, Orwell's novel was "the hottest literary property in town."[69] A new movie was in the pipeline, it added— co-produced by Marvin Rosenblum's widow, Gina.[70]

Nineteen Eighty-Four

Winston Smith: John Hurt
O'Brien: Richard Burton
Julia: Suzanna Hamilton
Charrington: Cyril Cusack
Parsons: Gregor Fisher
Syme: James Walker
Tillotson: Andrew Wilde
Tillotson's friend: David Trevena
Martin: David Cann
Jones: Anthony Benson
Rutherford: Peter Frye
Waiter: Roger Lloyd Pack
Winston as a boy: Rupert Baderman
Winston's mother: Corinna Seddon
Winston's sister: Martha Parsey
Mrs. Parsons: Merelina Kendall
William Parsons: P.J. Nicholas
Susan Parsons: Lynne Radford
Inner Party speaker: Pip Donaghy
Whore: Shirley Stelfox
Instructress: Janet Key
Artsem lecturer: Hugh Walters
Man in white coat: John Hughes
Shouting Prole: Robert Putt

Soup lady: Christine Hargreaves
Guards: Garry Cooper, Matthew Scurfield
Patrolmen: John Golightly, Rolf Saxon
Eurasian soldier: Ole Oldendorp
Executioner: Eddie Stacey
Man on station: Norman Bacon
Youth leader: John Foss
Party members: Carey Wilson, Mitzi McKenzie
Telescreen announcer: Phyllis Logan
Washerwoman: Pam Gems
Aaronson: Joscik Barbarossa
Goldstein: John Boswall
Big Brother: Bob Flag
Written and directed by: Michael Radford
Producer: Simon Perry
Production designer: Allan Cameron
Director of photography: Roger Deakins
Music: Eurythmics and Dominic Muldowney

15

A Merry War (1997)

It's probably fair to say that the big-screen version of *Keep the Aspidistra Flying*—renamed *A Merry War* for the American market, from a line in the book about Comstock and Rosemary's relationship—is one of the more contentious adaptations of Orwell, at least in the UK. Whatever the literary purists were expecting in 1997, it wasn't a romantic comedy.

Stateside critics were more enthusiastic (in *Time* magazine's view, it was one of the ten best movies of the year) and in 1999, once the dust had settled, screenwriter Alan Plater and director Robert Bierman recorded a commentary for a U.S.–only special edition DVD.[1] Plater, echoing comments he'd made in print at the time of the film's release, joked that Bierman had "betrayed" him by shooting his script "almost syllable for syllable. So if it doesn't work, who do I blame?"

This, remember, was one of Britain's most respected screen dramatists, a man who'd won Baftas and an International Emmy. "His name guaranteed a quality of humour, heart and humanity," wrote *The Guardian* when he died in 2010, aged 75, "usually matched by high standards of acting and production values."[2]

"Orwell did the social message and Alan did the wit," is how his widow Shirley Rubinstein characterizes the *Aspidistra* movie, but the reaction in their home country was disappointing to say the least. "The kind of comment I remember was sort of 'the dead hand of public money,'" she says, alluding to its Arts Council funding. "There seemed to be an attitude to it before people had even seen it. It opened the London Film Festival and we sort of got a feeling there that it was not going to be liked."[3]

So, what happened? For the full story, we need to step back another 13 years, to that most Orwell-centric of times: 1984.

The Outline

Bierman bought the rights to *Keep the Aspidistra Flying* in the early eighties—"my favorite Orwell book," he calls it on the DVD.[4] Casting

157

around for someone to write the film, his first thought on watching *The Crystal Spirit*—a thrilling work, he thought, based on the less-than-promising scenario of "author writes book"—was "here's a man who understands Orwell."

In February 1984, Plater agreed to write a treatment and two draft scripts. His aptitude for penning adaptations was well known by this point, with credits such as the 1977 film *It Shouldn't Happen to a Vet*, based on James Herriott's memoirs; Yorkshire TV's 1980 serialization of JB Priestley's *The Good Companions*; and Anthony Trollope's *The Barchester Chronicles*, which garnered rave reviews for the BBC in 1982. Five years later, memorably, he would script a BBC mini-series of Olivia Manning's *Fortunes of War*—the epic that introduced Kenneth Branagh to future wife Emma Thompson.

Interviewed by the author of this book in 2000, Plater explained his philosophy. "If you do a classic like *The Barchester Chronicles*, you're honoring Mr. Trollope," he said. "But if you're doing, say, *A Very British Coup*, which is not a good book,[5] you're redeeming it. It becomes halfway to being an original piece of work."[6]

Rubinstein remembers his working methods well. "He would read the original time and time again," she says. "For something as big as the Trollope, the *Barchester*, or for *Fortunes of War*, he would do an enormous time chart with characters, showing where they came in and out. Make sure he didn't forget anybody. You needed fewer characters than were in the book, so deciding who to conflate, who to drop…. And then he would start writing. But he would soak himself in the writer of the original. He said it was a different set of muscles from an original. What you had to do was climb inside it and shine a light for a modern audience. That's what he did with *Aspidistra*, or tried to do. Obviously people didn't feel that the film quite worked and we've never really been sure why."

Plater's treatment for the proposed film, held in the archive at Hull History Centre, is lively, thorough and remarkably perceptive. Take this opening line: "Orwell's novel was first published in 1936. Its central character, Gordon Comstock, is an anti-hero supreme—an Angry Young Man, twenty years ahead of the fashion."

He went on: "Comstock is not merely angry. He is, in Orwell's own words, 'a snivelling, self-pitying little beast' dedicated to the overthrow of practically everything. He is a self-confessed poet, but hates books and their writers, with the exception of Lawrence and Joyce, 'before he went off his coconut.' He hates money and capitalism, but has equal loathing for the trendy socialists seeking to destroy them. He hates middle-class conformity and respectability, epitomised by his own family, and is haunted, on a daily basis, by aspidistras, symbol of all that he despises. Periodically, he looks to the skies, praying for the arrival of aeroplanes with high-explosive bombs to destroy the universe, so that mankind might start again with a clean sheet."

Comstock's "highly personal Odyssey" was the novel's narrative core, argued Plater. "He throws up a successful career as an advertising copywriter to become a poet. His supplementary ambitions are to avoid the money-trap, and persuade his girlfriend, Rosemary, to go to bed with him. Towards the end of his period in the wilderness, she does so though, predictably, it is a fairly joyless experience. Rosemary becomes pregnant, Comstock marries her, gives up his poetic ambitions, returns to the advertising agency, but *insists*, in a final act of perverse defiance, that they should have an aspidistra in their home.

"In Gordon Comstock, whining self-pity achieves a kind of nobility. He is a unique and remarkable comic character in a world dominated by poverty, unemployment, the lust for respectability and the fear of war. He fails, but does so with style, booze and bad grace. He *doesn't* behave like a true-blue Englishman, and that is perhaps his greatest triumph."

Plater's early suggestions were "an opening shot at how Orwell would have told his story if he'd been working with a camera," and one of his first steps was to discard the book's back-and-forth timeline. "The novel contains a lengthy 'story-so-far' section in Chapter 3. In the film, part of this—Comstock leaving the New Albion—moves to the head of the story. In dramatic terms it is the natural beginning. Thereafter the film proceeds in natural time sequence but with the option of brief flashbacks concerning the Comstock family, built into the scenes between Gordon and Julia."

"The cinematic style will echo Orwell's prose style: simple, direct, crystalline, with a good journalist's eye for precise visual detail. The characters in the novel tend to spend too much time walking about, talking and brooding—especially brooding, in Comstock's case. In the film, they will be placed in physical situations that add point to the story—thus, Comstock and Rosemary will play out their love story in settings that they can afford to visit: public parks and transport, station waiting rooms, bus shelters, alleyways, cheap tea shops, all smelling strongly of the 1930s.

"Above all, the film is conceived as a comedy, though the laughter should scratch a little. Wherever possible the comedy will be visual, and all the dialogue will have to work its passage." This, wrote Plater, implied a visual style somewhere between Buster Keaton and the pioneering Scottish documentary-maker John Grierson.

Key images would recur. "The posters created by New Albion will crop up everywhere, reminding Comstock of his past and possible future; the bombs will fall whenever he calls upon them; and there will be aspidistras in every window and across all the land.

1

1   1930'S LONDON MONTAGE (LIBRARY MATERIAL)

(TITLE SEQUENCE)

Sequence of shots drawn from archive sources establishing
the place, which is LONDON, and the time, which is 1934,
with jolly music to match: perhaps Jessie Matthews singing
'Over My Shoulder'...

Out of the general scene-setting, a visual theme develops:
the stark contrast between rich and poor. The Upper Crust
whooping it up in the West End; the Lower Orders surviving
by the skin of their teeth down the East End. All this is
presented slightly tongue-in-cheek; not so much earnest
documentary style as a parody of that style.

Against the images we hear the voice of GORDON COMSTOCK,
struggling poet and human being.

                    COMSTOCK
                  (Over)
          Though I speak with the tongues of men and
          of angels, and have no money, I am become
          as a sounding brass or a tinkling bloody
          cymbal. And though I have the gift of
          prophecy, and understand all mysteries,
          and all knowledge; and though I have all
          faith, so that I could remove mountains,
          and have no money, I am verily sod all.

2   EXT. NEW ALBION PUBLICITY COMPANY DAY

ESTABLISHING SHOT New Albion Publicity Company, a piece of post-war
Britain born prematurely in the early 1930's: a three-storey
office building not quite in the centre of London.

The voice of COMSTOCK is heard, preaching his sardonic message.

                    COMSTOCK
                  (Over)
          Money suffereth not, and is kind; money
          envieth not; money beareth all things,
          believeth all things, hopeth all things,
          endureth all things.

Now we see the man himself, GORDON COMSTOCK, gazing from a first
floor window. He is twenty-nine years old, frayed in all departments,
with a hopeful heart and a melancholy mind. He relishes misery and
is made nervous by prospects of joy.

Page one of Alan Plater's first draft of *Keep the Aspidistra Flying* (photograph by David Ryan, courtesy estate of Alan Plater).

"The stanzas of *London Pleasures* will be used as a running narrative commentary throughout, again with comic intent, and of course the love story will be given proper emphasis. Comstock and Rosemary are capable of having fun amidst the gloom, and we will share it with them.

"At its heart, the film will celebrate James Thurber's dictum about the Dignity of Man: 'It is only when he falls down that we realise how straight he can stand....'"

The First Draft

With his playful wit and distinctive take on the world, Plater's dramatizations were anything but workaday. To illustrate this, Rubinstein namechecks Reginald Hill, author of the Dalziel and Pascoe crime novels he adapted for the BBC. Hill used to "go through the script, saying: 'Did I write that or did Alan?' And when he'd found [a line] he'd written, it was bingo."

The earliest *Aspidistra* script, which sticks more closely to the novel's plot than the finished film does (sometimes to its detriment), is a case in point. It's jokier and more warm-hearted than Orwell, but right from the opening titles—a slightly tongue-in-cheek montage of archive footage, overlaid with a jolly Jessie Matthews–like soundtrack—it makes a serious, socialistic point: that in mid–1930s England, the upper classes were living it up while the lower orders were struggling to survive.

At the New Albion Publicity Company, graphic designer Rosemary is working on the Bovex hot drink account. Comstock, *en route* to the office of their dullard boss, Mr. Erskine, takes one look at its Corner Table character—a bespectacled clerk in a cafe—and damns him as a "little rat-faced monster." He's rude to Erskine too, responding to his offer of a pay rise by blurting out his resignation, almost by accident. The executive takes this in his stride, musing good-naturedly that poetry and advertising aren't so different—they're the same words, only in a different order.[7]

Breaking the news to Rosemary, Comstock quotes Wordsworth—"Bliss was it in that dawn to be alive, but to be young was very heaven!"—and flings out an arm, spilling a pot of paint. Twenty-nine isn't young, she retorts, in a line that won't survive the casting of 39-year-old Richard E. Grant. With money borrowed from his long-suffering sister Julia, he calls on his benefactor Ravelston, who's lounging in bed with his caustic, sexually voracious girlfriend, Hermione. The suave champagne socialist and magazine publisher, fresh from printing Comstock's poem about dying prostitutes, secures him a job in a Hampstead bookshop—much to the disgust of Hermione, who regards Comstock as "a little turd."

On the advice of new boss McKechnie—a benign, white-bearded Scotsman—Comstock looks for lodgings in Willowbed Road, close to the shop. Drawn to the window with the biggest aspidistra, he rents a room from what Plater calls the "malignantly respectable" Mrs. Wisbeach. Two fellow tenants, lost from later drafts, are Flaxman, a fat, lecherous sales rep who's been thrown out by his wife, and Lorenheim, a fatalistic, largely taciturn European. They're a double act, essentially: while Lorenheim frets about the prospect of fascist bombing raids, Flaxman chirrups that he'd be happy to die drunk, "with a tit in one hand and a bum in the other."

Gordon, meanwhile, suffers one disappointment after another. Turning up at the Ritz hotel—where critic Paul Doring is hosting a literary gathering, according to Ravelston—he finds a roomful of rabbis, as the event has been rescheduled. Yelling: "Go and fuck yourself!" at Doring over the phone, he sulkily heads home to torture his aspidistra with a burning cigarette.

To put the spark back into their relationship, he and Rosemary arrange a trip to the countryside by train, financed by Julia; the £5 he's borrowed in total was supposed to be her Christmas money. On the big day, the lovers visit a high-class hotel, eat the cheapest meal they can get away with and, merry on claret, find an alcove in the forest where Rosemary strips off. Gordon, being thoughtless, hasn't brought condoms, so she pushes him away in annoyance. Presently, she changes her mind and drags him into a barn, but this time it's Comstock who cries off, whimpering about the eightpence in his pocket. "Poverty castrates a man," he moans.

The next night, at a cheap alehouse, he rants at Ravelston about women, the intelligentsia and people with an income of more than £500 a year. Refusing the loan of a tenner, he slinks off, fantasizing about bombing raids. But a day later, his luck changes. He's having breakfast when it happens, listening to one of Flaxman's limericks.

> There was a young couple of Aberystwyth
> Who united the parts that they kissed with
> And as they grew older
> They also grew bolder
> And united the parts that they good morning Mrs. Wisbeach....

A surprise $50 check has arrived from an American magazine, prompting a night on the town with Rosemary and Ravelston at one of London's swankiest restaurants. Gordon emerges boozed up and boorish, mauling Rosemary until she slaps him, dragging Ravelston into a drinking den and picking up a couple of hookers. With his mortified pal in tow, the revelers take a cab to a hotel, where Comstock instantly blacks out. Waking up in a police cell, and missing the £5 he planned to give Julia, he is fined by a magistrate and bailed out by Ravelston.

When a newspaper court report costs Gordon his job and his lodgings, the only work Ravelston can find for him is in poverty-stricken Lambeth. He rents a squalid room from a Mrs. Meakin—a friendly old lady who more or less offers to sleep with him—and is comforted by the knowledge that he can't sink any lower. This nihilism, coupled with his decision to give up writing, horrifies those closest to him. But when Comstock comes home one evening, he finds Rosemary in his room, ready and willing to spend the night. Next morning, they share a stilted conversation. "Clearly," says the script, "their love-making has not been an occasion of majesty and joy."

The script ends, much as the finished film does, with copywriter Comstock bringing an aspidistra home to his pregnant wife. In the draft version, though, a rousing *Rule Britannia* strikes up. The camera pulls out, out, out, until the Comstocks are microscopic—"much as he suspected all along," writes Plater.

A Long Time in Limbo

"Refreshingly simple, this bit," the screenwriter wrote in May after consulting his backers. "Consensus view is that everything's fine up to the Great Pissup, but gathers speed and rushes a little too eagerly to the end of the movie thereafter." Other alterations included a "slight change of emphasis in Erskine—his genuine concern that he's losing his best copywriter" and the addition of an undertaker "out of Joe Orton" to the Lambeth sequences. "He and Gordon compare notes daily on books sold and stiffs buried—the serious subtext being that what Gordon has come to terms with is the certainty of his own mortality and *that's* always good for a few laughs." The final scenes also required work, such as "a Gordon bathing, shaving and cleaning himself up sequence, so that we see the lower-middle-class man restored" and a "going into work sequence where Gordon demonstrates his near-genius as a copywriter—his knowing sellout to the System."

A rewrite duly appeared in July, but wasn't taken up. No one was interested in making the film. "It was on the shelf," says Rubinstein, "with the not-abandoned projects, as it were."

Finally, in 1995, Bierman approached producer Peter Shaw, owner of United British Artists (UBA), a company he'd formed in 1983 with John Hurt, Maggie Smith, Albert Finney, Glenda Jackson, Harold Pinter, Diana Rigg and Richard Johnson. Impressed with the script, Shaw felt confident he could find the money. Knowing that Bierman had the interest of Richard E. Grant and Helena Bonham Carter, he agreed to arrange the financing and distribution.

Shaw wrote to Plater in January 1996, enclosing a draft of the screen-play that UBA was promoting and setting out plans to shoot the picture in Dublin that summer. Returning to the project, Plater wrote: "It's always a little alarming to be confronted with a piece of work written some time ago, but I cannot tell a lie: I enjoyed reading the screenplay. It seems to have caught that characteristic Orwell stance: merciless observation redeemed by irony and the merest hint of compassion. And all a bit dark, which seems to be the spirit of our times: can't imagine why. It's also funny and about the only thing I know about audiences is they enjoy laughing.

"Here as elsewhere, he's better at depicting men than women. Rose-mary is a bit of a doormat and we should honour the changes that have taken place since the 1930s by clarifying her motives a little. It isn't enough to say she loves Comstock. Why does she love him? We probably need to be told. My instinct says she loves him because she loves the rebel and the outsider—there's something of the rebel in her, long subdued. There are lots of ways we might explore this—e.g. (and I'm improvising) supposing at the end she paints a beautiful but sardonic picture of the aspidistra and hangs it over the fireplace[8]? Maybe an end shot comprising picture, baby, Rosemary, Comstock and the *real* aspidistra, already with its first cigarette burn? Graft that on to the line: 'The Comstocks are on the march again' and we'd have a nice complex resolution that doesn't betray Orwell or any-one else.

"Otherwise, I'd love the chance to do a personal polish, with special reference to the end section, Rosemary in general (bearing in mind it's already twenty years *after* the suffragettes) and a few grace notes along the way, including a lovely Bill Naughton line I'd like to pinch for Mrs. Meakin's speech on p84:

> "'and a public wash-house on the Lambeth Road. I go there on my birthday. *Whether I need a bath or not.*'"

Pre-Production

Tightening the screenplay, which at that juncture exceeded two hours, Plater axed peripheral characters and played up the romantic comedy angle. Out went flabbier scenes—the "poverty castrates" sequence, Comstock and Ravelston's heart-to-heart in the alehouse, the fantasies about bombing raids—and in came the Lambeth undertaker, "Orton." Gordon's exploitation of his sister was toned down (in the movie, he makes of point of returning her Christmas money on his wedding day) and the dalliance with prostitutes (one of Orwell's cliché scenes, he argues on the commentary) pretty much erased. When Bierman objected to the f-bomb, which cropped up twice, Plater found alternatives. First for the chop was the "Go and fuck yourself!" line: when Doring bleats that the cancellation should have gone out on the grapevine, Comstock suggests instead that he stick his grapevine up his rectal orifice.[9]

The idea of Rosemary lying naked in the countryside also bothered Bierman, as it might make shooting Comstock's side of things more difficult. "The other way is to put her in underwear, this may be funnier," he told Plater in one of his notes. Writing to Bonham Carter's agent in December 1996, Bierman stressed that the actress wouldn't have to bare all and that Plater's rewrites would "give Rosemary a more significant role" in the story. She would, he promised, be "a star illustrator" whose career would flourish in Gordon's absence.

Plater states on the DVD that "a kind of non-story" in the papers, "that we had rewritten the part to make Helena's character more of a feminist"[10] had upset her. The truth, says Bierman, is that she had asked, rightly, if her part could be expanded. Orwell's Rosemary is a doormat, replies Plater; her relationship with Gordon wouldn't convince a modern audience. Bierman agrees, pointing out that in his copy of the novel, the two don't meet in person until page 131.

Making Merry

After Shaw's plans for Dublin fell through, shooting took place in London in the spring of 1997. Locations included the Institute of Directors' basement restaurant in Pall Mall (Julia's tea shop), St. Pancras Station (filmed throughout the night, when it was closed) and an East End street off Brick Lane (doubling for Lambeth). The New Albion's exterior, with "Blair Bros" delivery van, was in Holborn, not far from the West End; its art deco interiors were in Bethnal Green town hall, an East End landmark.

Trade journal *Screen International* put the budget at £6m ($9.5m), half of it supplied by the American sales and distribution outfit Overseas Filmgroup and the rest shared between the Arts Council of England (ACE) and UK distributor First Independent Films.[11] ACE's contribution—in effect an interest-free loan from the National Lottery, recently introduced by the government—was crucial. "Putting the money together for a film like this is tortuous," Shaw told the magazine. According to Bierman, Overseas Filmgroup salvaged the project after a crisis with domestic backers a week before filming. In a flurry of phone calls and faxes, he pulled off a deal in two days—"a miracle," he says on the DVD.[12]

Production wrapped in April at the end of a six-week shoot and Plater, as Rubinstein remembers it, "was just very excited it was going to be made." The couple adored the cast and crew. "Helena was perfect, and Richard, lovely Harriet Walter [as Julia]—well, all of them—and Bob [Bierman] just loving the material and the spirit of Orwell that pervaded it all. I think it was better than it was assessed at the time."

Given his upbringing in Swaziland's British expatriate community, leading man Grant already had the accent and mannerisms of a 1930s Englishman—and, says Bierman, looked eerily like Orwell when he wore a moustache for a camera test. (He removed it when the make-up ladies told him it was a turn-off.)

The shoot had its ups and downs, of course. Day one, with Grant and Bonham Carter strolling towards the Hampstead shop,[13] was disrupted first by a helicopter, which buzzed them until Bierman called air traffic control, and then by a man who walked into a shot naked. A "very famous" actor, cast as McKechnie, was fired for turning up drunk at rehearsals.[14] And when aspidistras proved impossible to find in the UK, the crew was forced to import them from the Netherlands.

Another challenge for Bierman was an obligation to cast as many disabled actors as possible to meet ACE's diversity quotas. His solution was to place a one-legged man outside a bank, playing a First World War veteran begging for cash. Comstock, who's there to convert his $50, cheerfully obliges.

For a time, Bierman considered a modern-day setting, as he wasn't interested in making a period film *per se*. The trouble was that no one in the nineties yearned to be a famous poet. The film's detractors accuse him of making its Depression-era setting too colorful, too pretty, but he disagrees, citing Madame Yevonde's sumptuous color photography as evidence that the thirties weren't as drab as we imagine. He also defends the changes to Orwell's plot: Gordon's night with Rosemary, for example, is shown to be a happy experience to "give them some hope."

The Reception

At a gala evening on 6 November, *Keep the Aspidistra Flying* opened the London Film Festival. One of the guests, Richard Blair, assured Bierman that "dad would have loved it."

The publicity effort that followed centered largely on Grant, who was open about his indifference to Orwell. Speaking to *The Observer*'s Lynn Barber, he said Plater's screenplay improved on the "relentlessly nihilistic" novel. Barber, one of Fleet Street's star writers, thought she and the actor had hit it off famously, but learned through his PR that he'd hated the whole experience. Miffed that she hadn't asked enough about the film, he ruled out any more interviews.[15]

On *Moviewatch*, a Channel Four youth show, however, he did describe the story in a roundabout way: "I think it's a classic case that still persists now of somebody who's middle class stabbing themselves for being middle class. Trying to be working class but never succeeding."[16]

The adaptation, starring Richard E. Grant and Helena Bonham Carter, met with scorn when it opened 1997's London Film Festival. Critics saw it as a fusty, smug, glorified TV movie (copyright First Independent).

Two champions of the film hailed from Tony Blair's Labour government, which had cut short 18 years of Conservative rule in May and was still enjoying a honeymoon with voters. At the festival's opening, culture secretary Chris Smith—reminding journalists and movie folk that Orwell and the prime minister shared a surname[17]—used it to promote the British film industry, predicting that in the 21st century, the UK would become *the* center of film-making. Unfortunately, wrote *The Guardian*'s Jonathan Romney, *Keep the Aspidistra Flying* was a "fusty" echo of a bygone age. "It's one thing to depoliticise Orwell, something else again to come up with such a smugly reactionary trifle as this."[18]

Future prime minister Gordon Brown, then overseeing the economy as chancellor of the exchequer, also showed a keen interest in the film. In a piece for *The Times* headlined "The chancellor keeps the aspidistra flying," Melvyn Bragg commented on the annual *Spectator* lecture,[19] given by Brown that year, in which he'd addressed the issue of Britishness—in particular, "what Orwell called the British Genius."[20] Bragg struck a positive note, about Brown at least ("Like his hero Orwell, he has told it like it is"[21]), but others at *The Times* loathed the picture. Critic Geoff Brown labeled it "small and archaic" and "the most pointless British film of the year,"[22] and colleague Daniel Britten thought Orwell must be turning in his grave: "The man who proclaimed that truth is more important than politics has now had his novel … turned into the sort of trivial romantic comedy that he despised."[23]

"A key problem," wrote *Sight & Sound*'s Claire Monk, who thought the script was superb, "is that the liberal-bourgeois preoccupations which are supposed to provide *Aspidistra* with its central dramatic substance are now such well-worn themes of British literary drama, the film risks seeming like a pastiche."[24] At *The Independent*, Matthew Sweet considered it "unremarkable but efficient period film-making, crucially energised by a performance of battery-acid tartness by Richard E. Grant."[25]

Empire magazine's Darren Bignall thought the film deserved the same attention as Orwell's better-known works, praising its "sprightly and sweet-natured" qualities.[26] *Screen International*'s Sheila Johnstone was another admirer, writing: "Prospects look bright for this well-designed, highly entertaining piece with fans of sophisticated comedy and heritage drama."[27]

At the mass-market *Daily Mail*, though, Christopher Tookey took exception to the film. In a column headlined "Why do our movies still live in the past?" he wrote that Plater's script was a failure, riddled with anachronisms; that Grant, overacting manically as he recycled his character from *Withnail and I*, was almost impossible to like; and that Bonham Carter, soldiering on gamely, had little to work with in terms of character. This was, he believed, a disastrous festival opener: "There is the antiquarian obsession with the minutiae of a mythical past, an unconscious snobbery, a failure to involve us with its characters, and an air of having been made for television, with no thought of the movie-going public."[28]

The following April, Tookey resumed his attack in a double-page spread lambasting the Arts Council's Lottery panels. "Fool Britannia" blared the headline, "(Or how the British film industry took £150 million of your money and produced two dozen turkeys)." Alongside flops such as *Photographing Fairies, Stella Does Tricks, The Secret Laughter of Women, Crimetime, Wilde* and *My Son the Fanatic,* he damned *Keep the Aspidistra Flying* as a doomed attempt to turn "Orwell's gloomy, social-realist novel into light romantic comedy." From a £3.2 million budget, the *Mail* claimed, not a penny of the £1 million grant had been repaid.[29]

Arthouse Fayre

"I think the reviews were probably mixed,"[30] says producer Peter Shaw. "No one was ecstatic about it, that's for sure, except—and I think this is a very important 'except'—it got very good reviews in America. It got better reviews in America than it did in the UK. I have a feeling that UK critics in a sense were getting fed up with semi-classics—which I suppose anything from George Orwell would be considered as—being turned into films which they probably considered to be a bit old-fashioned by the standards of what the nineties was pressing forward to try and achieve. Whereas in America, they just took the film for what it was, and in fact they gave it a different title. I like the title. It's not George Orwell's but it's a good title—a good, commercial film title. I think the British critics were very stuffy about it, to be honest, and couldn't see it for what it was."

Time's "best of 1997" top-ten list placed the "splendid adaptation" seventh, saying that Grant "struts and mopes majestically."[31] *Entertainment Weekly* gave the film an A-minus, calling it "a dissection of class struggle as pointed as in any Mike Leigh movie."[32] Ty Burr in *The New York Times* thought it "a sprightly, proto-yuppie farce"[33] and *LA Weekly*'s Ella Taylor enjoyed "a wickedly clever piece of satirical fun."[34]

This was a "wistful, witty movie," wrote *Boxoffice*'s Susan Green, that "skillfully balances the humor and sorrow of Gordon's predicament."[35] "It's always fun to see people full of themselves fail," snickered the U.S. edition of *GQ*,[36] while Ed Kelleher at *Film Journal International* thought Bierman and Plater captured "much of Orwell's vitriol and perhaps more importantly, his heart."[37]

"I always liked the film," says Shaw. "I thought Richard E. Grant was very good in it. I thought Helena was fine. I thought Bob did a pretty good job. It could be classed a bit pedestrian, I suppose. It could be classed a bit old-fashioned in a way, but it's quite an old-fashioned subject, isn't it? The trouble is—and we knew this at the time, everybody involved knew this—a film of this nature, on this subject matter, is bound to be considered a bit of an arthouse film. It's difficult to break a subject like this out of that and to get really wide distribution. We were destined for the arthouse-type audiences as opposed to getting into the multiplexes."

A Merry War
(a.k.a. *Keep the Aspidistra Flying*)

Gordon Comstock: Richard E. Grant
Rosemary: Helena Bonham Carter
Ravelston: Julian Wadham
Erskine: Jim Carter
Julia Comstock: Harriet Walter
Hermione: Lesley Vickerage
Mrs. Wisbeach: Barbara Leigh Hunt
Mrs. Meakin: Liz Smith
McKechnie: John Clegg
Cheeseman: Bill Wallis
Mrs. Trilling: Lill Roughley
Old woman: Dorothea Alexander
Old man: Peter Stockbridge
Beautiful young man: Grant Parsons
Paul Doring: Malcolm Sinclair
Lecturer: Derek Smee
Ravenscroft waiter: Ben Miles
Head waiter: Richard Dixon
Barmaid: Eve Ferret
Policeman: Roger Morlidge
Magistrate Croom: Roland Oliver
Orton the undertaker: Roger Frost
Dora: Dorothy Atkinson
Barbara: Harri Alexander
Factory girl: Lucy Speed
Librarian: Joan Blackham
Cabby: Roy Evans
Customer: Maggie McCarthy
Girl in Modigliani's: Lone Vidal
Man at club: Steven Crossley
Screenplay by: Alan Plater
Directed by: Robert Bierman
Produced by: Peter Shaw
Production designed by: Sarah Greenwood
Director of photography: Giles Nuttgens
Music composed and conducted by: Mike Batt

16

Animal Farm (1999)

The technique may have fallen out of favor somewhat, but for a time in the nineties, animatronics was all the rage in Hollywood. Programming robots to mimic living creatures wasn't exactly new—Disney had put animatronic birds through their paces in 1964's *Mary Poppins*[1]—but it took the genius of Steven Spielberg to appreciate its potential. At the same time as pushing computer-generated imagery (CGI) to new peaks, his 1993 dinosaur epic *Jurassic Park* boasted a full-sized tyrannosaurus rex stuffed with 4,000kg of electronics.[2]

Two years later, *Babe* charmed audiences with its tale of a cute little pig who dreams of being a sheepdog. The special effects by Jim Henson's Creature Shop—founded by the Muppet maestro and supervised by a British design graduate, John Stephenson—drew widespread acclaim, so it's small wonder that before the millennium was out, the film business would revisit Orwell's farmyard fable.

Robert Halmi, chairman of Hallmark Entertainment, commissioned a script in 1996.[3] "Halmi was an extraordinary character,"[4] says Stephenson, who made his directorial debut on the resulting TV movie. "He was snaffling up as many classics as he could—he did *Alice in Wonderland*, he did *Gulliver's Travels*. I think he went to the bestselling-books-in-the-world list, the classic books, and just nicked stuff off the top of that and said: 'We're going to make a film of it. He was producing quite good-quality films and all of the television networks in America were clamoring to get his stuff because there was nothing else quite like it. He could get the finance very, very easily. It really was a bit of a merry-go-round because I think he relied on the continuity in order to make the finance work. He could never just stop, so he bounced from one story to another."

By this stage, Hallmark and the Creature Shop were close collaborators. "I'd done a lot of work already on things like *The Odyssey*.... Hallmark were very much a part of us," says Stephenson. "Then Robert Halmi offered me *Animal Farm* to direct, which was great. I was absolutely thrilled and did

Hallmark's animatronic *Animal Farm*, screened on Ted Turner's TNT network in the U.S., was released theatrically in parts of Europe and Asia (copyright Hallmark Entertainment, TNT).

it the only way I knew how. I doubt that I would do it the same way again but at that particular point in time, it was the way to go. I'm quite proud of it, really, but I think it looks terribly dated."

A Shaggy Dog Story

Aimed at a mainstream audience, rather than literary pedants, the film tinkers with Orwell's story but retains its spirit for the most part. For one thing, it's told in flashback, as sheepdog Jessie—a minor character in the novel, afforded the role of narrator here—hides from Napoleon's spies with her friends. One stormy night, in an ominous pre-title sequence, they witness the farm crumbling and collapsing about their ears.

Years before, their human masters had set a beastly precedent. The first time we see oafish Farmer Jones, largely played for laughs by gaunt Pete Postlethwaite, he's threatening Boxer the carthorse with the glue factory for failing to plow straight. Corpulent neighbor Pilkington, who turns up for dinner with his brassy wife and cruel, piggy twin sons, is if anything even more objectionable. He's here to pressure Jones into paying off a debt or giving up the deeds to Manor Farm.

Old Major's speech, pared down by scriptwriter Alan Janes and voiced by Peter Ustinov, sounds undeniably noble in this sleazy, degraded environment. But as he leads the animals in an internationalist anthem, *Beasts of the World*, the buffoonish Jones (in bed with Mrs. Pilkington while her husband sleeps off the booze) investigates the disturbance, trips in the dirt and blasts him dead with his shotgun.

The subsequent uprising resembles the book's, but with an added barn fire. And while some may wince at Jones's fifties television (which shows American commercials), the scene in which the animals explore his farmhouse is at pains to reflect Orwell's prose. The horsehair chair, the bed filled with feathers, the raw hams hanging in the kitchen—even the lithograph of Queen Victoria gets a nod.

True to form, Napoleon drives Snowball into exile, sticks Old Major's flyblown skull on a pole, develops into a paranoid despot and trades with the human beings he purports to hate. (Mr. Whymper is absent, admittedly, but another of Jones's neighbors, Farmer Frederick, turns up looking like Hitler.[5])

Wallowing in alcoholism and corruption, the pigs in the house subvert the animals' seven—that's right, seven—commandments and terrify the farm with the help of Jones's home movie equipment. As the show trials commence, spin-doctor Squealer records them as lurid newsreels.

When the book's last paragraph does appear, it's six minutes before

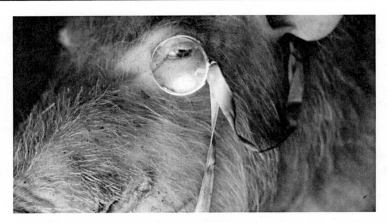

In a departure from Orwell's novel, Squealer (voiced by Ian Holm) makes propaganda films to boost Napoleon's regime (copyright Hallmark Entertainment, TNT).

the credits. Jessie peers into the farmhouse, sees Mr. and Mrs. Pilkington hobnobbing with Napoleon and his cronies and—as a windowpane warps the faces of man and pig—says: "I can't tell the difference between them!"

There's more to come, however. Finding "some animals are more equal than others" daubed on the barn, Jessie pokes her head inside and sees outrageous propaganda projected on the wall. Singing like a diva, a duck is praising Napoleon to the skies while the pig, dressed in a suit and standing on his hind legs, waves imperiously at the crowds. Ducks and sheep, sycophants all, chant: "Four legs good, two legs better." It's Soviet agitprop, the Nazis' Leni Riefenstahl and Hollywood's Busby Berkeley, all rolled into one.

Napoleon announces that henceforth, the farm will devote itself to weapons and walls—at which point we're back where we started, years later. The swine lie dead, snouts sticking out of the mud, as the rain-lashed farm falls apart. Jessie and her friends, returning from exile, are elderly but optimistic—and one bright day, there's cause for hope. Smiling, clean-cut American human beings—mom, pop and two little blond boys—swing by in an open-topped convertible to take ownership.

"Now at last we shall be free," says the Border collie, as the radio in the car plays Fats Domino's *Blueberry Hill*.

"Every day was a challenge"

In the beginning, American writer Martyn Burke produced a draft script. "He kind of Disneyfied it," says Stephenson, "and then Alan Janes, who's a very intelligent man, came along. He was determined, as was I, to try, in spite of the American influences, to keep it as true to the original as we possibly could…. It's quite a difficult thing to make work as a film. So he did that, and I thought the script was fantastic—except for the new ending, which again was an American insistence." Updating the story was inevitable, he says. "I think we had to. We were basically not capable of doing the story exactly as it was written. Technically, it wasn't possible."

The decision to have Jessie narrate came out of Stephenson and Janes' discussions. "Hopefully it didn't damage it too much. I think it worked reasonably well. I mean, it sort of demands a narration anyway and it was difficult to decide whose mouth we should put that narration into. There were other options: Farmer Jones's wife was one of them, I seem to remember. No, I thought it worked all right because [Jessie] could bounce in and out of the action—I'm happy with that." He is less pleased with a CGI rat, who offers black market goods in the manner of a Second World War spiv. "It looked absolutely terrible," he admits. "The rat was the first CG character that Cinesite, who are now massive—they did things like *Golden Compass* and the Bond films—had ever done, and it looks like it, in my view. I think in retrospect, maybe the comedy rat wasn't the world's greatest idea."

A mooted location near Melbourne, Australia, failed to live up to expectations, so Stephenson and his crew settled on Luggala, a valley owned by the Guinness estate in County Wicklow, Ireland. Their shoot, commencing August 1998, was to last 14 weeks. Seventeen years earlier, director of photography Mike Brewster had worked there on John Boorman's film *Excalibur* and been impressed by the quality of its light, which changed palpably from season to season.

The idea, Brewster explained, was that the setting would start off "golden and lush" to reflect the animals' optimism. "They think they are going to look after themselves and create a society where they won't be mistreated and everything will be wonderful. Of course, it's not like that—they become more and more abused, so we wanted the climate to look bleaker and bleaker."[6]

According to Stephenson, up to 120 real-life animals were used. "It was a huge undertaking. Massive. Every day was a challenge, but if you go to the interior of the barn, for instance, there's a speech by Old Major and you've got all the animals in the barn, all lined up. Now of course, 90 percent of those animals were the real thing. I tried to use the real animals as much as I could. Well, obviously you can't put sheep, cows, chickens, pigs, rabbits, ducks, whatever—they just don't stand there all next to each other and behave."

As Brewster told *American Cinematographer* at the time: "Mixing humans, animals and animatronics safely and effectively takes patience and tenacity, and [Stephenson is] brilliant at coping with pressure. The real animals are just that—real animals. The goat won't stand next to the dog. The two horses don't like one another much. Sheep are sheep, and the donkey does his own thing, not yours."[7]

"I had a sort of anamorphic lens camera," says Stephenson, explaining the set-up. "I had a very long, letterbox-shaped image on my camera, which I had up high in the barn, and then I introduced four cows. Locked the camera off, turned over, then I introduced six sheep, then 20 chickens, and I did them all separately, one after the other, so that I could composite the whole thing together in post. But then, of course, it would have been a bit boring because there'd be no move on it—it'd be a locked-off image. This wasn't shot on a digital camera, this was shot on 35mm film. So what I did is, I went into a green-screen stage and I shot some foreground elements to put into that shot and I did just a little panning move across the foreground elements. In other words, they would then change in perspective as the fake camera move was applied to the long, anamorphic-shaped box that I'd shot the rest of it in. I could then just move gently across the length of this shot that I'd created … and the beams and the bits and pieces in the foreground would shift in perspective."

The ousting of Farmer Jones, besieged by animals as he runs to his car, was "absolute mayhem" according to Stephenson. "There's animals moving in every direction and of course, we had to shoot all that separately as well. There's lots and lots of layers. Hundreds of bits of compositing involved. A lot of rotoscoping had to be done to get rid of operators and performers with the green screen. It was pretty complicated putting it all together. That number of animals in that number of shots, and making them talk, it had its moments of mayhem. Very, very complicated stuff. Great fun, though.

"I'd recently been working on the film *Babe*, which preceded it. What I loved about this one was that it was very, very earthy. It had a sort of realism about it which was very exaggerated because we were up to our knees in mud and dirt and rain, and everything had sort of mucus and sweat. It was very visceral, the whole thing, and I quite liked that about it. I think it allowed the animatronics to fit into the film a little more comfortably."

For the layman, then, how do animatronics actually work? "They're intricate pieces, almost like watchmaking," says Stephenson. "They're sculpted out of clay and molded very accurately. You then make a skeleton and a core which the skin, which is made out of latex or silicon, sits on. Then to the skeleton you add various forms of bulk and stretchy materials to simulate muscles, and then you use a whole range of activators, from electric servo-motors to bicycle cables. Anything and everything—in *Animal Farm* there's quite a lot of hydraulic activators embedded in the creatures. All of that is run through a computerized control system so that you can gang up all the actuators into recognizable moves and expressions. The talking part of it is computer-controlled as well, so in some instances you'd use a face-reading rig, which copies the movement of somebody's lips and transfers that to the mechanics inside the beastie. It's very time-consuming and expensive."

The technology was also restrictive, as Brewster noted in a 1999 interview. Keeping the electronics dry and hiding the hydraulics was a challenge in itself, and shooting some of the bigger animals, which didn't have a rear half, limited the number of camera angles they could use. "You normally poke the head out between real animals," said the director of photography.[8]

If he were making the film today, Stephenson wouldn't bother with animatronics. "That technology is unnecessary and well out of date," he says. "Trying to create living creatures mechanically is quite a tough call. We were quite good at it at that stage of the game but soon after that, I had about 90 CG artists working for me."

An example of *Animal Farm*'s CGI comes when Snowball is perched on a ladder, daubing the commandments on the barn. As the digital pig descends six or seven rungs, it looks a little primitive to modern eyes, though *American Cinematographer* thought the effect "intercut seamlessly with animatronic and real animals."[9]

Before filming, Irish actors recorded the story as a radio play,[10] "because of the voice technology. A lot of the big speeches had to be pre-recorded so that we could make the mouth shapes." Stephenson assembled an illustrious cast for the finished product, including Patrick Stewart, Kelsey Grammar, Paul Scofield, Julia Ormond, Ian Holm and Julia Louis-Dreyfus. "They were all very keen to get involved," he says.

"It's a very easy film to criticize"

The movie aired on Ted Turner's TNT network on 3 October 1999, ahead of a theatrical release in parts of Europe and Asia. *Variety* called it "serviceable but charmless."[11] Other than savaging the ending, *Time* magazine was more charitable, praising some of the imagery as "ingenious" and the ducks' musical number as "a perfect and hilarious imitation" of Soviet propaganda.[12]

Stephenson thinks the film has dated "but that's because of the technology we were using. There are some performances in there that I like very much. There's some bits of animatronics that I find almost impossible to look at. There's some bits of CG—for instance, with Jessie the sheepdog, her mouth is obviously post-production with CG, but we had to replace her mouth and her head for all her talking scenes and I think that works pretty damn well. Talking about animatronics, there are some scenes with Boxer the horse where it was a remarkable piece of work. There are lots of scenes where you think you're looking at a real horse and you wouldn't have realized that it's animatronic.

"I have mixed feelings about it. To be honest, I don't think anything that I've ever been involved with I would look back and think: 'Wow, didn't I do a good job, isn't that brilliant?' I think everything has its time and I find it very, very difficult to look at these days. I wouldn't look at it by choice and I'm not particularly happy with it, but at the time I don't think there was anyone around who could have done a better job, quite frankly. The way it's cut, the way it's lit, a lot of the camera work, all of it is actually dictated by the technology we were using. It's a very, very easy film to criticize but it was a very, very ambitious thing to try and do at that particular point in time. But I have to say, I absolutely loved doing it. The crew were just fantastic, they were amazing, and they definitely went the extra mile with us. We were filming in the most atrocious conditions quite a lot of the time."

On budget DVD, the film's reach has been remarkable. "It's everywhere," says Stephenson. "In every university in the world there's a copy of that film. Funnily enough, it gets played in the cinemas in places like Poland, and for some reason it does quite well in Italy."

As the conversation draws to a close, the Creature Shop veteran—awarded an OBE[13] in 2000 for services to the computer animation industry—underlines just how demanding it is to emulate real life forms. "What I didn't talk about was the fur and the hair on those creatures. It was immaculate. With the pigs, the hairs were all put in individually—they were all punched into the skin basically, one at a time. It's an amazing piece of craft.

"When we were shooting the animatronics, the crew would fall around me one by one because I had to be so specific to get just that one little moment, and I would be doing 30 or 40 takes of each little thing until I got it absolutely right. That's why I think the Irish crew were amazing. I'm not sure I could have made that in England, actually. I don't think they would have put up with me."

Animal Farm

Snowball (voice): Kelsey Grammar
Squealer (voice): Ian Holm
Mollie (voice): Julia Louis-Dreyfus
Jessie (voice): Julia Ormond
Benjamin (voice)/Jones: Pete Postlethwaite
Boxer (voice): Paul Scofield
Napoleon (voice): Patrick Stewart
Old Major (voice): Peter Ustinov
Farmer Pilkington: Alan Stanford
Mrs. Jones: Caroline Gray
Mrs. Pilkington: Gail Fitzpatrick
Mr. Frederick: Joe Taylor
Dennis: Jimmy Keogh
Eric: Noel O'Donovan
Farmers: Gerard Walsh, Jer O'Leary
Pilkington's sons: Sean Fitzsimons, Conor Kirwan

Additional voices: Charlie Dale, Amanda Symonds, Louise Gold, Paul Mark Elliot, Jean Beith, Nicole Tibbels, Tim Whitnall, Brian Gulland, Hannah King, Tim Merton-Laight, Charlotte Merton-Laight
Screenplay by: Alan Janes and Martyn Burke
Director: John Stephenson
Producer: Greg Smith
Executive producer: Robert Halmi, Sr.
Production designer: Brian Ackland-Snow
Visual effects supervisor: Angus Bickerton
Music: Richard Harvey

17

George Orwell:
A Life in Pictures (2003)

Shown on BBC Two on 14 June 2003[1]—11 days shy of Orwell's centenary[2]—this ingenious drama-documentary admits from the off that because there's no footage of the author, its makers have cooked up their own. In scenes occasionally reminiscent of the Woody Allen mockumentary *Zelig* (1983) or director Robert Zemeckis's *Forrest Gump* (1994), comedy actor Chris Langham portrays Orwell in a string of vintage-film pastiches designed to shed light on his life and times.

"I think most of the major channels were planning Orwell documentaries of one kind or another,"[3] says its director, producer and co-writer, Chris Durlacher. When a TV executive who knew of his admiration for Orwell mentioned that the BBC was touting for ideas, "I jumped at the chance and immediately I said: 'Well, we've got to make it all about the essays and journalism. It's the story that people don't tell so much.'"

As a framing device, the film turns Orwell's 1946 essay *Why I Write* into a televised interview. Clearly modeled on the BBC's *Face to Face* (1959–62)—in which ex-politician John Freeman quietly, and sometimes mercilessly, grilled public figures—the sequences place Orwell's prose into Langham's mouth.

It quickly becomes apparent that this is the documentary's *modus operandi*. As narrator Barbara Flynn states: "The pictures are invented, but every statement Orwell utters is his own." There are clips, too, from Nigel Williams' *Arena* programmes, Melvin Bragg's *The Road to the Left* and Jack Bond's *George Orwell 1903–1950*. Over the course of 90 minutes, then, this quirky biography covers the following milestones:

Such, Such Were the Joys: Orwell's damning verdict on St. Cyprian's, the minor boarding school he attended, was considered too libelous to publish in his lifetime. Reimagined by Durlacher, it's a confessional piece, shot in color, in which the essayist recalls the shame of wetting the bed.

A Hanging: Serving in Burma with the Indian Imperial Police, Orwell was sickened by a prisoner's execution. In a fictitious radio interview, accompanied by a filmed reconstruction, he explains his disenchantment with British colonialism.

Orwell's poor health: A public information film, devoid of literary quotes, that shows a doctor examining the writer for tuberculosis.

Down and Out in Paris and London: Publisher Victor Gollancz unveils its hotshot new author with a promotional film in which he dresses up as a tramp.

Bookshop Memories: Looking back on his Hampstead days for a first-person documentary, Orwell bemoans the tendency of lunatics and paranoiacs to frequent bookshops.

The Road to Wigan Pier: The author takes an exhausting trip down a mine to see life at the coalface first-hand. Once recovered, he visits a slum house in Sheffield, where he measures the dimensions of the rooms and examines the appalling diets of local people.

Married bliss: Silent, color home movies of Orwell and his new wife Eileen, rearing (and milking) a goat outside their rented cottage in rural Wallington, Hertfordshire.

Homage to Catalonia: In a newsreel from the Spanish Civil War, a reporter speaks to "one heroic Briton" intent on joining an anti-fascist militia. Later, in documentary footage from the frontline, Orwell shivers in a trench and explains the secret of making a perfect cup of tea. Returning for a time to Barcelona, a city he'd idealized as the model of a workers' state, he is dismayed to find communists clamping down on dissent. Ultimately, having been shot in the throat on combat duty, he is forced to flee with Eileen to France before the Stalinist authorities murder him.

England Your England: A propaganda short, based on the patriotic essay of 1941, that points out the English people's love of flowers, hobbies and individual liberty. Not to mention tea.

Pacifism and the War: Orwell debates two pacifists ("the writer and critic Derek Savage" and "the poet and sexologist Alex Comfort"), becoming increasingly agitated as he argues that their stance is objectively pro-fascist.

Arm the People: Rejected by the army for health reasons, the author joins the wartime civil defense force, the Home Guard. Using the text of a letter in 1940, Durlacher dresses Sergeant Orwell in combat fatigues as he advises the public on how to repel a German invasion.

The Lion and the Unicorn: Speaking to a village hall gathering, Orwell calls for a revolution against the moneyed class.

Working for the BBC: Two years as a reluctant government mouthpiece.

Animal Farm: The as-yet-unpublished anti–Stalinist fable wins the praise of an American newsman. "In an exclusive interview," he says, "Brit George Orwell gives us the lowdown on this showdown hoedown." While children on stage enact extracts from the book, Orwell explains its genesis and the antipathy of British publishers.

Some Thoughts on the Common Toad: A nature film drawn from the 1946 essay.

Adopting a baby: Another home movie, this time of the Blairs in their London flat with their new son. When Orwell—an enthusiastic whittler—hands the child a large knife, Eileen snatches it away.

Creating Order Out of Cologne Chaos: Reporting from the devastated German city.

Eileen's last letter: Written in hospital, the day she died in a routine operation.

Politics and the English Language: Alone at home in 1946, Orwell types his seminal essay on bunkum.

A letter of proposal: Suddenly rich from the success of *Animal Farm*, and aware that his bleeding TB lesion might kill him, Orwell asks young neighbor Anne Popham to marry him, even though they barely know each other. He says he is desperately lonely. Like other women he asks, she turns him down—though just before his death, Sonia Brownell will relent.

Nineteen Eighty-Four: To tell the story of Orwell's time on Jura, director Durlacher fashions an ersatz arts documentary, *The Last Man in Europe*. Interviewed by a very proper female journalist, Orwell expresses a degree of dissatisfaction with his final novel and—sitting up in bed, dressed in a jacket and scarf—describes totalitarianism in all its horrors. There's a simple moral to be drawn from this, he says, turning to the camera. "Don't let it happen."

At the time of writing, a clip of the film's last two minutes has been watched hundreds of thousands of times on YouTube. To judge from the comments beneath it, some viewers think Langham is Orwell himself.

On a Woolworths Rose and a Prayer

More than a decade on, Durlacher is justifiably proud of his work. The BBC's Orwell centenary film was a prestigious project, after all. "There were lots of people competing to make it, so I came up with the idea of: 'because there's no archive film of him, let's create the archive.'

"Before I even wrote a script, the first thing I did was write an archive report," he says. "When you're making a documentary, one of the things you might do is hire an archive researcher who will then give you an archive report, which is a couple of sheets of A4 typed up with, you know: 'We found a film can of this, and there's this'—there's a roll number, a description of the film, the title of the film, some information about the dates on it and what sequences might be relevant to the film that you're making. So the first thing I did was, I just wrote a completely fake archive report. I had roll numbers, I had dates of all the films that were made and little vignettes of the kinds of things that Orwell is seen in. It was totally imaginary. I wrote that and I said: 'Look, that's my pitch.' They liked that idea and asked for a longer treatment and eventually we needed to write a script."

Along the way, squabbles about the budget nearly killed the project. "They were offering a fraction of the money we needed to make the film that was on paper and I said, 'Look, if that's what they're doing, I'm not interested.' Normally you say, 'OK, we'll somehow cut our cloth,' but this time I said, 'This is a really important piece of work, we only get one opportunity, so let's do it right.' They had to double or triple the amount of money available—I can't remember exactly, but they were way off.

"Everything went dead for another few weeks while they hummed and hawed over whether to go ahead with it. I remember I went to stay with my sister for a weekend. She lives in Cambridgeshire, and I said: 'Let's go to Orwell's cottage.' I went to Wallington in Hertfordshire and the Woolworths roses that he planted are still in the front garden. I held on to one of the roses and I made a funny little prayer to myself and Orwell—not that I believe in prayers working or anything like that—but I prayed that we would get the go-ahead. I think about ten minutes later the phone rang, and we got the green light."

On the recommendation of a friend, Durlacher asked a young screenwriter, Paul Whittington, to collaborate. "We were making it on a documentary budget, so we couldn't afford to get some big-shot screenwriter in. We wrote it together, basically. We'd pass drafts to one another. He might deal with one period of years, do a first draft of that one, I might deal with another and then I would pass my draft to him. We did it like that simply because time-wise, we had to get it out pretty fast because Orwell's centenary was coming up and also that kind of writing is sometimes easier if there's two people.

"Writing the script was similar to making any documentary or drama script. You have to make some tough decisions about what you're going to leave out and find the points in his life that are relevant to the story you're trying to tell. I always had a specific story in mind. I know it's a sort of cradle-to-grave biography, it covers his whole life, but it actually isn't just that. It always had a point. I was trying to reveal the emotional and intellectual journey that Orwell went on that led him to sit down and write *Nineteen Eighty-Four.*"

With an editorial line in place, Whittington and Durlacher had to consider what sort of archive material was available. "We shot some bits of archive and then embedded them in other bits of archive. The truth is that with each sequence, we just tried to be imaginative. I know quite a lot about film history and I've since made another documentary about the early documentary movement. It's very familiar territory to me, it's another enthusiasm of mine, so I thoroughly enjoyed myself creating those pastiches. We gave complete back stories to all of them." Armed with this information, director of photography Jeff Baynes shot each segment with the technology and techniques of the era in question.

In large part, the success of the film hinged on who would play Orwell—and here it's worth remembering that in 1983, *The Crystal Spirit*'s producer shied away from approaching comedy actor John Cleese. By contrast, Durlacher and his team were overjoyed when 53-year-old Langham, a former *Muppet Show* writer then best known for playing the lead in a spoof documentary show,[4] took an interest in the role. "We certainly weren't going to go for a lookalikey," says the director. "The voice was tricky because it's quite a dissociative voice and we were worried about that. We wanted somebody who could carry it, but it's a documentary and so you don't have access to the big stars on our budget. Also, the kind of program we were making, they don't act in them.

"I think the choice was great. Chris Langham gives a brilliant performance. I know why I chose him but I didn't have a logic in my head when I was looking for him. In fact, casting generally is a bit more random than that. When we first met, we talked about his father, and it was the conversation we had about that that led me to think he would be right for the part. He told me a story, and it was just a slight story, but it was the same sort of story that I could imagine George Orwell telling about his dad. He didn't open up about the inner workings of his relationship with his father, but he told me a couple of stories and they just sort of reflected a similar kind of sensibility to my sensibility, and also it felt right. I mean, it is instinct, casting.

"I think one of the reasons in the end why he worked was that he had a background as a comedian, which meant that he was used to performing on his own. Chris also is a really good dramatic actor, whereas perhaps John Cleese is more of a … just a comedian. I always felt confident that Chris had the acting chops to pull it off. The truth is, we felt lucky to have him."

The film portrays Orwell as a wise, principled and brave eccentric, a man of boyish enthusiasms and, to use the vernacular of the British upper classes, a silly ass. Was the characterization discussed in these terms with

Langham? "Everything would have come out of the script," says Durlacher. "Chris Langham's never read anything by Orwell, never did read anything by Orwell, so his only frame of reference was the script. We certainly didn't want to paint Orwell as just being some kind of intellectual action man who was always right about everything, because he was a mass of contradictions, and we always wanted somehow to let some of those contradictions bleed through.

"An actor's quite comfortable with that because they want to play rounded characters, so Chris never really minded…. I mean, there's that scene where he was playing with a Bowie knife with a child in the room. I'd read about that in one of the biographies of Orwell and I always thought that was quite telling. Would you invite that guy round for tea? Orwell wasn't necessarily a character who you'd want to have round for tea or be your close friend or have as a neighbor, but he nevertheless was a hero to everybody who was making that film. Certainly to me."

As Orwell's first wife, Mary Roscoe leaves a lasting impression. At times she's used as light relief, almost rolling her eyes at some of her husband's pronouncements, but her reading of Eileen's final note to her husband is almost unbearably poignant. "She had very little to work with as a performer because she never says anything—in the archive that we were using, she never would have said anything," says Durlacher. "We tried two or three times to find a way to give her some dialogue, but we couldn't. I think Mary did a fantastic job, having a presence in the film. Definitely."

The vast majority of the filming was in a studio, or—when the Burmese man is escorted across a yard to be hanged, stepping aside to avoid a puddle, for instance—in the grounds of the studio. In fact, the coal mine from *The Road to Wigan Pier* was made out of plastic. "[That sequence is] based on a film called *Coal Face*, which is a seminal film in the history of documentaries," says Durlacher. "I cut the archive first and I left little holes where I knew I was going to put the scenes that I was going to shoot. It's not a particularly difficult thing to build, a little black wraparound. There's a lift scene in it as well—I think that's the goods lift from the studio."

One of the film's central elements—the *Face to Face* interview—was very much an eleventh-hour decision. "We tried everything. We were going to have a *Big Brother* kind of interview, we had all kinds of crazy ideas. At the last minute, I came up with the John Freeman idea. The set's so easy, luckily—it's just a couple of black drapes and an armchair. But because it's the inner monologue, really, of the film—he talks about his motivation, directly, about why he writes—it was always going to be quite important and it was always going to have that role in the film where you come back to it three or four times."

On location in the countryside, Durlacher supervised scenes such as Orwell milking a goat. "I think I did that on a publicity day." Out of the blue, he wound up shooting material on Super 8 for what became *Some Thoughts on the Common Toad*. "That wasn't planned. I just said, 'Go on Chris, go off into the woods,' and I shot some stuff." In the end, it turned out to be his favorite sequence, "probably because it's one of my favorite pieces of his writing. At heart, it's his optimism that attracts me most to Orwell."

Asked about technical trickery, Durlacher is quick to point out that: "It was untricky. That was the trick, to be not tricky. These days people would process it, using all kinds of computer graphics to age the thing. The old archive was shot on film. Film's got less grainy and cleaner but essentially it's the same, so we got the most grainy film we could find. We used only lenses that they would have back at the time. In some cases, we used pretty much the same camera, although not always."

He mentions telecine, the process by which film is transferred to video-tape for broadcast. "These days nobody uses film any more, but then, people were using film and you would go straight from the negative on to tape and it would be electrostatically cleaned so there'd be no dust in the way. We did two things. First of all, we made a print, and you get a bit of grain by that process. It was difficult to find somebody who'd make a print, nobody was making prints any more. Then we left the film camera with the print in it lying around open on the floor for a couple of days, so we let some dust get on it."

Different Kinds of Jerk

Two weeks before *A Life in Pictures* went out, BBC Two's snooty arts show, *Newsnight Review*, previewed the documentary. Of the three cultural critics on its panel, only one had reservations about it.

Alkarim Jivani, television editor for the London listings magazine *Time Out*, said that next time he saw a picture of Orwell, his brain would register Langham. It was, he remarked, "a triumph over the tyranny of television, which says: 'No pictures, no program.'" To Jivani's mind, the show was both a spirited documentary on Orwell and a tribute to British documentary film-makers such as John Grierson. Every scratch, hiss and tick on the soundtrack seemed authentic.

Jude Kelly, former artistic director of the West Yorkshire Playhouse, called the film "breathtaking" and Langham "brilliant." It showed, she said, that Orwell was a brilliant journalist, writer, novelist and thinker, "and also probably a complete jerk to live with." But music critic Paul Morley was unconvinced. It was "a beautiful piece of embroidery" and Langham should be knighted for it, he said (four years before possession of child pornography destroyed the actor's career), but its "patronizing" tone and "tedious" modern techniques irritated him. "It was just very, very tepid and a little bit too polite."[5]

The print media disagreed. "Such, such a joy," gushed *The Guardian*, singling out Langham for his "captivating" performance. "He communicated Orwell's genius, his honest exuberance (retain one's childhood love of trees and toads, he advised), his heartfelt political views and his sadness and his cynicism, expertly," added reviewer Gareth McLean.[6]

The *Daily Express*'s Robert Gore-Langton thought the screen Orwell was "a hoot," labeling him "a dry stick in tweeds with a passion for the proletariat."[7] Paul Hoggart, for *The Times*, marveled at "the media studies exercise to end them all,"[8] while the *Daily Mail*'s Peter Paterson mused that Durlacher "may have changed the rules for bio-pics."[9] In *The Independent*, Thomas Sutcliffe appreciated its affection and respect for its subject, adding: "If even half of today's arts documentaries showed as much originality and inventiveness in their approach, we'd be lucky."[10]

Durlacher's film received three Bafta nominations: for best editing, factual (Steve Stevenson), best visual effects (Aidan Farrell and Barney Jordan) and best photography, factual (Jeff Baynes). It went on to scoop the Grierson Award for Best Documentary on the Arts, the Bronze World Medal for Docudrama at the New York Film Festival and an International Emmy for Outstanding Arts Programme.

"We cleaned up with this one," says Durlacher, "and it's very nice too."

George Orwell: A Life in Pictures

George Orwell: Chris Langham
Why I Write Questions: Michael Fenton Stevens
Derek Savage: Tom Goodman-Hill
Alex Comfort: Andrew Bone
Eileen Blair: Mary Roscoe
Jura Interviewer: Rebecca Front
Narrator: Barbara Flynn
Screenplay: Paul Whittington and Chris Durlacher

Produced and directed by: Chris Durlacher
Executive producer: Emma Willis
Film editor: Steve Stevenson
Original music: Daniel Pemberton
Archive research: Debbie Townsend
Production designer: Patrick Bill
Art director: Hannah Spice

18

The South Bank Show (2003)

June 2003 saw the publication of two weighty biographies—Gordon Bowker's *George Orwell* and DJ Taylor's *Orwell: The Life*—only one of which came with a television spin-off. As David Taylor remembers it, the book "was fixed up in about 1999" with a September 2002 deadline for submission. "As soon as 2002 came along, and I was actually writing the book—which had to be written at quite a lick—I was fishing around to get a TV thing on the back of it."[1]

London Weekend Television's *The South Bank Show*, the long-running arts magazine program hosted by Melvyn Bragg and broadcast on ITV on Sunday nights, seemed a sensible port of call. "I'd known Melvyn on and off for years and he'd always been very supportive," says Taylor, "although I did try one or two independent production companies. I had some dealings with Wall to Wall, but they were making that drama-documentary with Chris Langham that came out around the same time. In fact, I managed to get some money for advising them on that, so I did quite well.

"I suppose what I was trying to achieve was to put a mini-biography of Orwell on screen, talk to the people who were still alive … it was over 50 years since his death, so they were all getting on a bit. Ventilate a few new discoveries: people I'd found, things I'd discovered, people I'd talked to. And, I suppose, just put my own spin on it. The really unfortunate thing was that one or two of the people I'd found by that point were just too old, too decrepit, even to appear on screen. There was a wonderful old gentleman called George Summers who actually fought with Orwell over a woman in the early thirties on Southwold Common, but by the time we got to making the film, he was 93, and he died soon afterwards. It would have been great to have got him there in front of the camera, saying: 'I hated his guts, I thumped him.'"

Bragg—"an Orwell nut," in Taylor's words—lent a tremendous amount of support and encouragement to him and his director, Leo Burley. He had, after all, made *The Road to the Left* 32 years earlier. "His line was, 'You've written it, you have these theories, go ahead and do your thing. We will guide you and if we think we have to, we will rein you back.' It was immensely kind of him and I was more or less given my head."

Taylor, who was born in 1960, was roughly the same age as Burley and the two "had similar cultural interests, shall we say. In the book, there are some little musical jokes: the chapter about when he was working at the BBC is called *London Calling*—you know, the Clash song. And as you doubtless know, the Jam once did a song called *The Eton Rifles*. In doing the soundtrack, we tried, in a very tongue-in-cheek way, to work up the idea of the 'punk Orwell.'"

This meant that in the original rough cut, the sound of *The Eton Rifles* livened up newsreel footage of the 1921 Eton wall game. "And then when we had wartime stuff, we had the Clash doing *London Calling*. I remember walking up the steps of the studio in Soho, hearing this blasting out and thinking, 'We're never going to get away with this.' Of course, we didn't. Melvyn heard it, said: 'What is all this crap? We're not having all of this.' And so we started with Holst or something like that. I tried, and we had some fun. There was this kind of punk Orwell trying to surface, but he was squashed by Melvyn when it got to the production stage."

Keeping It Real

Often referred to as *The Real George Orwell*—a phrase used by Bragg in his introduction, but never spelled out on screen—the program[2] assembles a cast of characters both familiar and new, along with clips from the BBC spanning 30 years.[3] To begin with, Taylor eulogizes Orwell at his grave in Sutton Courtenay, Oxfordshire. He was, says the biographer, "a piece of moral litmus paper," part of the popular consciousness, and so influential— so prescient, it seems—that in 9/11's aftermath, pundit after pundit asked: "What would George have thought?"

Equally important, he tells viewers, is the question of *how* George thought—which takes us to the Orwell Prize ceremony in London. As the newly knighted Sir Bernard Crick mingles with journalists and publishers, *The Guardian*'s Polly Toynbee makes a speech. The real strength Orwell showed was his "searing eye for cant," she says, and while it may be tempting to second-guess him on issues such as Iraq, it's essentially a futile act. In the audience, one of the judges listens with interest. It's Alan Plater.

Across London, Taylor drops in on UCL's Orwell Archive, where Peter

Davison, editor of *George Orwell: The Complete Works*, doesn't envy his attempts to find new biographical material. Out on the road, he meets Orwell's one-time drinking buddy, the novelist Peter Vansittart, who says his friend used to use the phrase "let's have a pint" to sound more working class; Dora Hammond (née Georges), the daughter of a Greek Cypriot in Southwold, to whom a lovestruck Eric Blair wrote the sadly lost *Ode to a Dark Lady*; and Susannah Collings, whose mother spurned the "too cynical" Eric in favor of his friend Dennis. In a Collings family photo album, a previously unknown snap of Orwell on a beach leaves Taylor goggle-eyed.

Another segment dissects Orwell's questionable opinions about Jews and speaks to Denzil Jacobs, a Jewish Londoner who at 19 was part of the same Home Guard platoon as Orwell. From conversations they'd had, Jacobs considered the man an ally, so was "quite amazed" after the war to read some of his less guarded opinions. Davison points out that many Britons in those days were "careless about the way they spoke of Jews." Adam Phillips, a psychoanalyst, accepts that Orwell is "running the risk of being antisemitic," but defends him on the basis that he's interested in prejudice. He's asking questions about why antisemitism has persisted.

Back at UCL, Taylor boggles at one of Orwell's razor blades and a homemade Christmas card from son Richard, who's on hand to talk about his father's love of tobacco. Once, on Jura, Orwell casually handed him a lighter and let him puff on a pipe, putting the boy off smoking until his adolescence came around. And it's to the Hebridean island that the film goes next. "He was quite sure that there was going to be an atomic war," says Jacobs.

Happily, the producers have hired Ronald Pickup to read the show's literary extracts—and here he is on screen, in scenes from *The Crystal Spirit* (or *Orwell on Jura*, as it's titled here). Inside Barnhill, Taylor confides that he's always been suspicious of writerly presences, but that "here on Jura, Orwell's scent is very strong." He guides us through the house, lingering in the room where Orwell wrote; and at Downing College, Cambridge, meets David Holbrook, one-time boyfriend of housekeeper Susan Watson.

The writer, poet and Emeritus Fellow, who'd clashed with Orwell in 1946, thought him a "self-destructive" man who "destroyed everything that connected him with the mainland.... It was a very strange atmosphere." He is by no means an admirer of *Nineteen Eighty-Four*, which he glimpsed on a typewriter when its title was *The Last Man in Europe*. "It seems to me paranoid," he says, a little wearily. "I suppose some of it's come to pass."

While filming at Barnhill, biographer David Taylor started to understand the bleakness of Orwell's last days on Jura (photograph by David Ryan).

Unfinished Business

Looking back now, Taylor becomes animated at the memory of Jura. "You just got an idea of the remoteness and the sequestration of it, and I suppose the bleakness of it too," he says. "We were there on a summer's day and it was absolutely flooded with rain, and you had some idea of what it was like to have lived there. Sitting there in winter in the bleak little back bedroom, with the paraffin heater on, chain-smoking Capstan Full Strength and dying while trying to write this—forcing yourself to write this.

"He needn't have flogged himself like that. I'm not saying he could have saved his life, but he could have lived longer if he hadn't, you know, literally killed himself to finish it. If he'd sat out the winter and waited for somebody to come and type up the second draft under his supervision, he needn't have put himself through all that. Have you read the diary entries of late 1948? They're absolutely appalling: it's all kind of, 'Pain inside very bad. Pain inside very bad. Tried to walk in garden. Typed all afternoon. Pain inside very bad.'

"When he came out of hospital in the middle of 1948, the doctors thought he wasn't in too bad a shape. They thought they'd patched him up quite well and there was a possibility of his being what the medical people called 'a good chronic.' If he'd taken it easy and done a little bit of work here, a little bit of work there and not agitated himself, he could have lived a few years longer, possibly, but he didn't. He forced himself to finish *Nineteen Eighty-Four*. Finished typing his final version and then literally opened a bottle of wine and then collapsed and was taken away to hospital. There's a kind of fatalism about it, which is very typical of Orwell."

The show went out on 27 July 2003. Five weeks later, news broadcaster ITN[4] announced that *South Bank Show* researcher Phil Windeatt and associate producer Jonathan Levi had discovered the first confirmed footage of Orwell, playing the Eton wall game, in the Pathé news archive.[5] Taylor acknowledged this in an afterword to his paperback edition, reworked as an article for *The Guardian* the following February. More than one of his interviewees, he added, "found that a television camera acted as a powerful stimulant to memory." Vansittart, for example, recalled his history master taking him to a 1939 conference, organized by pacifists and attended by the likes of Orwell, Richard Rees and Rayner Heppenstall.[6]

By and large, making the documentary was "very knackering but rewarding," says Taylor. "*The South Bank Show* is an hour, so that's 52 minutes of film.[7] I'm telling you, we shot 13 hours of film, which I gather is standard for the format. It seemed to me extraordinary. The director would say, 'Oh, we need some more stuff from so-and-so in Southwold, we've got to go down there.' So you'd spend a day going to Southwold, doing an interview, coming back and then none of it would be used. But this is how TV works. I've had similar experiences with the BBC, where you think, 'How can they spend all this?'"

Still, the reaction pleased him. He was especially flattered when the writer Beryl Bainbridge, in a piece for *The Observer* to mark *The South Bank Show*'s move to Sky Arts in 2009, named it as one of the highlights of a 30-year run on ITV.[8] "I think a million people watched it," says Taylor, "which is pretty good, I was told, for a Sunday night in August about somebody literary."

From time to time, film clubs ask him to attend screenings of the documentary. "I'm glad it's still there," he says. "It's another brick in the Orwell path, I suppose."

The South Bank Show,
season 26, episode 19

Written and presented by: David Taylor
Produced and directed by: Leo Burley
Edited and presented by: Melvyn Bragg
Extracts read by: Ronald Pickup

19

Orwell Against the Tide (2003)

In the words of producer-director Mark Littlewood, *Orwell Against the Tide* is "a film about George Orwell from the freedom fighter perspective."[1] With near-enough dramatizations of passages from *Homage to Catalonia* and highly charged comments from philosophers Richard Rorty and Noam Chomsky, the international co-production wears its radical sympathies on its sleeve.

The mood is set in the opening few minutes, when Stanford University's Professor Rorty posits that wherever people are struggling for political freedom, they will recognize figures like O'Brien and institutions like the Ministry of Truth. "Wherever the high are oppressing the low," he says "there will be something that Orwell has diagnosed." Professor Chomsky, from the Massachusetts Institute of Technology, is no less forceful. "Orwell is not writing about classical Athens," he says. "We are living in the world that he was working in, writing about, commenting on and so on."

Littlewood's world—or at least his immediate locality—is Scotland, where he co-founded Pelicula Films in 1971.[2] Working with media students from the University of the West of Scotland in 1999/2000, he heard about the Orwell centenary from their lecturer, Tony Grace. In Littlewood's opinion, his schoolteachers had presented Orwell's work in the most boring, unimaginative way possible. Over the years, he'd thought about exploring another side of the author for the benefit of a non-academic audience.

"I suppose it was my idea, really," says Grace, "and we sort of developed it together. I wrote the treatments and the initial scripts. It had a fairly protracted development."[3]

With the promise of funds from the European Commission and Scottish Screen, Littlewood trekked around the film festivals of Europe, securing modest contributions from eight countries. One of the main selling points was the involvement of Chomsky, who'd met Grace on a visit to Scotland years earlier and was happy to grant him an interview. Backers were hard to find, but just as Littlewood was on the verge of giving up, Barcelona-based independent film-maker Oriol Porta signed on as co-producer, bringing his Catalan film crew on board. It was, says the director, a turning point.

Grace's recollection is slightly different. "The key person was a guy called Jordi Ambros, who was commissioner for TV3 Catalonia. The influence he had in the European documentary community was substantial, so a lot of people then followed on."[4]

The last pre-production challenge—copyright—took Littlewood to the London headquarters of AM Heath, which represents the Orwell estate. Ushered into a lawyer's office, he explained that he was a cash-strapped documentary-maker who wanted permission to quote from everything Orwell had written. The lawyer's eyes widened, then widened some more, until at last he granted the rights for £250, much less than the sum Littlewood had in mind.

Perhaps, he thinks, the lawyer was impressed by the "bold thoroughness" of his proposal. "He later told me that he'd had to pacify Hugh Hudson, director of *Chariots of Fire*, who had already paid a small fortune for the exclusive rights to make a feature film of *Homage to Catalonia*," he says. "He'd explained to Hudson that any dramatization I might do wouldn't really be dramatization, but more what he called 'a creative realization of reality.'"

In May 2003, *The Scotsman* reported that the film would cost £300,000, be shown as part of Scottish Television's *Artery* series (making it the most expensive documentary the company had ever commissioned) and air in at least ten other countries. According to Littlewood, it would concentrate on Orwell the man, bringing out his humor and humanity. "He was a freedom fighter with great physical and mental courage," the newspaper quoted him as saying, "and not quite the dowdy old man in a sports jacket who appears in the photographs at school."[5]

Viva España

From his birth in Motihari, India, to his burial in a quiet Oxfordshire village, the film provides a comprehensive overview of Orwell's life. Pathé's film of the 1921 Eton wall game, so narrowly missed by *The South Bank Show*, "just happened to come as were putting the thing together," says Grace.

In some respects, though, it is decidedly less conventional than its predecessors. For a start, roughly half of its 55-minute running time is devoted to Spain, because Grace (who'd developed a fascination with the civil war during his postgraduate research on Orwell) considers it "a turning point" in the author's life and thinking. Leaving aside its short dramatizations of

Nineteen Eighty-Four's torture scenes, it's also devoid of dialogue to all intents and purposes, relying on narrator Siobhan Redmond to explain the context of its splendid archive footage. As Orwell, Scottish actor John Kay Steel looks and sounds authentic, but the only time he speaks is when he's reading passages in voiceover.

Considering his avowed anti-imperialism, few Orwell documentaries are quite as hard-hitting about the empire Eric Blair grew up in. Here, however, Chomsky notes with calm authority that his father Richard, a civil servant in charge of opium harvests in India, helped to run the biggest narcotrafficking trade in history. Rorty, filmed in Paris, brings up the oppression of the Burmese and says that Blair's police duties gave him material for the rest of his writing career.

In one of the film's few real scoops, the POUM Youth's former general secretary, Wilebaldo Solano, reminisces about 1937 Barcelona. "He arrived at the barracks," he says, "and people wondered about this man who seemed so dull and then so shy." Yet thanks to his Burmese days, Blair knew more about military discipline and weapons than most of his comrades. Sequences shot around Monflorite evoke the atmosphere of the Aragon Front, as Steel reads accounts of the classless militia, lice infestations, parties in a commandeered country house and shouted boasts about delicious buttered toast (designed to make the enemy troops feel jealous). Orwell's reluctance to shoot a fascist who'd just been to the toilet is amusingly conveyed. His bullet to the throat, less so.

As his time in Spain is curtailed, and his friend Bob Smillie dies at the hands of the communist secret police, the documentary makes a point of examining Orwell's attitude to Scotland. Earlier, it had noted that St. Cyprian's School was strangely in awe of Scottish culture, because only the richest families in England could vacation there. It also mentioned that in Orwell's novels, Scots were often the most unsavory characters. But he was full of admiration for Smillie, a fearless, 22-year-old Glasgow University student. "Orwell," says the narrator, "would never again profess to hate the Scots."

Terrible Times

Made on a shoestring and scored by Jim Prime from the band Deacon Blue, *Orwell Against the Tide* aired on Scottish Television on 17 November. South of the border, it had a Leicester Square premiere, a screening at Oxford University and public showings at *The Guardian* newspaper offices in London. Bafta Scotland nominated it for a documentary award.

The film is a reminder, in many ways, of the febrile atmosphere in 2003, when opposition to the U.S.-led invasion of Iraq was at its peak. Rorty warns that Orwell's worst nightmares "may come true in the old democracies as a result of terrorism"—one of several remarks that Grace thought might date the film. "Unfortunately," he says, "many of the comments [he and Chomsky] make seem almost more relevant than they did at the time."

Orwell Against the Tide

Writer/co-producer: Anthony Grace
Produced & directed by: Mark Littlewood
Writer/editor: Andy Boyd
Music: Jim Prime
George Orwell: John Kay Steel

Eileen Blair: Natalie Haverstock
O'Brien: Melvyn Williamson
Winston: Raymie Day
Big Brother: Joe MacFadyen
Narrator: Siobhan Redmond

20

Peaceforce (2011)

Politics has changed drastically since the CIA subverted Orwell's works to use as Cold War propaganda; when the young take to the streets today, it's usually to oppose racism, imperialism and injustice. The 2010s have yielded two short adaptations so far, and it can't be a coincidence that both are of *Shooting an Elephant*.

The 1936 essay is a powerful, deceptively simple tale, based on an incident in 1920s Burma. Faced with a rampaging creature that has trampled a coolie to death, police officer Eric Blair is reluctant to kill it, knowing that the animal is valuable and that its attack of 'must' has passed. But as a crowd of at least 2,000 is willing him on, and would laugh and jeer if he simply walked away, he feels has no choice but to gun it down.

"It really affected me, the story," says Danish director Peter Gornstein.[1] "I think it's a brilliant essay in so many ways. It describes the essence of humanity, basically: the conflict between what you're supposed to do—the man you'd like to be—and the man you're actually going to be most of the time. It takes a lot of courage to not do what's expected of you. In that sense, the story really fascinated me."

Filming a literal adaptation wasn't feasible, though. "With the settings that were available to me, I couldn't just take a guy and put him in khaki shorts and run him out into the Danish forest—that wouldn't really work in the middle of winter, although I would have loved to have done it as a period piece [in Asia]. The only option left available to me was to set it in a post-apocalyptic scenario, which could still embody the story and the spirit and make it spectacular in a different kind of way."

Utilizing his experience as a concept artist at Sony Pictures Imageworks, where he'd contributed to movies such as *Starship Troopers*, *Contact* and *Jumanji* in the nineties, Gornstein wrote a treatment set in 2032, in a devastated Denmark where capitalism had run its course. Working closely with writer David Sandreuter, he expanded this into a 19-minute mini-epic called *Peaceforce*.

Make no mistake about it, this is *Shooting an Elephant* with English and Danish dialogue. But instead of British imperial policemen, there's Peaceforce—"like a revamped United Nations," says the director, though the film is deliberately vague about their status. All you need to know is that they're flustered troops in a compound, with Union Jack shoulder flashes, who strive to maintain order among the angry, starving Danes.

After the locals pillage Copenhagen's zoo and slaughter most of its animals for food, word comes through that an elephant is charging around a neighborhood that's already been reduced to rubble. Daniel, a young soldier from Denmark who fled with his family to the UK as a boy, is sent to investigate and realizes before long that the wretches standing behind him view the leathery mammal as their next meal.

"I wanted to keep the essence of the story, about the destruction of this magnificent beast," says Gornstein, "and being put in a situation where you know what you're about to do is wrong, but you're kind of forced to do it. It's the whole dilemma of the human condition. I took the idea of this guy who gets further and further away from his comfort zone in his lust for adventure, and then finally ends up in a place where the adventure turns out to be a nightmare. He's forced to do what he sees as the wrong choice—but it could potentially be his neck on the line rather than the elephant's, right? It's easier to do what you know is wrong than to do what you know is right."

Not-So-Wonderful Copenhagen

Filming took place over 12 days in 2010, across four locations.[2] The main one, in the middle of the Danish capital, was the only part of the city that hadn't been modernized or revamped. "Right now, that's luxury condos, all that stuff, but at that point it was still industrial wasteland. The whole thing was shot around the same building, but we just moved the camera around because that's all the dystopian stuff that was left. The last day of the shoot, they came in with bulldozers and tore the whole thing down."

The climactic scene, in which Daniel shoots the behemoth, is brutally convincing, so much so that animal hired to play it—a circus performer called Lara—appears to act out its death throes. "That's all editing magic. We were promised by the circus guy, the elephant trainer, that Lara would lay down and do whatever we asked of her, but it turns out that elephants have a mind of their own and do whatever the hell they want to do.

"There are only six elephants in all of Europe that you can actually use for this kind of stuff and I don't even think it's legal any more. I think they changed the law. What is really going on is Lara is standing there and she has her family, which is two other elephants, right outside of the frame because they don't like being alone." On a bitterly cold Scandinavian day, the crew found a way to cajole Lara into lying down for the camera. "I think she had an OK time," says Gornstein. "She got several buckets full of carrots."

One of the producers, Swedish baroness Beatrice von Schwerin, reminisced about the film for the website Tinsel Town News Now in 2016. This was her first producing credit, and she knew that if she could overcome the film's challenges—of cast, crew, locations, extras, children, animals and elaborate visual effects—then she could cope with anything. As she recalled, the elephant sequence was shot over two days (one for the creature, the other for the extras) in a field outside the city: "Every now and then during the shoot, we'd have our star [elephant] head over to the others for some down time. It was a great and exciting day for both us and the elephants," she said.[3]

The VFX by matte painter Ivo Horvat took almost ten months to complete.[4] Having been present on location, he submitted stunning work from his base in Los Angeles, including aerial shots of Daniel's armored vehicle on patrol in a ruined Copenhagen.[5] The film-makers were lucky, he told digital artists' site Renderosity in 2011, because "we lined up locations like a modern-day industrial power facility that had a lot of grime and machinery and a ruined factory that was almost completely destroyed. We could never have art directed or built sets like that with all those crooked chimneys, debris and blast holes."

Force of Nature

In February 2011, *Peaceforce* premiered at the International Short Film Festival in Clermont-Ferrand, France: "the world's biggest and most esteemed festival for short films," according to the Danish Film Institute.[6] Judges awarded it the Prix Canal+, thereby guaranteeing that Canal+, the premium cable TV channel, would buy it for broadcast in France and Spain. "It was quite a sensation," says Gornstein. "I think they paid €50,000 for it, which was unheard of. It was a bit of a buying bonanza at the time. I was very popular for a couple of days; I felt like a movie star."

The film was nominated for a Robert (a Danish Oscar) and played at the Marché du Film in Cannes, Toronto's Worldwide Short Film Festival and the London Film Festival, among others.[7] "It got a very positive reaction. It was quite overwhelming for a while but then it kind of died down, as it does with short films, especially science-fiction short films." Since Netflix started streaming its own shows, he says, these post-apocalyptic stories are very much in fashion.

"I did send it to the Oscars and it did get shortlisted, but it didn't win," he adds. "That was a shame."

Hang on—it's good to be shortlisted, surely? "Yeah," he shoots back. "But it's better to win."

Peaceforce (2011)

Daniel: Cyron Melville
Jesper: Henning Jensen
Rolf: Anders Hove
Selma: Silja Byske
Soldier: André Babikian
Captain: Søren Poppel
Elephant: Lara
Graying woman: Simone Kamilla Karrebæk

Dying man: Simon Maach
Written by: David Sandreuter
Directed by: Peter Gornstein
Produced by: Jonas Allen, Peter Bose, Beatrice von Schwerin
Production designer: Thomas Bremer
Music by: Kristor Brødsgaard, Vagn Luv

21

Shooting an Elephant (2016)

As the clamor over *Peaceforce* faded in continental Europe, a former professional sportsman in the United States joined forces with an Academy Award nominee to conjure up a more traditional, straightforward *Shooting an Elephant*. Since Orwell's essay[1] is a succinct one, audiences had to be satisfied with another short.

In the age of video streaming sites (and, the more curmudgeonly might argue, reduced attention spans), that's not necessarily a bad thing, though. Short films have enjoyed something of a renaissance since the turn of the millennium, with young audiences in particular embracing the format. It also helps that they don't cost the earth and that film-makers with something to prove can appeal directly for cash online.

Juan Pablo Rothie, the film's Venezuelan-American director, first latched on to Orwell's writing at high school. Born in 1985, he was already something of a globetrotter, migrating to India with his family at the age of seven and to the Philippines four years later. After studying film at the University of Southern California and playing squash professionally for several years, Rothie set his heart on bringing *Shooting an Elephant* to the screen. He gained the Orwell estate and Richard Blair's support, but was issued with strict guidelines about how it should be adapted.

Feeling a little overwhelmed, he sought guidance from one of *Toy Story*'s Oscar-nominated screenwriters, Alec Sokolow, who'd employed him as a researcher in his USC days. In July 2013, the two launched a crowd-funding campaign on the website Kickstarter for $100,000, earmarking $75,000 to production, $20,000 to post-production and $5,000 to presenting the film at festivals.

"George Orwell's one of the reasons I became a writer to begin with, and here's Orwell becoming Orwell on the page," said Sokolow in the campaign video. "It's brutal, it's honest, it's funny and it's scathing social criticism—against the British Empire, against the Burmese and even against

In the short film *Shooting an Elephant*, Barry Sloane plays Orwell as he was in the 1920s: a British imperial policeman, faced with a dreadful dilemma in Burma (copyright Tusk Pictures).

himself." The screenplay, he added, was "not commercial. This is passion. This is, I think, the best thing I've ever done."[2]

With 99 backers pledging $42,568 in total, the campaign failed to meet its target. Feedback was mostly positive, says Rothie, but some prospective donors "were put off by the title and subject of the film. I read a lot of messages from uninformed people wondering why I wanted to make a movie where an elephant would be killed."[3] (For the record, no animals were harmed.)

Other film-makers warned him that shooting a period piece on a short-film budget, never mind in a foreign location, was an impossibility. "My own cinematographer told me a cautionary tale of his colleague getting killed during a shoot involving an elephant," says Rothie. "That said, we succeeded in garnering interest for the project and found Orwell fans around the world willing to support our endeavor. So, we decided to seek private solicitations to raise some of the funding and then relaunch another Kickstarter campaign with lower funding requirements."

The new appeal in December 2013 altered the branding message by headlining Orwell and using a working title, *Beast*. Setting the bar at $15,000, after cutting the budget to $80,000, it was a resounding success, with 152 people contributing $25,309.

"Orwell is an immortal, extraordinary author whose ideas are in some ways more relevant today than when he wrote them," says Rothie. "Alec's credits—*Toy Story, Evan Almighty, Garfield*—legitimized the project and framed our telling of this story in a respectful, conscientious sort of way.... That said, it was a unique challenge to overcome the initial shock of the title and subject. I knew it was a lot to ask a backer to look deeper into themes, so I positioned our marketing effort to focus on the beautiful imagery of Burma and elephants."

He framed the subject as an important, neglected personal memoir. "Alec and I both wrestled with the meaning of this story, and throughout this journey it has meant different things to us," he says. "It is no doubt a scathing criticism of imperialism, with a narrator voice as the anti-hero in his own story. On a personal level, it's about the fatal flaws in our egos." Moreover, the tale reminds him of the "tragic police violence that happens every day around the world."

Rather like Blair in Burma, the director was desperate to avoid looking a fool. "I constantly felt the pressure and pride consume me," he says. "When failing to fund on Kickstarter, and while facing my crew and production team, the fear and need to avoid humiliation horrified me. I felt deeply moved by the struggle that Orwell articulated in such a universal way."

Blue-Eyed Boy

Helped by angel investors—actor Alan Alda, his photographer/writer wife Arlene and media proprietor Mort Zuckerman among them—Rothie was determined to make a film that everyone would be proud of.

"After the second and successful Kickstarter campaign, we had sufficient funding to make it, but not where I wanted to do it," he says. "I had researched several stunning locations in India with elephants—the Kerala, Assam and North Bengal regions—but my line producer could not make the numbers work. It was simply too expensive and too big of an endeavor for a small, short film. So we scouted Nepal and it turned out to be an even more magnificent canvas.

"Casting was a long and challenging process. It was more about finding an Orwell than 'the' Orwell. But that still meant a lot. I knew I needed a name with the chops to pull off Orwell, no matter the size of the film. I did extensive research on Orwell's physical characteristics and spoke with biographers including Gordon Bowker and Peter Stansky, who gave all of the little details that I needed to make sure I had a grip on this character. He had to be British, blue-eyed, very tall.

"My casting director and I approached many actors for the role but

Director Juan Pablo Rothie settled on Barry Sloane as Orwell after consulting biographers about the young Eric Blair's physical characteristics (copyright Tusk Pictures).

they were either unavailable or uninterested in working on a short. I understood that not just anyone is willing or able to fly across the world to a remote village in Nepal to shoot a film with a wild animal. I needed someone who would embrace the challenge. I met with Barry Sloane and knew he was up for the challenge."

When the area around the capital, Kathmandu, proved unsuitable for a period piece, Rothie moved the production to an elephant sanctuary in Chitwan National Park. "To relocate the entire production on a few days' notice to an unscouted area seemed absurd," he says. "However, after quick research, a lot of luck and extraordinary teamwork, we were able to move production to Chitwan—25 minutes away by plane, seven hours by van— two days before filming, recast our elephant and village of extras and secure the locations needed to begin our first day of production.

"I'm so thankful we made the decision to relocate, as it was in Chitwan that we found our magnificent elephant. I remember driving for hours on multiple days to all the possible locations where we could find elephants, feeling helpless and lost. We needed a big elephant with massive tusks, and it turns out that is almost impossible to find these days in Asia, which is very sad. Sure enough, though, our local guide took us to a breeding center as a final attempt at finding an elephant and there he was in all his glory. His name is Dipendragod and he is the most beautiful creature I've ever laid eyes on. I remember he was twice the size of all the other elephants and had a history of violence, so we were advised to not approach him too suddenly. This would be a challenge, given that in our story there would be a mob forming around him."

For crew and villagers alike, the filming was an eye-opener. "No one had ever seen cameras and every day we had huge crowds hovering around the set. It enhanced the tonal experience that I was trying to achieve, with our lone officer feeling pressured by an ever-growing mob. Plus, there wasn't much we could do about it. We were using their homes, their schools and their markets.

"We shot the elephant sequences inside an elephant sanctuary because our elephant could not be transported too far from his comfort zone or he would become frightened and violent. As it turned out, he was very well behaved and allowed us full access without any issues at all. Our elephant was our star and made everyone happy to be around him. I think he really enjoyed being on camera."

Time constraints made for "a brutal and extraordinary experience," the director admits. "Having cut down our shooting days because of the relocation, we were struck with torrential rains from an early monsoon season arrival that cut our shooting schedule again, by half, into three-and-a-half days. Given most of the shots were exteriors, we had to go with the weather every day to make the best of our time. I learned a lot about making movies: mainly the truth that in every project, one faces unique challenges."

During a fraught shoot at Chitwan National Park in Nepal, director Rothie cast a huge, magnificent elephant with a history of violence (copyright Tusk Pictures).

Muscular

The finished film, made with advice from *A Merry War* director Bob Bierman, makes Orwell's points forcefully but is by no means a slavish retelling. A scene in which two crusty officers upbraid Blair for fraternizing with the natives owes much more to Sokolow than Orwell, for instance.

Sloane, dressed in pith helmet and jodhpurs, is the most youthful, rugged and muscular Orwell to date. He neatly conveys Blair's frustration—with the Burmese, the British and himself—and his appalled indecisiveness when called upon to shoot the beast. David Kaye, on narration duties as Orwell the essayist, provides the calm, thoughtful perspective of an older man.

Rothie, working from Sokolow's succinct script, capably evokes the weariness, disgust and exoticism of the original essay. He was especially pleased when the film made it on to the official selection list at New York's Tribeca Film Festival in 2016—an honor for a first-time director. "I've received so many messages and emails regarding the project," he says. "Journalists, professors, Orwell fans, even teachers interested in showing the short at school."

Shooting an Elephant

George Orwell: Barry Sloane
Narrator: David Kaye
Commissioner Westfield: James
    Oglethorpe
Ellis: Murray Robertson
Ma Mla May: Shilpa Maskey
Veraswami: Anup Baral
Ko S'Law: Jeewan Adhikary

Dead coolie: Deepak Adhikari
The elephant: Dipendragod
Written by: Alec Sokolow
Directed by: Juan Pablo Rothie
Produced by: Juan Pablo Rothie, Alec
    Sokolow, Daljit D.J. Parmar
Production designer: Pradip Redij
Music by: Greg Kuehn

22

Assorted Orwell

Release (BBC2, 28 September 1968)

To mark the imminent publication of the four-volume *Collected Essays, Journalism and Letters*, this BBC magazine program devoted eight minutes to an interview with Michael Foot. The letters in these books aren't exactly illuminating, says the managing director of *Tribune* and future leader of the UK's Labour Party, but the essays illustrate how Orwell set about achieving his main ambition: to turn political writing into an art. Foot recalls the influence of Rudyard Kipling, James Joyce, Jack London and Henry Miller; reading Joyce in particular left Orwell feeling like a eunuch, trying to pass muster as a baritone or bass. Foot adds that like Kipling, his friend "tried to make everything understandable to everybody"—and to that extent, achieved his goals. "Politics and art do occasionally nod to one another nowadays."[1]

It's My Pleasure: Alan Price on George Orwell (BBC2, 18 June 1982)

Alan Price, the founder and former keyboard player of the Animals, went to school in Jarrow, a town in North East England ravaged by the Great Depression like its North Western counterparts in *The Road to Wigan Pier*. As he set about composing a musical based on the Jarrow Crusade of 1936, when 200 men marched to London to protest about unemployment, he immersed himself in Orwell's work, marveling at the author's sensitivity to injustice and unsentimental love of England.[2]

Enlisting the help of film director Lindsay Anderson—whose *O Lucky Man!* (1973), sprinkled with on-camera performances from Price, is more than a touch Orwellian—he compiled a program of songs and readings for the BBC's *It's My Pleasure* show. The playlist included *Poor People, Citizens*

207

of the World and *England, My England* but, to some people's surprise, not *Jarrow Song*, his top-ten single from 1974.[3] Anderson, whose British Raj upbringing bore some similarities to Orwell's, performed the readings.

"It's all very relevant and prescient, but dully presented," sniffed *The Observer.*[4] The *Daily Express* agreed that Anderson's segments were ponderous, "but Price packages it neatly with some bluesy, social comment songs of his own that make the medicine go down very nicely."[5] In spite of the show's failings, wrote the *Daily Mail*, Price's "patent sincerity" shone through.[6]

1984 Revisited (CBS, 7 June 1983)

Nearly seven months ahead of the year itself, Walter Cronkite hosted an hour-long *CBS News* special exploring how, perhaps, the world was beginning to resemble Orwell's nightmare. In addition to the U.S., the veteran newsman's quest took him to England, Denmark and Switzerland. A computerized construct of Big Brother—an amalgam of Hitler, Stalin, Mao, Mussolini and Ayatollah Khomeini's faces—watched over him in the studio.

The show itself is nothing if not varied. British novelist Anthony Burgess, whose 1978 book *1985* took its inspiration from Orwell, scoffs at the idea that *Nineteen Eighty-Four* was a prophecy. "It was just a kind of toy, a kind of game, a horrible game that Orwell was playing." Cronkite, who isn't so sure, investigates the rise of modern surveillance (from CCTV to electronic banking), the corruption of language ("Peacemaker" missiles) and the rewriting of history (such as the Soviets erasing Trotsky or the Japanese school textbooks that leave out the Rape of Nanking).

American critics had kind words for the special, with *Variety* calling it "gripping" in parts[7] and *The New York Times* applauding its seriousness and sense of responsibility.[8] Fleet Street's denizens, on the other hand, were damning when it aired on BBC2 on 25 August. The *Financial Times* dubbed it "third-rate,"[9] while *The Guardian* dismissed it as an "instant guide to world repression, torture and the spread of electronic communications, with a light garnish of biography about Orwell."[10]

1984: A Personal View of George Orwell's Nineteen Eighty-Four (ITV, 22 January 1984)

Returning to one of his pet topics, Anthony Burgess presents this 25-minute Thames TV schools program on Orwell's last novel. "The book shocked a lot of people. The various adaptations that were made of the book shocked even more," he says, after a clip of Rudolph Cartier's Two Minutes Hate. Now that 1984 has arrived, there's an uneasy feeling it might come true—or that it would have come true had the novel not been published.

For a while, Burgess concentrates on Orwell's personal qualities, characterizing him as a staunchly English, largely self-taught man of action, though arguably mistaken about Empire. (Burgess, who served in Malaysia, thought the British did a lot of good.) He could sympathize with the working class and fight for them in Spain, but he couldn't identify with them. The corduroys he wore were "a kind of proletarian fancy dress."

Only now, says Burgess, are we beginning to see what *Nineteen Eighty-Four* was really about. The Labour government of 1945 had promised a fresh start, but by 1948, bankrupt Britain was even more short of food than it had been in the worst days of the war. Razor blades and cigarettes were scarce. London was grimy and bombed out, with a constant smell of cabbage in the air. In many respects, it's a book about 1948, overlaid with the trappings of a totalitarian state.

There's little sign that Orwell was right: the British can say and read what they like and Big Sister Margaret Thatcher seems intent on paring back the state, not expanding it. The worry for Burgess is that an organization will emerge from beneath, not above. That it will say: "Britain is a great country, kill the blacks and the Jews." Its leader, in effect, will be Big Brother—but he'll be too smart to call himself that.

Four Episodes from 1984 (1985)

Written and directed by New York University film student Marshall Peterson, *Four Episodes from* 1984 links together scenes from or inspired by the novel. It runs for nearly 30 minutes. "The film was never released commercially and only shown at a few student film festivals, and as a demo for the cast and crew," says Peterson.[11]

"Syme's Arrest," set about halfway through the book, shows the lexicographer and his wife asleep in twin beds and monitored by a camera on the wall. Thought Police fling open the door, assault him with a baton and drag him away.

Columbia University's Low Memorial Library provides the backdrop for episode two, "The Ministry of Truth." Here, Winston Smith (John Nowak, a young, fair-haired man dressed in the blue dungarees of the Outer Party) and O'Brien (thin-faced, balding Alan Leach, wearing black dungarees and speaking with the film's most creditable English accent) have a coded conversation about the "unperson" Syme and the latest Newspeak dictionary.

Winston and Julia (Jayne Bentzen) ponder their inevitable capture in "The Room Over Charrington's Shop." When the action switches to "The Ministry of Truth" at roughly the 12-minute mark, the film becomes unintentionally funny, for British viewers at least. Smith's cellmates speak pure Dick Van Dyke at times. "It was my little girl," says his sleep-talking neighbor, Parsons. "She listened in at the keyhole and nipped off to the patrols the very next day. Pretty smart for a nipper of only seven, eh?"

Much better are the grimly powerful torture sequences that dominate the second half. In a murkily lit operating theater—part of Goldwater Memorial Hospital on Roosevelt Island, if you're wondering—Leach is genuinely chilling as the merciless Inner Party zealot. The film's young director deserves kudos too, not least for the illusion that O'Brien's hand, held in front of Winston's face as he's losing his mind, consists of five fingers and a thumb.

Beautiful Lies (BBC2, 15 August 1992)

Paul Pender's scintillating, edifying chamber piece, directed by Jim Gillespie and shown as part of BBC Scotland's *Encounters* series, is as much about H.G. Wells as it is about Orwell. In 1941, *Horizon* published a short essay[12] by Orwell that acknowledged his boyhood hero's status as a literary inspiration and visionary, but took him to task for failing to understand the visceral appeal of the "screaming little defective" in Berlin. This 53-minute play dramatizes a dinner Wells attended at Orwell's London apartment in St. John's Wood soon afterwards, when the two writers squared off against each other.[13]

At first the atmosphere is cordial, but tensions arise when Wells (Richard Todd) writes off the Nazis as a "pack of madmen" who won't last. Orwell (Jon Finch) and his wife Eileen (Natasha Morgan) beg to differ. Once Eileen has gone to bed, the discussion becomes heated, as Wells insinuates that Orwell (to judge from his *Mein Kampf* review of March 1940) may have a sneaking regard for Hitler. He slams down the latest issue of *Horizon*, containing the essay—*Wells, Hitler and the World State*—that's so offended him.

In placatory tones, Orwell tries to explain himself. He suggests that those who see Hitler as the Antichrist are closer to the truth than those, like Wells, who consider him a figure from comic opera. Wells, who's been privy to a list of Britons who'll be executed in the event of a Nazi invasion, retorts that he is close to the top of it; Orwell features too, probably because of his activities in Spain.

The younger man persists. He thinks that Wells fails to grasp fascism's spiritual appeal, believing instead that "man is governed by sweet reason." He unfurls a wall map showing the extent to which German tanks have overrun Europe. Wells is ashamed that he "invented" the tank in *Anticipations*, his 1901 book of scientific prophesies. "In retrospect, I should have called it *Abominations*," he says.

At heart, he resents Orwell as one of the "old-school-tie brigade." Granted, Blair was only a scholarship boy at Eton, but he's still benefited from his Old Etonian chums; whereas "Bertie Wells," the son of a gardener and a housemaid, is "a jumped-up draper's assistant," in spite of his scientific training and literary achievements. Orwell's line that he's "a shallow, inadequate thinker" in his old age has wounded him.

You're my literary father, Orwell protests. Indeed, says his guest—just look at your latest novel, *Coming Up for Air*, which is "Wells watered down." And where did you get that pen name, George Orwell? It's a lot like Herbert George Wells, isn't it?

Taking a breather on the balcony, the men calm down. You're a coming writer, says Wells. When your essay is included in a book, I'll be remembered as an old man perplexed by the modern world.

With another dinner guest, the poet William Empson (Patrick Ryecart), they relax and play darts in the lounge. The dartboard, inside a cupboard door, is fixed to a photo of Hitler in lederhosen, so that should a projectile go astray, it will more than likely pierce his gonads. To the tune of *Colonel Boagey*, the trio sing "Hitler has only got one ball."

There's an air raid. A German bomb hits the next street, causing Orwell's bookcase—its titles arranged bookshop-style, alphabetically by author—to topple over.

Recovering on the balcony, Wells and Orwell reach a rapprochement. Destroying suburbia in *The War of the Worlds* was fun, the old man admits, but these real-life bombardments bring nothing but personal anguish. The next war will be atomic: "another of my damned anticipations." Before they part, Orwell agrees that when the time comes, he will write Wells's obituary. His generous assessment of the man, for the *Manchester Evening News* in 1946, provides the play with its ending.

In reality, six months after the dinner party, the two clashed over an article of Orwell's in *The Listener*.[14] "Read my early work, you shit," exhorted Wells in a personal letter.[15] In *Beautiful Lies*, the insult emerges from his mouth.

Down and Out in Paris and London (Channel Four, 29 March 1993)

Screened as part of Channel Four's *Gimme Shelter* season looking at homelessness in the UK, this hour-long documentary[16] follows in Orwell's footsteps 70 years after his book of reportage came out.

Unlike Orwell, travel writer Nick Danziger doesn't linger in Paris. He highlights the police's zero-tolerance approach to vagrancy, then moves on after less than nine minutes of screen time. In London, he stays in a cheap bed and breakfast and says he can identify with Orwell as he attended a fee-paying school in Switzerland. "Coming from a privileged background," he adds, "you do feel guilty, especially when you know how other people are living."

Sleeping in the cold under a noisy bridge, he encounters Edinburgh-born Alan, an eloquent young man with a thick russet beard who by his own admission enjoys getting drunk a lot. The Scotsman is familiar with *The Spike*, Orwell's essay from his tramping days, and knows how life has and hasn't changed under the post–1945 welfare state. Close by in Whitechapel, Danziger tracks down "Leeds Ronnie," a bluff, mutton-chopped Yorkshireman who says the fresh air keeps him young as he beds down behind the post office night after night.

Violence, alcoholism and life-changing misfortune are ever-present. As a child, Ronnie suffered beatings from his drunken "wicked bastard" of a father. The marriage of Rosie, an ex-nurse living in a St. Mungo's hostel, fell apart when she discovered her husband wearing women's clothes. Tears streaming down her cheeks, she talks about destitution, the fiancé who raped her and why she's too ashamed to contact her children.

Near the end, and in defiance of a Home Office ban on filming, Danziger reveals the vile state of a government-run resettlement unit—a spike, as it was called in Orwell's day. The beds, carpets and furniture are filthy; some of the residents are mentally disturbed; and to everyone's disgust, a drug addict's syringe lies abandoned under a bath full of stagnant water.

Summing up, Danziger says he will never again judge homeless people by their appearance. "Their wounds are internal." The documentary, directed by Rob Rohrer, uses Orwell as a hook and little more, but the readings by Jonathan Pryce at least convey the spirit of his book.

Me and the Big Guy (1999)

A straight-up parody of *Nineteen Eighty-Four* by American writer-director Matt Nix, this nine-minute short stars Michael Norton as the annoyingly effusive Citizen 43275-B. The joke is that he seems to enjoy see-ing Big Brother (Dan Kern) on the telescreen at home every night, treating him as a confidante and regaling him with the banal events of his working day. In frustration, the dictator levels with him. "Let me explain something here. Big Brother is a name we use to suggest an omniscient totalitarian presence. It's not supposed to be taken literally! I'm your oppressor, not your friend!"

Great Books: George Orwell's 1984 (The Learning Channel, 11 October 2000)

It misquotes the opening line in the first few minutes, but this install-ment of executive editor Walter Cronkite's *Great Books* series is a passable introduction to Orwell's life, worldview and most famous novel. Bernard Crick and novelist Margaret Drabble handle the biographical and literary stuff, while acclaimed science-fiction author David Brin describes *Nineteen Eighty-Four* as "one of the most powerful self-preventing prophecies of all time."

In what looks like an effort to seem relevant, writer-producer Ned Judge's documentary goes off at several tangents, however. A segment examining threats to privacy makes a fuss about telephone sales people's nightly phone calls to U.S. households; and Marvin J. Rosenblum, holder of the screen rights to *Nineteen Eighty-Four*, frets that a demagogue might come to power and use personal information on databases to persecute minorities.

After futurist Ray Kurzweil discusses the relentless rise of computing capacity—opening the door, perhaps, to non-biological intelligences watch-ing over the populace—social psychologist Philip Zimbardo points out that it takes very little prodding to make human beings act like fascists. In an experiment at Stanford University in the seventies, Zimbardo divided stu-dent volunteers into "prisoners" and "guards"—with soul-sapping results.

The show borrows the iconography of Michael Radford's movie—includ-ing the Ingsoc symbol and Bob Flag's face as Big Brother—and dramatizes scenes from the book with its own cast. Curiously, these are interspersed with clips from the film itself, meaning John Hurt, Suzanna Hamilton and Richard Burton alternate with more obscure actors in the same roles.

The love scene in the countryside is shot like a soft porn movie, with a cheesy electric guitar soundtrack. In the Ministry of Truth fiction depart-ment, Julia maintains a machine that churns out paperbacks of *Nympho Nights*. And on Winston's telescreen at work, the state executes "Comrade Rosenblum," an enemy of the people, for plotting to assassinate Big Brother.

Was that last example a joke? Judge for yourself. In September 2000, a month before the documentary aired, Marvin Rosenblum sued the U.S. version of *Big Brother*—the reality show, in which contestants confined to a house are monitored around the clock—for alleged copyright infringement. At the time, he was attempting to develop a computer game and sell a television show based on the novel. The case was settled in 2001.

A History of Britain: The Two Winstons (BBC One, 18 June 2002)

For the 15th and final part of his BBC series, historian Simon Schama compares and contrasts the lives (and works) of Orwell and Winston Churchill. Both were privileged, to varying degrees; both rebellious, courageous and iconic. The Old Etonian socialist despised the British Empire; the maverick Tory cherished it. Yet, when it mattered most—as fascism threatened to obliterate everything they held dear—they were fierce patriots. "They not only wrote the history of their times," says Schama in his introduction, "they lived it."

The Real Room 101 (BBC Four, 14 June 2003)

Calling it "Big Brother Night," the BBC devoted the best part of a Saturday evening to Orwell's centenary. After *George Orwell: A Life in Pictures* on BBC Two, it aired a half-hour rumination on the Ministry of Love's most notorious torture chamber, this time on BBC Four (which then repeated Rudolph Cartier's classic). "Was there a real Room 101?" asks director Jonty Claypole's documentary, gathering comments from Michael Radford, John Hurt and David Taylor along the way. Former Beirut hostage Terry Waite recalls his own ordeal, and is thankful he wasn't eaten alive by rats; novelist Margaret Attwood marvels at the concept of an individualized "worst thing in the world"; and there's a good deal of speculation on the extent to which authoritarian sadists at St. Cyprian's School—and, in adulthood, Orwell's lying for the greater good at the BBC Eastern Service—influenced *Nineteen Eighty-Four*.

It's long been thought that Orwell took the name "Room 101" from an office in Broadcasting House. Ahead of a renovation that would do away with the room, the BBC invited Turner Prize-winning artist Rachel Whiteread to take a cast of it—to "memorialize this space," as she put it—and so a chunk of the program chronicles her progress. With the Iraq War in its early stages, the show ends on a topical note, as veteran Labour politician Tony Benn suggests that Orwell's cautionary tale is morphing into reality under George W. Bush and Tony Blair.

Orwell Rolls in His Grave (2003)

If anything, the opposition to Bush is even more pronounced in Robert Kane Pappas's feature-length documentary film, which argues that the independence of American news media has been shamelessly undermined by right-wing politicians and their corporate cronies. Referencing *Nineteen Eighty-Four* (and briefly *Animal Farm*), Pappas damningly compares turn-of-the-millennium journalists to Winston Smith at the Ministry of Truth. The lobbying industry, the abandonment of impartiality rules and the gobbling up of media outlets by a handful of giant businesses has, he contends, had a chilling effect on public debate.

There's an extensive discussion of the disputed presidential election in 2000—Al Gore was robbed, Pappas concludes—and an assertion that the subsequent invasion of Iraq was straight out of Big Brother's "permanent war" playbook. Driving the narrative are comments from, among others, disillusioned ex-journalists, academics, maverick investigative reporters, Vermont senator Bernie Sanders, actor Tim Robbins and film-maker Michael Moore. Robbins, incidentally, would direct a stage play of *Nineteen Eighty-Four* in 2006; a proposed film version failed to get off the ground.[17]

Maazel—1984 (2008)

Savaged by the critics when it opened at London's Royal Opera House in 2005, composer Lorin Maazel's *1984* received a DVD release three years later. The American conductor, who was 75 at the time of the premiere, had been talked into writing the opera—his first—by the director of the Bavarian State Opera, whose subsequent death threw the project into limbo. Through a new company, Big Brother Productions, Maazel salvaged the production with a personal cash injection of about £400,000. In picking up nearly half the costs, the Covent Garden venue was accused of squandering taxpayers' money on a vanity project.[18]

For the Orwell buff, there's actually much to enjoy. Maazel and his stage director, Robert Lepage, accentuate the story's epic quality, helped by Carl Fillion's gloomy, evocative sets. Herd-like crowds, with a quasi-religious mania, sing of their hatred for Big Brother's enemies; Julia and

Winston's tragic love story fits the genre like a glove; Jeremy Irons lends a steely tone to the telescreen propaganda; and O'Brien's torture chamber is a veritable Frankenstein's laboratory.

Admittedly, not all of it works—the cringeworthy addition of a choir of street urchins in the prole sector brings to mind *Oliver!* more than Orwell— and the casting is a tad eccentric. A muscular Simon Keenlyside transforms Winston Smith into a bare-chested beefcake, while Nancy Gustafson is a frumpier Julia than we're used to. What's more, in a society where food is rationed, it's amazing how well-fed Parsons, Charrington, O'Brien and some of the proles look. Brian Large directed the video version.

Damien O'Keeffe as Winston Smith and Ben Eagle as O'Brien, with a projection of John Hurt as Big Brother, in Paper Zoo's stage production of *1984*, adapted by Alan Lyddiard (copyright Jim Moran).

1984 (2009)

This isn't a production in its own right, but a video backdrop to a play that toured the North of England. That said, it's worth mentioning for its link to Michael Radford's *Nineteen Eighty-Four* movie. The story begins in 2008, when Paper Zoo Theatre Company in Bradford, West Yorkshire, revived Sir Peter Hall's musical of *Animal Farm*, first staged in 1984 at the National Theatre, London. The National Media Museum, also in Bradford, was so impressed that it commissioned a live version of *Nineteen Eighty-Four* by playwright Alan Lyddiard for the novel's 40th anniversary. "We tend to do one production a year. It's a very small company," says the play's director, Stuart Davies.

The venue was the museum's Pictureville Cinema, which meant a movie screen would provide a backdrop to the action. "It was either the face and shoulders of John Hurt as Big Brother, who was slowly looking round the audience as if he had his eye on them, or it was CCTV, as though Winston Smith was being followed around in his daily life," says Davies.

"We were all sitting round one day [discussing what form the play would take] and I remember thinking, 'We need something on the screen where we haven't got CCTV, because it's not appropriate for the whole play and we don't just wanted a blank light screen.' Somebody said, 'What about Big Brother permanently? Not like a picture, but something animated? Just moving around and surveying the audience.'

"Almost off the cuff, someone said: 'It would be great to get John Hurt because he played Winston Smith in the film.' We all laughed." Even so, a diligent colleague emailed Hurt's agent.

"John Hurt responded within a couple of days, personally, saying, 'That sounds like a great idea and I'll be pleased to do it. If you meet me in the Science Museum in London, I'll give you two hours of my time and you can film me,'" says Davies.

Martin Knowles, who directed the film sequences, was nervous about giving Hurt instructions, but the star put him at his ease. "He said at the time he likes to help out aspiring companies and young actors," adds Davies. "He didn't see the production, but he did come up to Bradford to meet us." So, how was the play received? "We got much bigger audiences than we normally do."[19]

Orwell in Catalonia (2012)

Part of a site-specific virtual reality installation, this short, surrealist documentary by American Andy Fedak was filmed in a Spanish bunker where Orwell saw combat. "During the filming of this area, dark clouds gradually formed and a sudden hailstorm overtook us," says Fedak, an assistant professor of animation at California State University, Fullerton. "The film begins with this hailstorm, and then continues until the last stone is melted—a direct metaphor to the anarchistic worldview, which at present is slipping away in history."

Wildflower (2014)

Film-maker Gary Wilkinson turns the spotlight on his fellow Tynesider, Eileen O'Shaughnessy, depicting Orwell's first wife as one of history's unsung heroines.

Northern Ballet Presents 1984 (BBC Four, 28 February 2016)

Nearly six months after its West Yorkshire Playhouse premiere, and three months in advance of its UK tour ending in London, BBC Four screened this unusually dystopian ballet, starring Tobias Batley as Winston, Martha Leebolt as Julia and Javier Torres as O'Brien. "My ambition is to tell this story without words," says choreographer Jonathan Watkins, in a two-minute introduction outlining the genesis of the ballet—which means that, barring the rather intense score by Alex Baranowski, this is the first silent adaptation of Orwell.

23

Not-Quites and Near-Misses

Let's discard the Orwell documentaries for a moment, and with them the docudramas about his life. Let's concentrate on the adaptations alone. To date, there have been four feature films, five television plays, a TV movie that had a limited theatrical release, two short films about elephants and, if we're being completist, a student film made up of isolated scenes.[1] That's 13 dramatizations in total, six of them *Nineteen Eighty-Four*.

You might think, from this, that film-makers aren't much interested in Orwell—in which case, you'd be mistaken. In the course of writing this book, it's been frustrating to learn of the projects stuck in "development hell." But not every admirer takes the purist or literal route. A plethora of movies and TV shows owe a recognizable debt to Orwell, whether their creators will admit it or not.

His first two novels have yet to make it to the screen, though not for want of trying. Arthur Penn, director of *Bonnie and Clyde*, was reportedly working on *Burmese Days* when he died in 2010, aged 88. The movie, from a screenplay by British writer Hugh Stoddart, was first announced as far back as 1993, with Matthew Modine and Helena Bonham Carter tipped to star.[2] Similarly, a TV movie of *A Clergyman's Daughter* was scheduled to go before the cameras in 1983 under the guiding hand of Alvin Rakoff, director of the award-winning *A Voyage Round My Father*.[3] Its script, by John Peacock, was refashioned as a BBC radio play ten years later.[4]

Oscar-winner Hugh Hudson has long cherished the idea of filming *Homage to Catalonia*. It looked like he was close to succeeding when, in 2009, *Variety* reported that Colin Firth and Kevin Spacey would appear in *Catalonia*, a drama by Australian screenwriter Bob Ellis about Orwell's relationship with his charismatic commander, Georges Kopp.[5] Speaking at the Sofia International Film Festival in 2012, Hudson conceded that Firth had grown too old to play Orwell, who was 29 when he went to Barcelona. Describing the film, he said: "It follows his personal story of a war reporter who becomes a fighter, risks his own life, risks the life of his wife, because she joins him in Spain. This puts their marriage on the rocks, and still their marriage survives the huge pressure."[6]

Films about the Spanish Civil War are rare, so when director Ken Loach made *Land and Freedom* in 1995, it wasn't difficult to find allusions to Orwell in the press. True, Jim Allen's script is about an Englishman (a working-class Liverpudlian, played by Ian Hart) who joins the POUM and is betrayed by the Stalinists. But it isn't *Homage to Catalonia*, any more than it's Ernest Hemingway's *For Whom the Bell Tolls*.

In director Terry Gilliam's *Brazil* (1985), Jonathan Pryce plays a government nebbish in a world of bureaucracy gone mad. Gilliam originally pitched the movie as "Franz Kafka meets George Orwell" (copyright Universal Studios).

Brazil, released in 1985, is another film that draws frequent comparisons to Orwell, only this time with good reason. When director Terry Gilliam first pitched the story to Paramount, who turned it down, he described his Pythonesque satire—about a government nebbish (Jonathan Pryce) in a grimly amusing world of bureaucracy gone mad—as "Franz Kafka meets George Orwell."[7]

There's nothing wrong with a knowing nod and wink, of course. Take, for example, 1992's *Chain of Command,* a *Star Trek: The Next Generation* two-parter in which our hero, Captain Picard, falls into the hands of a Cardassian torturer. The alien tries to "break" Picard into telling him that a row of four lights is in actuality made up of five. As the story ends, the rescued captain admits to a crewmate on the starship *Enterprise* that at his lowest ebb, he did indeed see five.[8]

So, when does homage cross the line into plagiarism? It's a question that sometimes preoccupied the late Marvin Rosenblum, Chicago lawyer and holder of *Nineteen Eighty-Four*'s screen rights. Let's look finally, then, at one of the most famous commercials in American history: the "1984" ad, by agency Chiat/Day, that launched the Apple Macintosh home computer.

Directed by Britain's Ridley Scott, who'd made his name in the cinema with sci-fi blockbusters *Alien* and *Blade Runner,* the 60-second TV spot is unquestionably a mini-masterpiece. Many think it aired only once, on CBS, during the XVIII Super Bowl on 22 January 1984; and in terms of nationwide exposure, this is correct. The truth, however, is that it debuted in Twin Falls, Idaho, in December 1983 so that it would qualify for that year's advertising awards.[9]

The tone, at first, is depressing. Bald-headed figures in identical blue garments[10] troop through a tunnel lined with telescreens. They're androgynous automatons in a drab, blue-gray world. As they take their seats before a gigantic screen, filled with the face of a ranting, middle-aged, bespectacled Big Brother figure,[11] an athletic platinum blonde[12] in red shorts and a white tank top bursts in, pursued by four Thought Police in riot gear. Spinning like a discus thrower, the woman hurls a sledgehammer at the screen. In the instant Big Brother declares: "We shall prevail," it explodes, showering the audience in dust—and while the camera lingers on their stunned reactions, black text appears for the benefit of viewers in the real world. "On January 24th, Apple Computer will introduce Macintosh. And you'll see why 1984 won't be like '1984.'"

The $650,000 commercial, which was championed by Apple co-founder Steve Jobs in the face of staunch resistance from his board, had tested incredibly poorly.[13] But the sensation it caused—eschewing celebrity endorsements and introducing the notion of the Super Bowl ad as entertainment—meant that news shows couldn't stop talking about it. All this free advertising helped Apple to secure more than $150 million in sales in the Mac's first 100 days.[14] Rosenblum's response, while working on Michael Radford's film, was to fire off a cease-and-desist notice. Bombarded with calls from the media asking if the scene was from his movie, he wrote to Chiat/Day on 26 April, calling it "a blatant infringement of motion picture and other media rights I own." The "1984" in the tag line, he wrote, made it impossible to argue that this was "a vague allusion to an Orwellian society."[15]

In a 2009 piece for the *Dartmouth Law Journal*, Chicago attorney William Coulson, who has represented the Orwell estate, noted that the ad was true to the novel and very well done. Rosenblum "might have weighed the positive publicity the commercial would have generated for his upcoming film," he wrote. "But that was Rosenblum's, not Apple's, decision to make."[16]

Even though the lawsuit failed to materialize, this brief but devastating "1984"—named by *TV Guide* and *Advertising Age* as the greatest television commercial of all time—never aired again, except in clip shows. With hindsight, it heralded a new age for humanity of mass computerization and, perhaps, the surveillance society. Orwell's relevance, his prescience, is a constant feature of our lives, conveyed by visual media in ways that even he couldn't have imagined. But that, as they say, is another story.

Chapter Notes

Chapter 1

1. During a word from *Studio One*'s sponsor in 1951, Westinghouse spokeswoman Betty Furness suggested viewers might like to buy "this table model ... in a handsome mahogany cabinet, with a huge 17-inch screen."

2. According to IMDb.com. Three of the five Primetime Emmys were for Reginald Rose's play *Twelve Angry Men*, shown almost a year to day after *1984* on 20 September 1954.

3. According to Bobby Ellerbee of the TV history website eyesofageneration.com, *Studio One* was routinely broadcast from studio 41 above New York's main railway station, Grand Central Terminal (http://eyesofageneration. com/november-7-1948-studio-one-debuts-on-cbsthe-first-epi). Loring Mandel mentions the station too during the 1987 Paley Center seminar. However, in a piece for *The New Yorker* in 1995, writer Gore Vidal mentions attending a *Studio One* run-through at a converted theater on Tenth Avenue in February 1954. Gore Vidal, "How I survived the fifties," *The New Yorker*, 2 October 1995, 62–76.

4. A recording of the 17 November event is on the six-DVD, region 1 box set *Studio One Anthology*, released in 2008 by the Archive of American Television and KOCH Entertainment.

5. *Voices from the Archive: Studio One* (from *Studio One Anthology*.)

6. The anecdote about Kipling's *The Light That Failed* came from Mosel at the seminar. It was Swift who said the title was read aloud.

7. The House Un-American Activities Committee, part of the U.S. Congress, began to subpoena film industry professionals in 1947. http:// www.history.com/topics/cold-war/huac.

8. Schultz told this story at the 1987 seminar.

9. Rival series included *Goodyear Television Playhouse, Kraft Television Theatre, Philco Theatre* and *Robert Mongomery Presents*. According to English professor Lawrence Raw, a notable aspect of *Studio One* is that it "consciously

marketed itself as a 'quality' series." Lawrence Raw, "Form and function of the 1950s anthology series—*Studio One,*" *Journal of Popular Film and Television*, Summer 2009, 90–96.

10. C. Gerald Fraser, "Worthington Miner, producer in the early days of TV, dies," *The New York Times*, 13 December 1982, http://www. nytimes.com/1982/12/13/obituaries/worthing ton-miner-producer-in-the-early-days-of-tv-dies.html.

11. Mary Wickes played Mary Poppins.

12. Heston portrayed, among others, *Jane Eyre*'s Mr. Rochester (1949) and *Wuthering Heights*' Heathcliff (1950).

13. "Felix Jackson is dead; film producer was 90," *The New York Times*, 16 December 1992, http://www.nytimes.com/1992/12/16/obitua ries/felix-jackson-is-dead-film-producer-was-90.html.

14. Jackson's writing credits included the 1939 Jimmy Stewart Western, *Destry Rides Again*. He was married to singing star Deanna Durbin from 1945–50.

15. The show was "back on the microwave for a sixth season," according to the *Los Angeles Times* (21 September 1953, 30). How quaint the terminology seems now.

16. Sidney Lohman, "Notes from the studios." *The New York Times*, 6 September 1953, X9.

17. We'll be returning to *The March of Time* in the chapter on *Animal Farm* (1954).

18. "Loring Mandel interviews Paul Nickell," 5 October 1987, the Paley Center for Media, featured on the *Studio One Anthology* set.

19. Albert appeared in his own play, *The Love Nest*, with actress Grace Brandt on 6 November 1936. It was broadcast live from NBC's experimental television station, based in New York's Rockefeller Center. Gary R. Edgerton, *The Columbia History of American Television* (Columbia University Press, 2007), 53.

20. "Loring Mandel interviews Paul Nickell."

21. Chinese-American artist Dong Kingman provided the illustration.

22. The play doesn't have time for the scene in the novel in which Oceania switches alliances and brazenly pretends it has always been at war with Eastasia.

23. There's also a female telescreen voice, which ticks Winston off for not wearing his identification badge and is accompanied by a mist-shrouded, glaring pair of eyes.

24. Culp's first screen role, according to IMDb.com, was in CBS's *The Death of Socrates*, directed by Sidney Lumet in May 1953.

25. The prole quarter of the book.

26. Apart from the male telescreen voice, Charrington is the only nod to *Nineteen Eighty-Four*'s British origins.

27. 1 Spencer Lane in the script.

28. In fact, we don't see the rack until Michael Radford's feature film in 1984.

29. It looks like a neon sign in a nightclub, quite honestly.

30. John Rodden, "The Orwellian night of December 12," *Society*, April 2015, 159–165. Rodden's article is primarily concerned with the BBC adaptation shown in 1954.

31. Jack Gould, "Studio One presents masterly adaptation in opening program," *The New York Times*, 23 September 1953, 44.

32. This is according to *The Manchester Guardian*'s front-page report of 14 December 1954 (headlined "1984—and all that, No cuts in TV play repeat, from our London staff"). It contrasted the praise given to CBS's play with the condemnation directed at the BBC's effort more than a year later.

33. Speaking to TV and film historian Stephen Bowie in the final years of his life, designer Kim Swados singled out 1984 as "the one I'm very proud of." He added: "It was done as a stark, documentary-like, very frightening attempt to explore the anxiety that Mr. Orwell had about fascism." Stephen Bowie, "Voices from the studio," *The Classic TV History Blog*, 27 January 2009, https://classictvhistory.word press.com/2009/01/27/voices-from-the-studio.

34. Philip Hamburger, television reviews, *The New Yorker*, 3 October 1953, 84–89.

35. *Variety*, 23 September 1953, 33.

36. Bob Francis, *The Billboard*, 3 October 1953, 13.

37. "A 1984 specter on 1953 screens," *Life*, 5 October 1953, 115–118.

38. Rodden, *Society*, April 2015.

39. John Rodden, *George Orwell: The Politics of Literary Reputation* (Transaction Publishers, 2002), 274.

40. Val Adams, "The pessimistic television drama," *The New York Times*, 11 October 1953, X15.

41. "Tap Studio One as pix source," *Variety*, 30 December 1953, 1.

42. "John Paul Nickell: director during TV's golden age," *Los Angeles Times*, 20 May 2000, http://articles.latimes.com/2000/may/20/local/me-32099.

43. Loren Ghiglione, *CBS's Don Hollenbeck: An Honest Reporter in the Age of McCarthyism* (Columbia University Press, 2008.)

44. A series of Senate hearings, held between April and June 1954, to investigate conflicting accusations between the U.S. Army and Senator Joseph McCarthy.

45. Susan Hallaran McKenzie, email to David Ryan, 22 March 2017.

Chapter 2

1. Among them the novelist Anthony Burgess, in a schools program from 1984 (see chapter 21.)

2. Food rationing ended only five months earlier.

3. In the BFI TV 100, a British Film Institute poll of 2,000 industry professionals in 2000, it emerged as the 73rd-best British show of the 20th century. It was the oldest entry on the list.

4. The British Broadcasting Corporation Annual Report and Accounts for the Year 1954–55 (HMSO 1955.)

5. Author Bill Warren, working from reports in the Hollywood trade press, reports that Charles K. Feldman bought the film rights shortly after the book's publication. Robert Maxwell and Bernard Luber did the same in 1951, planning to shoot a movie in England in 1952. In April 1954, the rights passed briefly to Frank McCarthy, who wanted Anthony Mann to direct his film in West Berlin. Warren, *Keep Watching the Skies! American Science Fiction Movies of the Fifties* (McFarland, 1982), 298.

6. BBC Written Archives Centre (WAC), T48/456/1, 10 February 1953.

7. Andrew Martin, BBC Genome blog post on Nigel Kneale, 18 December 2016, http://www.bbc.co.uk/blogs/genome/entries/c7325e7b-d63a-4843-bd35-f540384d0e5a.

8. BBC WAC, T48/456/1, 27 August 1954.

9. Cartier settled in the UK after a spell in Hollywood working with Billy Wilder.

10. Andy Murray, *Into the Unknown: The Fantastic Life of Nigel Kneale* (Headpress, 2006), 36.

11. *The Late Show*, BBC Two, 25 October 1990 (source: British Library Sound Server V0719/01.)

12. Murray, 36.

13. BECTU History Project, interview with Rudolph Cartier, http://historyproject.org.uk/content/0180.

14. BBC WAC, T5/362/2, 10 August 1954.

15. Andrew Pixley, "Big Brother is watching you," *TV Zone* 159, 50–55.
16. *Ibid.*
17. Albert Schweitzer.
18. BBC WAC, T5/362/2, 30 September 1954.
19. BBC WAC, T5/362/2, 8 October 1954.
20. BBC WAC, T5/362/2, 11 October 1954.
21. BBC WAC, T5/362/2, 22 October 1954.
22. *Late Night Line-Up*, BBC2, 27 November 1965.
23. BBC WAC, T5/362/2, 30 November 1954.
24. BECTU History Project.
25. Nigel Kneale, "The last rebel of Airstrip One," *Radio Times*, vol 125, no 1622, 12–18 December 1954.
26. Composed of footage from A-bomb tests.
27. Britain is, in effect, the 51st state of the USA.
28. In the novel, Winston Smith is 6079 Smith W.
29. In Kneale's script, Goldstein begins to speak like a bleating sheep, as happens in the novel. This was not attempted on screen until the play was remade in 1965.
30. BV-9001 Parsons T. on screen.
31. In the novel, the paperweight is coral.
32. Christopher Gullo, *In All Sincerity, Peter Cushing* (Xlibris, 2004), 59.
33. *Peter Cushing: A One-Way Ticket to Hollywood*, Tyburn Film Productions, Channel Four, 4 June 1989.
34. "TV repeat for Orwell play as planned," *The Daily Telegraph*, 14 December 1954, 8.
35. BBC WAC, T5/362/2, 13 December 1954.
36. "Nineteen Eighty-Four," *The Times*, 13 December 1954, 11.
37. "Peter Black's Teleview," *Daily Mail*, 13 December 1954, 4.
38. "Orwell's Nineteen Eighty-Four" *The Manchester Guardian*, 13 December 1954, 5.
39. RPMG, "Orwell novel adapted," *The Daily Telegraph*, December 13, 1954, 9.
40. Philip Phillips,"1984—and all this horror," *Daily Herald*, 13 December 1954, 1.
41. "Protest storm on TV horror," *News Chronicle*, 13 December 1954, 1.
42. David Holloway, "That Big Brother will lurk in my set," *News Chronicle*, 13 December 1954, 3.
43. "1984: Wife dies as she watches," *Daily Express*, 14 December 1954, 1.
44. "A million nightmares," *Daily Express*, 14 December 1954, 4.
45. "Battle of 1984—BBC is doing it again," *Daily Sketch*, 14 December 1954, 1.
46. "Horror? I say well done (says Candidus)," *Daily Sketch*, 14 December 1954, 4.
47. "No BBC retreat in 1984 row," *Daily Sketch*, 14 December 1954, 24.
48. James Thomas, "BBC will repeat all of 1984," *News Chronicle*, 14 December 1954, 3.
49. Alison Macleod, "BBC means to repeat its horror comic," *Daily Worker*, 14 December 1954, 1.
50. "Don't chain the BBC," *Daily Herald*, December 14, 1954, 4 editorial.
51. "Well done the Radio General," *Daily Mirror*, 14 December 1954, 2.
52. Peter Black, "Honest Orwell did not want to horrify," *Daily Mail*, 14 December 1954, 4.
53. "1984—and all that," *The Manchester Guardian*, 14 December 1954, 1.
54. "Wife dies as she watches," *Daily Express*, 14 December 1954, 1.
55. "Commons split over Sunday sadism," *Daily Mail*, 15 December 1954, 3.
56. "1984 in the Commons: BBC attacked and applauded," *The Manchester Guardian*, 15 December 1954, 1.
57. "Controversy over 1984," *The Times*, 15 December 1954, 5 Political Notes.
58. "Why they love 1984," *Daily Worker*, 15 December 1954, 1 editorial.
59. BBC WAC, T5/362/2, 1 November 1954. The Written Archives Centre holds the unused shots of Oxley, some of which—the clean-shaven ones in particular—make Big Brother look downright benevolent.
60. "Mrs. Big Brother says he's such a gentle man," *Daily Sketch*, 15 December 1954, 20.
61. Philip Phillips, "Even Big Brother helps with the washing-up," *Daily Herald*, 15 December 1954, 3.
62. "Big Brother is potting you now," *News Chronicle*, 15 December 1954, 3.
63. BBC WAC, T5/362/2, 15 December 1954. Interviewed on BBC Two's *The Late Show* in 1990, Cartier said he had two bodyguards in tow. "There were very threatening phone calls to the BBC because everybody thought this was a pro-communist, anti-fascist subject."
64. "He will debate on TV why he wants 1984 banned," *News Chronicle*, 15 December 1954, 3.
65. *Panorama* transcript, BBC WAC TV Registry talks scripts, 1936–1964.
66. John Rodden, *George Orwell: The Politics of Literary Reputation* (Transaction Publishers, 2002), 274.
67. *Panorama* transcript, BBC WAC TV Registry talks scripts, 1936–1964.
68. Oliver Wake, "Nineteen Eighty-Four (1954)—Myth versus reality," *British Television Drama*, 1 October 2014, http://www.britishtelevisiondrama.org.uk/?p=4722.
69. BBC WAC, T5/362/2, 16 December 1954.
70. "Please, this is not THE Mr. George Orwell…" *Daily Mirror*, 16 December 1954, 6.

71. Philip Hope-Wallace, *The Listener*, 16 December 1954, 44.

72. "Nineteen Eighty-Four and All That," *The Times*, 16 December 1954, 9.

73. Alison Macleod, "They should have faded Orwell—RIGHT OUT!" *Daily Worker*, 16 December 1954, 2.

74. Philip Phillips, "Yackety, yack, yack, goes the row," *Daily Herald*, 16 December 1954, 3.

75. Philip Phillips, "Big Brother watches Big Brother," *Daily Herald*, 17 December 1954, 1. In what looked like a mocked-up shot, the cover photo showed Roy Oxley watching himself on his TV at home.

76. "Head of TV drama gives warning," *The Manchester Guardian*, 17 December 1954, 16.

77. "1984 is spine-chiller of the future world," *The Sunday Mail (Brisbane)*, 19 December 1954, 2.

78. *Daily Herald*, 17 December 1954, 1.

79. "TV repeat of 1984 hits cinemas," *Daily Mail*, 17 December 1954, 1.

80. Philip Hope-Wallace, *The Listener*, 23 December 1954.

81. Reginald Pound, "1954 in retrospect," *The Listener*, 30 December 1954.

82. Edward Hulton, "The real George Orwell?" *Picture Post*, 8 January 1955, 5.

83. Llew Gardner "1984 will be grand—under socialism," *Daily Worker*, 18 December 1954, 2.

84. "TV repeat of 1984 hits cinemas," *Daily Mail*, 17 December 1954, 1.

85. BBC WAC R9/7/12, Audience Research Report: *Nineteen Eighty-Four*.

86. BBC WAC R9/35/3, Audience Barometer for 12 December 1954.

87. Wake.

88. BBC WAC R9/35/1, Audience Barometer for 2 June 1953. Oliver Wake estimates that ratings for the Coronation coverage varied from 15.7 million to 19.7 million.

89. BECTU History Project.

90. BBC WAC R9/7/12, Audience Research Report: *Nineteen Eighty-Four*.

91. BBC WAC R9/7/13, Audience Research Report: *The Creature*.

92. BBC WAC R9/7/12, Audience Research Report: *Nineteen Eighty-Four*.

93. "Letter from London," *Queensland Times*, 31 December 1954, 4.

94. "Play which rocked UK for Lux Theatre," *Sunday Times (Perth)*, 27 February 1955, 17.

95. *The Goon Show: Nineteen Eighty-Five*, BBC Home Service, 4 January 1955.

96. Peter Cushing, *An Autobiography* (Weidenfeld & Nicolson, 1986), 126.

97. *Peter Cushing: A One-Way Ticket to Hollywood*, Tyburn Film Productions, Channel Four, 4 June 1989.

98. John Fleming, interview with Nigel Kneale, *Starburst* No 16, 1979, 15.

99. Murray, 38.

100. It may be that Cushing is misremembering, since the rat scenes were recorded on film in advance, at least in part.

101. Cushing, 125.

102. Bernard Wilkie, *A Peculiar Effect on the BBC* (Miwk Publishing, 2015), 89.

103. Wilkie, 84–87.

104. Bernard Wilkie, "Wind me up, let me go," *Cult TV*, August 1997, 65.

105. Wilkie, 87–88.

106. Murray, 38.

107. Wilkie, 90.

108. The Mickey Mouse part of the story seems highly unlikely. Neither Cushing nor Wilkie mentions it in their memoirs and Cartier never brought it up in an interview. On the Thursday night repeat, recorded with an actual snowglobe, Cushing simply says: "It's beautiful." For a *Doctor Who*-related podcast in 2013, writer and comedian Toby Hadoke interviewed ex–BBC producer George Gallaccio, who reminisced about Paddy Russell, the pioneering female TV director who had been Cartier's assistant for a decade. "At Alexandra Palace they had two tiny little studios and they were using both of them," said Gallaccio, adding that the two were connected by a corridor. "This paperweight, somebody put it down in the corridor, and they couldn't, you know ... I remember Paddy had this story of panic, rushing around trying to find it." Again, it seems as though someone's memory is imperfect. The main performance of the play, of course, was at Lime Grove, not Alexandra Palace. *Toby Hadoke's Who's Round* 131 (Big Finish, 2013) https://www.bigfinish.com/releases/v/toby-hadoke-s-who-s-round-131-george-gallaccio-1370.

109. Rodden, 278.

110. Rodden, 281.

Chapter 3

1. Vivien Halas, phone interview, 26 March 2015.

2. John Halas's mother was Jewish.

3. Tony Shaw, phone interview, 26 February 2015.

4. *The Film Programme*, BBC Radio 4, 16 October 2014.

5. Tony Shaw, *British Cinema and the Cold War: The State, Propaganda and Consensus* (IB Taurus, 2001), 94.

6. Frances Stonor Saunders, *Who Paid*

the Piper? The CIA and the Cultural Cold War (Granta Books, 1999), 294.

7. Daniel J. Leab, *Orwell Subverted: The CIA and the Filming of Animal Farm* (The Pennsylvania State University Press, 2007). "Hunt's claims to have been involved in the filming do not hold up," writes Leab in his preface (page xvi). He considers the Clark Gable rumor on 41–42.

8. Shaw, 96.

9. Roger Manvell, *The Animated Film* (Sylvan Press, 1954), 11.

10. Leab, 70.

11. Leab, 69.

12. Manvell, 24.

13. Manvell, 25.

14. Manvell, 28.

15. Manvell, 29.

16. Manvell, 41.

17. Manvell, 11.

18. Leab, 61.

19. Iain F. McAsh, letter to *The Veteran*, issue 91, Spring 2001, 22.

20. "The amazing things that went on in this house," *Picturegoer*, 12 February 1955, 12–13.

21. Leab, 68.

22. Leab, 96.

23. Leab, 76.

24. Leab, 98.

25. *The Film Programme.*

26. The film's narrator, much in evidence early on, was Gordon Heath, a gay African-American based in Paris. He'd moved to Europe for its tolerance.

27. *A Stay Tooned Special: Down on Animal Farm*, screened on BBC1 on 22 July 1995, appears on the *Animal Farm* DVD and 60th anniversary Blu-ray.

28. Granada TV made three John Halas specials as part of its *Clapperboard* series, shown on the ITV network in July 1980. An interview is included on *Animal Farm*'s 60th anniversary edition Blu-ray.

29. An orchestral version accompanies the opening credits.

30. In the novel, he dies three days later.

31. Leab, 38.

32. Shaw, 101.

33. Leab, 85.

34. Leab, 110.

35. *Motion Picture Herald*, 26 January 1955, 4.

36. *Variety*, 26 January 1955.

37. Leab, 112.

38. *Picturegoer*, 12 February 1955, 17.

39. *Today's Cinema*, no 7181, 12 January 1955, 10.

40. Paul Dehn, "Cartoons grow up," *News Chronicle*, 14 January 1955, 6.

41. "Animal Farm in London," *The Times*, 12 January 1955, 7.

42. "Animal Farm on the screen," *The Manchester Guardian*, 12 January 1955, 3.

43. "Our London correspondence," *The Manchester Guardian*, 12 January 1955, 6.

44. CA Lejeune, "Pig business," *The Observer*, 16 January 1955, 10.

45. "Reg Whitley at the New Films," *Daily Mirror*, 14 January 1955, 4.

46. Thomas Spencer, "It's a s(ham) world," by *Daily Worker*, 15 January 1955, 2.

47. Fred Majdalany, "Their animals lack characters," *Daily Mail*, 12 January 1955, 3.

48. Dick Kisch, "Finch's big chance in UK film," *The Sunday Times* (Perth), 16 January 1955, 38.

49. Harold Conway, "Pig Brother has scared them," by *Daily Sketch*, 13 January 1955, 14.

50. Leab, 114.

51. Philip Phillips, "Big Brother pig is film horror," *Daily Herald*, 24 December 1954, 2.

52. Published by the Association of Cinematograph and Allied Technicians.

53. "A film technicians notebook."

54. At the Hammer Theatre in Wardour Street.

55. *The Cine-Technician*, no 125, May 1955, 6–8.

56. *Clapperboard* interview, July 1980.

57. Terry Staples, BFI Southbank *Animal Farm* program notes, November 2012.

Chapter 4

1. Tony Shaw, *Hollywood's Cold War* (Edinburgh University Press, 2007), 93; *The Times*, 15 November 1983.

2. Tony Shaw, phone interview, 26 February 2015.

3. Paul Tanfield, "Tanfield's Diary," *Daily Mail*, 3 February 1956.

4. "N. Peter Rathvon, industrialist and a film producer, is dead," *The New York Times*, 27 May 1972, 32.

5. Tony Shaw, *British Cinema and the Cold War: The State, Propaganda and Consensus* (IB Taurus, 2001), 230.

6. Shaw, *British Cinema and the Cold War*, 106. Speaking to gossip columnist Paul Tanfield in 1956, Rathvon was more ambiguous, remarking that "McCarthyism has not permanently harmed the States." "Tanfield's Diary," *Daily Mail*, 3 February 1956.

7. Frances Stonor Saunders, *Who Paid the Piper? The CIA and the Cultural Cold War* (Granta Books, 1999), 295.

8. Stephen Watts, "Shaping the world of

1984 to the screen," *The New York Times*, 24 July 1955.

9. Shaw, *British Cinema and the Cold War*, 106.

10. Thomas M. Pryor, "Movie is planned of Orwell's 1984," *The New York Times*, 25 September 1954, 11.

11. Lionel Crane, "Now 1984 will be filmed," *Daily Mirror*, 22 December 1954, 6.

12. "1984 film will be for adults only," *Daily Mail*, 22 December 1954, 3.

13. "Joan Fontaine's bright future," *The New York Times*, 6 February 1955, X7. Ms Fontaine claimed she'd been offered the lead role in *1984*.

14. Cecil Wilson, "1984 and all that doesn't worry Jan," *Daily Mail*, 14 June 1955, 6.

15. Dennis Fischer, *Science Fiction Film Directors 1895–1998, volume 1* (McFarland, 2000), 42.

16. *The Movies: Mr. Anderson's War*, BBC2, 8 May 1967. Transcript courtesy of the BFI, job no 5627/0077, interview with Terence Heelas dated 21 January 1967.

17. Michael Anderson, email to David Ryan, July 2015.

18. Will Murray, "Once in a Millennium," *Starlog* 146, November 1989, 16.

19. Ernie Player, "This British film must shock America—that's why 1984 is being made here with two Hollywood stars," *Picturegoer*, 2 July 1955, 14.

20. *Ibid.*

21. "1984," *Film Review*, April 1956, 6–7.

22. Or the former Nelson's Column, as a statue of Big Brother has replaced Admiral Lord Nelson.

23. *Picturegoer*, 2 July 1955.

24. Either that or New Zealand's parliament in Wellington, known as "the Beehive."

25. *The New York Times*, 24 July 1955.

26. *Ibid.*

27. *Picturegoer*, 2 July 1955.

28. As it was in *Studio One*.

29. Syme is relegated to a bit part like he was in *Studio One*.

30. Stonor Saunders, 296.

31. Stonor Saunders, 296; letter from Sol Stein to Peter Rathvon, 30 January 1955 (ACCF/NYU)

32. Stonor Saunders, 297, letter from Sol Stein to Peter Rathvon, 30 January 1955 (ACCF/NYU)

33. *Ibid.*

34. *Ibid.*

35. The script can be viewed in London at the British Library's Rare Books and Music Reading Room and the British Film Institute's Reuben Library, BFI Southbank.

36. Stephen Watts, "Noted on the British film scene," *The New York Times*, 18 March 1956, 131.

37. Shaw, *British Cinema and the Cold War*, 107.

38. Paul Tanfield, "Tanfield's Diary," *Daily Mail*, 2 March 1956.

39. Edward Goring, "The 'happy' 1984 film shocks Mrs. Orwell," *Daily Mail*, 27 February 1956, 5.

40. *Ibid.*

41. "In the picture," *Sight and Sound*, Spring 1956, 170.

42. Only one rat appears in the movie, in Charrington's room.

43. CA Lejeune, film reviews, *The Observer*, 4 March 1956, 11.

44. Harold Conway, *Daily Sketch*, 2 March 1956, 13.

45. Thomas Spencer, "1984's the big flop of 1956," *Daily Worker*, 3 March 1956, 2.

46. Derek Hill, *Sight and Sound*, Spring 1956, 198.

47. Maryvonne Butcher, "Past and future imperfect," *The Tablet*, 10 March 1956, 8.

48. *Kinematograph Weekly*, 16 February 1956, 18.

49. Isabel Quigley, "The rats in Room 101," *The Spectator*, 9 March 1956, 20.

50. *The Times*, 1 March 1956, 5.

51. "Orwell adjusted. Weakened warning in film of 1984," *The Manchester Guardian*, 1 March 1956, 7.

52. Robert Cannell, "Last night's TV," *Daily Express*, 6 March 1956, 6.

53. Andy Murray, *Into the Unknown: The Fantastic Life of Nigel Kneale* (Headpress, 2006), 103.

54. Edward Goring, "Can it happen here? No, you say…. Then you see this and wonder," *Daily Mail*, 1 March 1956.

55. "Reg Whitley at the New Films," *Daily Mirror*, 2 March 1956, 12.

56. Anthony Carthew, "Redgrave gives a course in cruelty," *Daily Herald*, 2 March 1956, 6.

57. *The Daily Film Renter*, 24 February 1956, 3.

58. *Today's Cinema*, 23 February 1956, 8.

59. *Historical Journal of Film, Radio and Television*, volume 20, number 4, October 2000, 476.

60. Bill Warren, *Keep Watching the Skies!: American Science Fiction Movies of the Fifties* (McFarland, 2010), 636.

61. AH Weiler, "The screen: '1984' opens; Adaptation of Orwell's novel at Normandie," *The New York Times*, 1 October 1956, http://www.nytimes.com/movie/review?res=9E0 1E4DA1E31E23BBC4953DFB667838D649E DE

62. *George Orwell 1903–1950*, BBC2, 20 November 1965.
63. Source for the four uncredited actors listed here is Michael R. Pitts, *Columbia Pictures Horror, Science Fiction and Fantasy Films 1928–1982* (McFarland, 2010), 179.

Chapter 5

1. BBC Written Archives Centre (WAC), T48/456/1, 20 May 1957.
2. In the seventies, David Bowie cast himself as Winston Smith in an abortive *Nineteen Eighty-Four* musical. His songs *1984*, *Big Brother* and *We Are the Dead*, written with the show in mind, surfaced on the 1974 album *Diamond Dogs*.
3. BBC WAC, T48/456/1, 22 May 1957.
4. BBC WAC, T48/456/1, 28 July 1959.
5. BBC WAC, T48/456/1, 21 December 1961.
6. BBC WAC, T48/456/1, 16 January 1962.
7. BBC WAC, T48/456/1, 15 November 1962.
8. *Daily Mail*, 8 February 1965, 3.
9. Marjorie Bilbow, "Marrying the right play to the right director," *The Stage and Television Today*, 22 April 1965, 10.
10. The play, about a haunted English village in the 18th century, ends on a twist: the "ghosts" are from a future nuclear war.
11. *The Road* was the second play that Morahan directed for the BBC. He went on the become head of plays at BBC Television from 1972–76.
12. Christopher Morahan, phone interview, 6 February 2015.
13. Robin Chapman, phone interview, 15 March 2015.
14. It was 1937.
15. Michael Williams, *Radio Times*, 4 November 1965, 11.
16. BBC WAC, T5/1545/1, 1 April 1965.
17. BBC WAC, T5/1545/1, 12 March 1965.
18. The locations were Jennings Wood near Burnham Beeches, a private field by the River Thames at Medmenham and the footpaths off Rotten Row, near Hambledon. BBC WAC, T5/1545/1, March 1965.
19. One wonders what Alfred Lynch, who was gay, made of Orwell's mincing stereotype.
20. Stuart Hood, "Orwelliana," *The Spectator*, 19 November 1965, 15–16.
21. BBC WAC, T5/1545/1, 25 March 1965. Documents suggest graphic designer Bernard Lodge painted Corner Table, but in an email to the author of this book on 22 August 2016, he refuted this. "What I did for the production wasn't an advertising animated poster, but it was a title sequence made from various photos of a town," he wrote. "I don't remember the town. I junked the photos soon afterwards."

22. Clive Elliott, phone interview, 13 June 2015.
23. Both men were Orwell's literary friends.
24. This is a stage direction in the script. Peckham is a working-class area of London.
25. Political correctness hadn't caught on in 1965.
26. Morahan cast Sydney Arnold, a 65-year-old comedy actor who stood less than five feet tall.
27. In the novel, it winds up down a drain. In the movie, Gordon tosses it into the Thames.
28. Peter Black, *Daily Mail*, 8 November 1965, 3.
29. Kenneth Eastaugh, "Passion grows among the aspidistras," *Daily Mirror*, 8 November 1965, 18.
30. Mary Crozier, *The Guardian*, 8 November 1965, 7.
31. Mary Crozier, "Political parleys," *The Tablet*, 13 November 1965, 18.
32. "Nostalgic view of 30's from George Orwell," *The Daily Telegraph*, 8 November 1965, 14.
33. Stewart Lane, *Daily Worker*, 13 November 1965, 2.
34. "Rebel poet's decline and fall," *The Times*, 8 November 1965, 14.
35. *Variety*, 17 November 1965, 46.
36. Hood, *The Spectator*.
37. Frederick Laws, "Drama and light entertainment," *The Listener*, 2 December 1965, 55.

Chapter 6

1. It didn't help that television was seen as an ephemeral medium, union agreements put a limit on the number of repeat screenings and few could imagine the nostalgia craze and home video market that took off in the eighties.
2. BBC WAC, T51/21/1, 14 April 1965.
3. Jack Bond interview, London, 29 March 2016.
4. Malcolm Muggeridge, "Orwell and his times," *Radio Times*, 18 November 1965, 5.
5. The scene was shot several times and transcripts exist of each take. Whenever the Beatles were mentioned, Muggeridge was in the habit of saying: "Those four unspeakable youths," a line that failed to make the final cut.
6. BBC WAC, T51/21/1, 9 August 1965.
7. *Radio Times*, 18 November 1965, 5.
8. *The Observer*, 28 November 1965, 25.
9. *The Listener*, 25 November 1965, 47.
10. John Rodden, *George Orwell: The Politics of Literary Reputation* (Transaction Publishers, 2002), 285.

11. BBC WAC, T51/21/1, BBC Audience Research Barometer of Viewing for 20 November 1965.
12. BBC WAC, T51/21/1, Audience Research Report, 29 December 1965.
13. www.bfi.org.uk/films-tv-people/4ce2ba 035fc55.

Chapter 7

1. Robin Chapman, phone interview, 15 March 2015.
2. In the novel, George can't remember the anti-fascist's name.
3. *Radio Times*, 18 November 1965, 14.
4. Christopher Morahan, phone interview, 6 February 2015.
5. Weekly repertory theatres used to stage a different play every week. It's another British tradition that has died out.
6. BBC Written Archives Centre (WAC), T5/1021/1, 5 July 1965.
7. BBC WAC, T5/1021/1, 5 July 1965.
8. BBC WAC, T5/1021/1, 7 July 1965.
9. BBC WAC, T5/1021/1, 5 July 1965.
10. BBC WAC, T5/1021/1, 2 July 1965.
11. John Glenister, phone interview, 4 June 2015.
12. BBC WAC, T5/1021/1, 10 August 1965.
13. BBC WAC, T5/1021/1, 20 August 1965.
14. Kenneth Easthaugh, *Daily Mirror*, 22 November 1965, 18.
15. LL, "Nostalgic visit that caught right mood," *The Daily Telegraph*, 22 November 1965, 16.
16. Maurice Richardson, *The Observer*, 28 November 1965, 25.
17. Frederick Laws, "Drama and light entertainment," *The Listener*, 2 December 1965, 55.
18. Philip Purser, "1984 in 1965," *The Sunday Telegraph*, 28 November 1965, 13.
19. BBC WAC, T5/1545/1, 10 June 1966.
20. Gerard Fay, "Never go back," *The Guardian*, 20 September 1966, 7.
21. Geoffrey Nicholson, *Daily Mail*, 20 September 1966, 3.
22. "Repeat of Orwell work well worthwhile," *The Times*, 19 September 1966, 6.

Chapter 8

1. BBC Written Archives Centre (WAC), T5/1724/1, 21 January 1965.
2. BBC WAC, T5/1724/1, 24 March 1965.
3. BBC WAC, T5/1724/1, 1 April 1965.
4. BBC WAC, T5/1724/1, 24 March 1965.
5. BBC WAC, T5/1724/1, 30 March 1965.
6. BBC WAC, T5/1724/1, 1 April 1965.
7. Christopher Morahan, phone interview, 6 February 2015.
8. Kim Newman, *Unrated*, http://www.unrated.co.uk/reviews/review_278.htm.
9. BBC WAC, T5/1725/1, accountant's record.
10. The play went out at 8 p.m.
11. *Radio Times*, 25 November 1965. The magazine used Orwellian imagery again for the New Year 1984 edition, when its cover illustration was of a recognizably Stalinesque Big Brother.
12. *Radio Times*, 25 November 1965, 13.
13. "Orwell keeps flying," *The Observer*, 7 November 1965, 23.
14. Letters and telegrams that the BBC retains to this day.
15. Kim Newman, *Unrated*.
16. BBC WAC, T5/1725/1, 15 July 1965.
17. Camber Sands beach, East Suffolk, appears in the pre-title sequence, showing the build-up to nuclear war. BBC WAC, T5/1725/1, 3 May 1965.
18. Dungeness nuclear power station in Kent doubled as the Ministry of Truth. BBC WAC, T5/1725/1, 10 May 1965.
19. The terraced housing, meant to be Victory Mansions, was in Doris, Street, Lambeth: BBC WAC, T5/1725/1, undated filming schedule for 17–21 May 1965. For Victory Square, Morahan filmed at a nearby waste area bordered by Goda Street and Ethelred Street. This was augmented by a 20-foot model of Big Ben: BBC WAC, T5/1725/1, 11 May 1965.
20. Winston's ID number is the same as it was in 1954. Other characters' numbers have changed, as has Julia's surname. O'Brien has a number on his upper sleeve: O'Brien G, PRL 412.
21. Are the telescreens linked to a team of quickfire sketch artists, who produce the drawings to order? How on earth would such a device work?
22. It's interesting how Shaps underplays Syme. In contrast with Donald Pleasence's interpretation, he's a timeserving inadequate rather than a swivel-eyed sociopath.
23. A 15-second snippet of the record, sung by Rita Cameron for composer Wilfred Josephs, is played in the scene. Later, Julie May (as Charrington's neighbor) sings a 45-second burst, offscreen, before the Thought Police bludgeon her. Cameron also sang the 41-second 'Chestnut Tree song.' BBC WAC, T5/1725/1, accountant's record.
24. Curled up on the floor, Winston is kicked and coshed, but the violence looks so fake, it's unintentionally comical.
25. Kim Newman, *Unrated*.

26. Peter Cushing, *An Autobiography* (Weidenfeld and Nicolson, 1986), 124.

27. Andy Murray, *Into the Unknown: The Fantastic Life of Nigel Kneale* (Headpress, 2006), 97.

28. Peter Black, *Daily Mail*, 29 November 1965, 3.

29. Philip Purser, "1984 in 1965," *The Sunday Telegraph*, 28 November 1965, 13.

30. LL, "1984 loses impact after 12 years," *The Daily Telegraph*, 29 November 1965, 14.

31. "Dr Who helps to rob 1984 of impact," *Daily Express*, 29 November 1965, 4.

32. Maurice Richardson, *The Observer*, 5 December 1965, 25.

33. Mary Crozier, *The Guardian*, 29 December 1965, 7.

34. BBC WAC, T5/1725/1, 31 December 1965, Audience Research Report: *1984*.

35. The play was shown on *NET Playhouse* on 19 April 1968.

36. Jane Merrow, phone interview, 23 May 2015.

Chapter 9

1. Essay by Melvyn Bragg, 2016, kindly supplied to the author.

2. Peter Fiddick, "Orwell: 'Nearer a saint than most," *Radio Times*, 9–15 January 1971, 9.

3. In his 2016 essay, Bragg wrote that Bergman "believed that the most powerful and endlessly fascinating part of the human being is the face."

4. In 1931, Huxley would write the other great dystopian novel, *Brave New World*.

5. Bragg approached Mailer as he was "working in the same area" as Orwell. "In fact, he's mad on him." *Radio Times*, 9–15 January 1971, 9.

6. Essay by Melvyn Bragg, 2016.

7. In the North of England, 'having tea' means eating an early-evening meal.

8. Mary Holland, "On the road with Orwell," *The Observer*, 17 January 1971, 23.

9. Michael Ratcliffe, "George Orwell at the Wigan crossroads," *The Times*, 11 January 1971, 7.

10. Kenneth Adam, "Lives of the great," *Financial Times*, 13 January 1971, 3.

11. Essay by Melvyn Bragg, 2016.

Chapter 10

1. Derek Granger, "Obituaries: Frank Cvitanovich," *The Independent*, 17 August 1995, http://www.independent.co.uk/news/people/obituaries-frank-cvitanovich-1596726.html.

2. Ian Cotton, "Why Orwell took the road to the dogs," *TV Times*, 13–19 October 1973, 10.

3. A little over 10 years later, this clip was re-used in Anthony Burgess's schools programme *1984: A Personal View of Nineteen Eighty Four*.

4. Musical interludes like these are a bold gamble on Cvitanovich's part. Or perhaps they're a 1973 phenomenon: *The Wicker Man*, which premiered in cinemas the following month, is about pagan Scottish islanders who sing folk songs at the drop of a hat.

5. *One Day While in the North Country* is Bob Davenport's own composition, based on traditional songs. The lyrics describe a pit accident but it's inspired by his 23-year-old father's death in 1933. A gas pipe exploded, destroying the family's house. Bob, who was ten months old, survived along with his mother.

6. The party leaders featured are Stanley Baldwin, Neville Chamberlain, Winston Churchill, Clement Attlee, Anthony Eden, Harold Macmillan, Hugh Gaitskell and Alec Douglas Home.

7. When the UK joined the European Economic Community on 1 Jaunary 1973, it was known as "the sick man of Europe."

8. Published in 1908.

9. Bob Davenport, phone interview, 13 October 2016.

10. The boundaries have since changed.

11. "Filmography and radio," *Morriston Orpheus Choir*, http://morristonorpheus.com/tv-and-film-appearances-of-the-morriston-orpheus-choir.

12. Sir Jeremy Isaacs, BFI event, London, 10 March 2016.

13. Helen Dawson, "Entertainments round-up," *The Observer*, 14 October 1973, 35.

14. Leonard Buckley, *The Times*, 17 October 1973, 11.

15. Peter Fiddick, *The Guardian*, 17 October 1973, 12.

16. Richard Last, "Orwell's compassion is given force," *The Daily Telegraph*, 17 October 1973, 14.

17. James Thomas, "Doling out the sympathy," *Daily Express*, 17 October 1973, 12.

18. Mary Crozier, *The Tablet*, 27 October 1973, 15.

19. Clive Gammon, "Orwellian insights," *The Spectator*, 19 October 1973, 57.

20. *TV Times*, 3–9 November 1973, 79.

Chapter 11

1. George Orwell, *Looking Back on the Spanish War*, *The Penguin Essays of George Orwell* (Penguin, 1994), 230–232.

2. He was born in the Tyneside town of Jarrow but moved to Hull as a child.

3. Shirley Rubinstein, interview in London, 23 May 2015.

4. Norman McCandlish, phone interview, 4 June 2015.

5. Newspaper reports at the time put Jura's population at 200. In his interview, director John Glenister remembered it as 120.

6. John Glenister, phone interview, 4 June 2015.

7. In the end credits, the BBC thanks Susan Watson, Richard Blair, Orwell's niece Jane Dakin, his brother-in-law Bill Dunn and the laird's wife, Margaret Fletcher, "for their help and advice."

8. Bernard Crick, *George Orwell: A Life* (Martin Secker & Warburg Limited, 1980.)

9. Alan Plater archive, Hull History Centre.

10. Ronald Pickup, interview in London, 31 May 2015.

11. Alan Plater, "Orwell on Jura," *The Observer Magazine*, 18 December 1983.

12. The estate house is known as Ardlussa.

13. Crick, 366.

14. Michael Hickling, "Orwell that ends well," *Yorkshire Post*, 31 December 1983, 8.

15. The original opening scene, showing Orwell visiting his wife Eileen's grave, was scrapped.

16. Nancy Banks-Smith, "Doubleplusgood view from Jura," *The Guardian*, 21 December 1983, 9.

17. Dennis Hackett, "Gripping snapshot," *The Times*, 21 December 1983, 9.

18. Elizabeth Cowley, "Pick of the day," *Daily Mail*, 20 December 1983, 16.

19. Ronald Pickup, interview in London, 31 May 2015.

20. Ronald Pickup, letter to David Ryan, 6 September 2017.

Chapter 12

1. *Radio Times*, 31 December 1983–6 January 1984, 1.

2. Christopher Priest, "The future isn't what it was," *Radio Times*, 31 December 1983–6 January 1984, 88–91.

3. *Radio Times*, 31 December 1983–6 January 1984, 29 listing.

4. *Radio Times*, 31 December 1983–6 January 1984, 71 listing.

5. Nigel Williams, phone interview, 12 October 2015.

6. In "Repeating the old lies," a 1999 article for *The New Criterion*, Orwell biographer Jeffrey Meyers claims that Frankford was an-

noyed that Cottman, rather than he, had been invited to Spain for the program. When interviewed by Meyers, Frankford grudgingly admitted that "POUM was all right."

7. The social security office, or welfare office.

8. Stewart Lane, "Dodging awkward aspects of Orwell," *Morning Star*, 4 January 1984, 2.

9. Lucy Hughes-Hallett, "The long road to Wigan Pier," *The Standard*, 30 December 1983, 22.

10. Julian Barnes, *The Observer*, 8 January 1984, 56.

11. Peter Kemp, "A nose for phoniness," *The Times Literary Supplement*, 20 January 1984, 62.

12. Christopher Dunkley, "Another week of pain and pleasure," *Financial Times*, 11 January 1984, 20.

13. Hugo Williams, *New Statesman*, 6 January 1984, 27.

14. Philip Purser, "Yesterday's today," *Sunday Telegraph*, 8 January 1984, 11.

15. *Arena* won best programme/series without category at the 1984 Baftas. Through a series of promotions, Alan Yentob went on to become the BBC's director of music and arts, the controller of BBC2, the controller of BBC1, the BBC's director of programs, the BBC's director of drama, entertainment and children's and the BBC's creative director.

Chapter 13

1. The line in Bernard Crick's biography is "You must let him play with his thingummy": *George Orwell: A Life* (Martin Secker & Warburg Limited, 1980), 347.

2. Crick, 357.

3. The letter, from 16 June 1949, was to Francis A. Henson of the United Automobile Workers: Sonia Orwell and Ian Angus, *Collected Essays, Journalism and Letters of George Orwell*, volume 4 (Harcourt Brace Jovanovich, 1968), 502. It recurs in 2003's *George Orwell: A Life in Pictures* (see chapter 17).

4. Leslie Megahey, "David Wheatley," *The Guardian*, 13 April 2009, https://www.theguardian.com/film/2009/apr/13/obituary-david-wheatley.

5. "An approach with potential but it has its pitfalls," *The Stage and Television Today*, 8 December 1983, 22.

6. Hall's best-known scripts were co-written with Keith Waterhouse.

7. The end credits state that Hall wrote *The Road to 1984* "in association with" Wheatley.

8. *The Stage and Television Today*, 8 December 1983, 22.

9. *Ibid.*

10. Roma Felstein, "A preview of the future 1984," *Broadcast*, 6 January 1984, 27.

11. Julia Goodman, interview in London, 14 October 2015.

12. Janet Dale, phone interview, 6 September 2017.

13. "In Granada's dramadoc on Orwell for 1984," *The Stage and Television Today*, 18 August 1983, 21.

14. "Fox to portray Orwell," *Screen International*, 20 August 1983, 14.

15. Alix Coleman, "Facing up to the prophet of doom," *TV Times*, 14–20 January 1984, 11.

16. Patrick O'Neill, "Orwell and little brother," *Daily Mail*, 19 January 1984, 22.

17. *Daily Mail*, 19 January 1984, 22.

18. *TV Times*, 14–20 January 1984, 11.

19. *TV Times*, 14–20 January 1984, 49 listing.

20. Christopher Dunkley, "A magnificent start to the year," *Financial Times*, 18 January 1984, 18.

21. Hilary Kingsley, "All's well, brother…" *Daily Mirror*, 20 January 1984, 17.

22. Jill Forbes, "News from Oceania," *Sight & Sound*, Spring 1984, 38.

23. Dennis Hackett, *The Times*, 20 January 1984, 7.

24. Orwell Society members visit Orwell's grave on the closest Sunday to his birthday. After meeting them, Janet Dale joined the society.

Chapter 14

1. "Orwell's 1984 rolls in London, first project of Chi film buff," *Variety*, 25 April 1984, 45.

2. William Langley, "Coming soon: 1984," *Daily Mail*, 17 July 1981, 4.

3. Lisa Dewson, "Big Brother is watching us in Nineteen Eighty-Four," *Photoplay*, December 1984, 14–15.

4. *Variety*, 25 April 1984, 45.

5. *Photoplay*, December 1984, 14–15.

6. Nan Robertson, "Orwellian saga," *The New York Times*, 13 January 1985, http://www.nytimes.com/1985/01/13/arts/orwellian-saga.

7. *Photoplay*, December 1984, 14–15. *Chariots of Fire*, released in March 1981, went on to win four Oscars, including Best Film.

8. The film, released in 1983, is about a woman in 1940s Scotland who has an affair with an Italian prisoner of war.

9. Simon Perry, phone interview, 22 October 2015.

10. Radford had read the book as a teenager. "It had been one of my favourite books when I was a kid, for a number of reasons. One, be-

cause of its political incisiveness and everything, but also because it was one of the few books that you could read when you were at school that had sex in it." *The Real Room 101*, BBC Four, 14 June 2003.

11. In the absence of a face-to-face interview, all of Michael Radford's lengthy comments in this chapter are taken from a public Q&A event at Oxford's Christ Church Cathedral School in 2009. The interview by Jean Seaton, director of the Orwell Prize (now the Orwell Foundation) was available on YouTube at the time of writing, entitled "Oxford 2009: Q&A with Mike Radford." https://www.youtube.com/watch?v=anA8wKWm1UE

12. O'Brien's apartment building, with an image of Big Brother on the front, is in reality Senate House, London, Orwell's original inspiration for the Ministry of Truth. "Senate House histories: on the screen," *University of London*, https://senate-house-histories.london.ac.uk/on-the-screen.

13. "A conversation with Michael Radford," 25 March 2017. Bill Banowsky interviewed Radford in Rome, days before a U.S.–wide screening of *Nineteen Eighty-Four* to protest the policies of the Trump administration. Their hour-long discussion was edited down to 15 minutes and shown at the end of the movie. The unedited version, which covers the same kind of ground as Jean Seaton's Orwell Prize interview, was uploaded to the *Violet Crown Films* website, http://violetcrownfilms.com.

14. "So this is what Orwell predicted!" *Film Review*, November 1984, 6–9.

15. Adam Pirani, "Welcome to 1984," *Starlog* number 88, November 1984, 78–80, 87.

16. *1984: Designing a Nightmare*, BBC2, 18 October 1984.

17. In the Banowsky interview of 2017, Radford remembers casting Scofield first, then approaching Connery, who instead returned to the role of James Bond in *Never Say Never Again*. He's clearly mistaken, as the Bond movie came out in 1983.

18. Ken Ferguson, "Life and John Hurt in 1984," *Photoplay*, October 1984, 12–13.

19. Fiona Kieni, *Metro* No 65, 7. The magazine was published by the Australian Teachers of Media (ATOM) with assistance from the Australian Film Commission.

20. Dominique Joyeux's interview with John Hurt, published in the French press and elsewhere in the eighties, appears on his website, http://100pages.me/film-writing/john-hurt.

21. *Photoplay*, December 1984, 14–15.

22. *1984: Designing a Nightmare*.

23. "Michael Radford on filming George Orwell's 1984," *Cinefantastique*, July 1985, 50.

24. According to Radford in his *Cinefantastique* interview.

25. *1984: Designing a Nightmare.*

26. Alexandra Palace's BBC studios, long defunct in 1984, had been used 30 years earlier for Rudolph Cartier's filmed inserts (see chapter 2).

27. Needless to say, the Docklands area has been redeveloped and is full of luxury flats. Radford says in his 2017 Banowsky interview that after seeing *Nineteen Eighty-Four*, Stanley Kubrick elected to use the same location as a substitute for war-torn Vietnam in *Full Metal Jacket* (1987).

28. The Roundway is near the town of Devizes (see themodernantiquarian.com for photos). In the film, it's also where Winston and Julia make love for the first time.

29. *The Two Minutes Hate* was shot in a grass-covered hangar at RAF Hullavington near Chippenham, Wiltshire. Hundreds of extras were paid £20 each and instructed to scream with rage like "a real Nazi fascist." The men were given quick, short haircuts at the Territorial Army Centre in Swindon beforehand. Barry Leighton, *Swindon Advertiser*, "Hundreds flocked to get heads cropped when movie stars came to town… but were you a hater?" 25 June 2014, http://www.swindonadvertiser.co.uk/news/11300158.Hundreds_flocked_to_get_heads_cropped_when_movie_stars_came_to_town_but_were_you_a_hater.

30. Despite its grisliness, *1984: Designing a Nightmare* aired at 7:30 p.m.

31. Keir and Louise Lusby, interview in Surrey, 10 April 2016.

32. Stephen Phillips, ITN news report, 8 October 1984. http://www.gettyimages.co.uk/license/673603912.

33. "Rats are basically very clean animals," special effects supervisor Ian Scoones told journalist Adam Pirani. *Starlog* number 88, November 1984.

34. Hurt told this story to Fiona Kieni (*Metro* No 65) and on *The Real Room 101*, BBC Four, 14 June 2003.

35. Burton insisted that O'Brien's boiler suit be handmade for him in Savile Row, London. *In Conversation with Michael Radford*, Sky Arts, 18 October 2013.

36. Lynda Lee-Potter, "Marriage … and Mr. Burton," *Daily Mail*, 12 June 1984, 18–19.

37. Melvyn Bragg, *Rich* (Hodder & Stoughton, 1988), 564.

38. Michael Billington, "A director's vision of Orwell's '1984' draws inspiration from 1948," *The New York Times*, 3 June 1984, http://www.nytimes.com/1984/06/03/movies/a-director-s-vision-of-orwell-s-1984-draws-inspiration-from-1948.

39. David Cann, phone interview, 18 May 2016.

40. *1984: Designing a Nightmare.*

41. Seaton interview, 2009.

42. Banowsky interview, 2017.

43. Philip French, "Doing Orwell proud," *The Observer*, 14 October 1984, 21.

44. *Variety*, 10 October 1984.

45. Julia Salamon, *The Wall Street Journal*, 17 January 1985.

46. John Hurt considered the anthem "senfuckingsational" and something that Elgar would have been proud of. http://100pages.me/film-writing/john-hurt.

47. Danny Peary, *Guide for the Film Fanatic* (Simon & Schuster, 1986), 301.

48. "They're like cavemen in a way. They're discovering something. There is something brutish about it," said Radford. *Cinefantastique*, July 1985, 50.

49. Peary, 301.

50. "'84' pulled from Venice; preem off until October," *Variety*, 1 August 1984, 7.

51. "'1984' comes to the screen," *Screen International*, 13 October 1984, 10–11.

52. *Screen International*, 27 October 1984.

53. Quentin Falk, *Daily Mail*, 12 October 1984, 26.

54. Arthur Thirkell, "Vision of despair," *Daily Mirror*, 12 October 1984, 6.

55. Nigel Andrews, "The historic voice of prophesy," *Financial Times*, 12 October 1984, 17.

56. Seaton interview, 2009.

57. Banowsky interview, 2017.

58. In the Banowsky interview, Radford says the flight was during the making of his 1998 film *B. Monkey.*

59. Seaton interview, 2009.

60. Banowsky interview, 2017.

61. "Year for Eurythmics," *Melody Maker*, 20 October 1984, 3.

62. "Directors anxious over '1984' soundtrack dispute," *Screen International*, 24 November 1984, 4.

63. Kimiko de Freytas-Tamura, "George Orwell's '1984' is suddenly a best'seller.," *The New York Times*, 25 January 2017, https://www.nytimes.com/2017/01/25/books/1984-george-orwell-donald-trump.

64. The same date Winston Smith started his rebellion.

65. Jillian Kestler-D'Amours, "Theatres to screen Orwell's 1984 in anti-Trump protest," *Al Jazeera*, 3 April 2017, http://www.aljazeera.com/news/2017/04/theatres-screen-orwell-1984-protest-trump-170403131200190.

66. *National Screening Day*, http://www.unitedstateofcinema.com.

67. Introduction by Michael Radford, http://violetcrownfilms.com.

68. Banowsky interview, 2017.

69. Tatiana Siegel, "In Trump era, '1984' is the hottest literary property in Hollywood," *The Hollywood Reporter*, 3 April 2017, http://www.hollywoodreporter.com/heat-vision/trump-era-1984-is-hottest-literary-property-hollywood-990730.

70. Marvin Rosenblum died in 2003.

Chapter 15

1. DVD International released *A Merry War* as part of its Prestige Collection in 1999. The commentary was recorded in London on 25 February.

2. Michael Coveney, "Alan Plater," *The Guardian*, 25 June 2010, https://www.theguardian.com/stage/2010/jun/25/alan-plater-obituary.

3. Shirley Rubinstein, interview in London, 23 May 2015.

4. Bierman was happy to contribute to this book, but thought the DVD commentary would be more helpful and comprehensive than an interview.

5. The 1988 TV version of Chris Mullin's novel *A Very British Coup*, screened by Channel Four, won four Bafta Awards and an International Emmy Award for Best Drama. http://www.imdb.com/title/tt0094576/awards.

6. David Ryan, "Plater's old-fashioned philosophy," *Highbury & Islington Express*, 7 April 2000, 23–24.

7. The line, which wasn't used in the end, riffs on a gag by Morecambe and Wise, the best-loved BBC double act of the seventies.

8. Rosemary does indeed paint a picture of an aspidistra at the end of the film.

9. In another change, the rabbis at the hotel were replaced with Catholic bishops.

10. Plater may have been referring to Luke Harding's story, "Movie reworks Orwell's angst," *The Guardian*, 14 April 1997, 3. It claimed that his script had "thrown out the doom and gloom" and turned Rosemary into "a sexually confident career woman." It went on to say she would lose Gordon's baby after refusing to marry him. Bierman told the paper: "What we have done is modernize the story elements. It is all about tonal quality. It is nothing to do with feminism whatsoever."

11. Louise Tutt, *Screen International*, 26 September 1997, 44.

12. *Ibid.* During filming, Bierman said he'd ignored Overseas Filmgroup's request that he "put bigger names in the film."

13. Not in Hampstead, but Woburn Walk, Bloomsbury. Simon James, *London Film Location Guide* (Batsford, 2007), 13.

14. The actor, playing bookseller McKechnie, was replaced by John Clegg.

15. Lynn Barber, "One minute he's laughing," *The Observer*, 9 November 1997, 92.

16. *Moviewatch*, Channel Four, 18 November 1997.

17. Philip French, "Vic, Bob and me," *The Observer*, 9 November 1997, 72.

18. Jonathan Romney, "Fusty festival opener fails to provide touch of class," *The Guardian*, 7 November 1997, 2.

19. Conservative magazine *The Spectator*, first published in 1828, is the oldest continuously published magazine in the English language.

20. Melvyn Bragg, "The chancellor keeps the aspidistra flying," *The Times*, 10 November 1997, 20.

21. Executive producer John Wolstenholme responded to Bragg's article with a letter to *The Times* published on 14 November (p23), noting that Brown also attended a London Film Festival reception for the film.

22. Geoff Brown, *The Times*, 27 November 1997, 35.

23. Daniel Britten, "Who needs Orwell that ends well?" *The Times*, 24 November 1997, 20.

24. *Sight & Sound*, November 1997, 44.

25. Matthew Sweet, *The Independent*, 30 November 1997, 8.

26. *Empire* issue 102, December 1997, 46.

27. *Screen International*, 17 October 1997, 37.

28. Christopher Tookey, "Why do our movies still live in the past?" *Daily Mail*, 28 November 1997, 44–45.

29. Christopher Tookey, "Fool Britannia (Or how the British film industry took £150 million of your money and produced two dozen turkeys)," *Daily Mail*, 28 April 1998, 36–37.

30. Peter Shaw, phone interview, 1 July 2015.

31. *Time International*, 29 December 1997–5 January 1998, 96.

32. *Entertainment Weekly*, September 4, 1998, http://ew.com/article/1998/09/04/merry-war.

33. Ty Burr, *The New York Times*, 30 August 1998, http://www.nytimes.com/1998/08/30/movies/film-down-and-out-on-the-sunnier-side-of-orwell.

34. Ella Taylor, *LA Weekly* and syndicated publications, June 1998, https://www.theatlantic.com/past/docs/ae/98jun/98junfil.htm.

35. Susan Green, *Boxoffice*, 1 April 1998, 199.

36. *GQ*, May 1998.

37. Ed Kelleher, *Film Journal International*, 1 April 1998, 72, http://www.filmjournal.com/merry-war.

Chapter 16

1. The Real History of Animatronics, Robo robotics.com, http://roborobotics.com/Anima tronics/history-of-animatronics.html.
2. Ron Magid, "Effects team brings dinosaurs back from extinction," *American Cinematographer*, June 1993, 46–52.
3. *Cinefantastique*, December 1999, 56–57.
4. John Stephenson, phone interview, 17 July 2015.
5. In the book, Frederick and Pilkington represent the Nazis and the Allies, respectively.
6. "A battle for the barn," *American Cinematographer*, October 1999, 72–81.
7. "Orwell that ends well," *In Camera*, April 1999, 4.
8. *Ibid.*
9. "Creature features," *American Cinematographer*, October 1999, 76.
10. *Cinefantastique*, December 1999.
11. David Rooney, *Variety*, 1 October 1999, http://variety.com/1999/tv/reviews/animal-farm-2-1117752212.
12. James Poniewozik, "Whitewashing the Farm," *Time*, 4 October 1999, 96.
13. OBE stands for Order of the British Empire.

Chapter 17

1. The transmission time was 9:05pm.
2. Orwell was born on 25 June 1903.
3. Chris Durlacher, interview in London, 24 March 2016.
4. The BBC's *People Like Us.*
5. *Newsnight Review*, BBC Two, 30 May 2003, http://news.bbc.co.uk/1/hi/programmes/newsnight/review/2956988.
6. Gareth McLean, *The Guardian*, 16 June 2003, B22.
7. Robert Gore-Langton, *Daily Express*, 16 June 2003, 45.
8. Paul Hoggart, "George Orwell: A Life in Pictures was a tour de force and a fitting tribute," *The Times*, 16 June 2003, Times 2 p19.
9. Peter Paterson, "Orwell … and good," *Daily Mail*, 16 June 2003, 45.
10. Thomas Sutcliffe, "Chapter and verse on literature's finest," *The Independent*, 16 June 2003, 21.

Chapter 18

1. David Taylor, phone interview, 11 January 2017.
2. Episode 19 of *The South Bank Show's* 26th season.

3. The program uses clips from Rudolph Cartier's *Nineteen Eighty-Four*, *The Road to the Left* (specifically, Joe Kennan's anecdote about Orwell collapsing down the mine) and *The Crystal Spirit: Orwell on Jura.*
4. *Channel Four News*, 2 September 2003, http://www.gettyimages.co.uk/license/6825401 90.
5. Frustratingly for Taylor, *The South Bank Show* has him peering at a different newsreel of the same game and failing to come up trumps. Another vintage film, of Southwold's local fair in 1930, includes a man who looks very like Eric Blair, though we'll probably never know for sure. Taylor thinks it's him.
6. DJ Taylor, "The ever-longer road to Wigan Pier," *The Guardian*, 21 February 2004, https://www.theguardian.com/books/2004/feb/21/georgeorwell.featuresreviews.
7. The rest of the hour was taken up with commercials.
8. Beryl Bainbridge, "Thanks for the memories, Melvyn," *The Observer*, 10 May 2009, https://www.theguardian.com/commentisfree/2009/may/10/melvyn-bragg-southbank-show-authors.

Chapter 19

1. Mark Littlewood's comments in this chapter come from email correspondence in January 2017 and notes he compiled when asked to speak at film screenings.
2. In 2008, Bafta Scotland gave Pelicula Films a special award for outstanding achievement in Scottish film. Littlewood set up the company with business partner Mike Alexander.
3. Tony Grace, phone interview, 27 January 2017.
4. The end credits run as follows: "A Pelicula film for Scottish Screen. Co-produced with Area de Television, Scottish Television, TV3 (Spain). With the support of the MEDIA Programme of the European Community and Institute Catala de les Industries Cultural. Made in association with RTE Ireland, YLE Finland, NRK Norway, VRT Belgium, SVT Sweden, SWR Germany."
5. "Orwell to be subject of £300,000 documentary," *The Scotsman*, 15 May 2003, http://www.scotsman.com/news/uk/orwell-to-be-subject-of-163-300-000-documentary-1-648 107.

Chapter 20

1. Peter Gornstein, phone interview, 1 June 2018.

2. Meleah Maynard, "Blurring the line between reality and fiction," *Renderosity*, 27 June 2011, https://www.renderosity.com/blurring-the-line-between-reality-and-fiction-cms-15672.

3. Lorraine Wilder, "A modern interpretation of Orwell in Peaceforce," *Tinsel Town News Now*, 25 November 2016, https://tinseltown-newsnow.net/2016/11/25/von-schwerin-a-modern-interpretation-of-orwell-in-peaceforce.

4. *Ibid.*

5. Maynard.

6. The Danish Film Institute (Det Danske Filminstitut), "Peaceforce wins at Clermont-Ferrand," 16 February 2011, https://www.dfi.dk/english/peaceforce-wins-clermont-ferrand.

7. Danish Film Institute database, *Peaceforce* listing, https://www.dfi.dk/en/viden-om-film/filmdatabasen/film/peaceforce

Chapter 21

1. The essay was first published in *New Writing*, No. 2, Autumn 1936.

2. Alec Sokolow, Kickstarter video, posted 25 June 2013. https://www.kickstarter.com/projects/1414558572/shooting-an-elephant-based-on-the-essay-by-george.

3. Juan Pablo Rothie, email to David Ryan, 11 April 2016.

Chapter 22

1. BBC Written Archives Centre (WAC) T53/237/1.

2. *Radio Times*, 12–18 June 1982, 75 listing.

3. Elizabeth Cowley, "Pick of the day," *Daily Mail*, 18 June 1982, 27.

4. Jennifer Selway, "The week in view," *The Observer*, 13 June 1982, 40.

5. Maureen Paton, "Tribute to an angry patriot," *Daily Express*, 18 June 1982, 25.

6. Mary Kenny, "The Price of patriotism," *Daily Mail*, 19 June 1982, 16.

7. *Variety*, 15 June 1983, 50.

8. John Corry, *The New York Times*, 7 June 1983.

9. Chris Dunkley, "1983: A watershed for television," *Financial Times*, 28 December 1983, 7.

10. Mick Brown, "Walt's faults," *The Guardian*, 26 August 1983, 10.

11. Marshall Peterson, email to David Ryan, 2 July 2015.

12. George Orwell, "Wells, Hitler and the World State," *Horizon*, August 1941; *The Penguin Essays of George Orwell* (Penguin, 1994) 188–193.

13. Recounted in the diary of Inez Holden, a mutual friend not included in the play, on 30 August 1941; Gordon Bowker, *George Orwell* (Little, Brown, 2003), 288.

14. Bernard Crick, *George Orwell: A Life* (Secker & Warburg, 1980), 294; DJ Taylor, *Orwell: The Life* (Chatto & Windus, 2003), 305.

15. Orwell diaries, 27 March 1942.

16. It's 50 minutes without the commercials.

17. "Tim Robbins to direct 1984," *Empire Online*, 13 January 2006, http://www.empireonline.com/movies/news/exclusive-tim-robbins-direct-1984.

18. Charlotte Higgins, "Covent Garden in row over vanity project," *The Guardian*, 2 May 2005, https://www.theguardian.com/uk/2005/may/02/arts.artsnews.

19. Stuart Davies, phone interview, 12 October 2015.

Chapter 23

1. *Four Episodes from 1984*, listed in the Assorted Orwell chapter.

2. *Screen International*, 21 May 1993, 7.

3. *Broadcast*, 4 April 1983, 15.

4. Transmitted on BBC Radio 4, 22 March 1993.

5. The story was taken up by other news outlets and widely reported on 18–19 May 2009. http://www.comingsoon.net/movies/news/55673-firth-and-spacey-to-star-in-catalonia.

6. "Hugh Hudson: Sport is a form of pure art," FilmFestivalswww, http://www.filmfestivals.com/blog/sofia_international_film_festival/hugh_hudson_sport_is_a_form_of_pure_art.

7. Aileen Doherty, "The Monty Python joker who won a guerilla war with Hollywood," *Daily Mail*, 21 December 1985, 7.

8. *Star Trek: The Next Generation, Chain of Command* parts one and two, 14 and 21 December 1992.

9. Andy Hertzfeld, co-creator of the Apple Mackintosh, claims that the commercial aired at 1am on 15 December. Andy Hertzfeld, "The original Macintosh:1984," *Folklore*, http://www.folklore.org/StoryView.py?story=1984. Tom Frank, who worked for the channel KMVT, says that as operator, he was under strict orders to transmit the ad during the last possible break on New Year's Eve. Chris Higgins, "The true story of Apple's '1984' ad's first broadcast … before the Super Bowl," *Mental Floss*, http://mentalfloss.com/article/29911/true-story-apples-1984-ads-first-broadcastbefore-super-bowl.

10. Scott and Chiat/Day recruited 300 extras, many of them real-life skinheads, for the three-day shoot in London. Tim Stenovec,

"Apple's iconic '1984' ad aired nationally for the first time 32 years ago today," *Business Insider*, http://uk.businessinsider.com/apple-1984-mac-ad-32-years-ago-2016-1.

11. David Graham, who played the Big Brother figure, voiced the Daleks in sixties episodes of *Doctor Who*. He is perhaps best known as the voice of Parker, Lady Penelope's chauffeur in the puppet show *Thunderbirds*.

12. Athlete, actress and model Anya Major had another brush with fame in 1985 playing Nikita, the Iron Curtain checkpoint guard in the Elton John music promo.

13. Fred Goldberg, *The Insanity of Advertising* (Council Oak Books, 2013). Goldberg, the Apple account manager at Chiat/Day, says the ad scored a five in market research. The average for a 30-second commercial was 29.

14. Kimberly Potts, "5 things you didn't know about Apple's '1984' Super Bowl ad (like how it almost didn't air)," *Yahoo TV*, 29 January 2015, https://www.yahoo.com/tv/bp/5-things-you-didn-t-know-about-apple-s-1984-super-bowl-ad-like-how-it-almost-didn-t-air-194148445.html.

15. "Orwell copyright court cases," *Orwell Today*, http://www.orwelltoday.com/readerorwellcopyrightcases.

16. William R. Coulson, "Big Brother is watching Apple: The truth about the Super Bowl's most famous ad," *Dartmouth Law Journal*, Vol VII, Winter 2009, http://www.gcjustice.com/Apple_Computers_Big_Brother.pdf.

Bibliography

By George Orwell

Down and Out in Paris and London (Gollancz, 1933).
Burmese Days (Gollancz, 1934).
A Clergyman's Daughter (Gollancz, 1935).
Keep the Aspidistra Flying (Gollancz, 1936).
The Road to Wigan Pier (Gollancz, 1937).
Homage to Catalonia (Secker & Warburg, 1937).
Coming Up for Air (Gollancz, 1939).
Animal Farm (Secker & Warburg, 1945).
Nineteen Eighty-Four (Secker & Warburg, 1949).
The Collected Essays, Journalism and Letters of George Orwell Volumes 1–4. edited by Sonia Orwell and Ian Angus (Secker & Warburg, 1968).
The Penguin Essays of George Orwell (Penguin, 1984).

Books

Bowker, Gordon. *George Orwell* (Little, Brown, 2003).
Bragg, Melvyn. *Rich: The Life of Richard Burton* (Hodder & Stoughton, 1998).
Crick, Bernard. *George Orwell: A Life* (Secker & Warburg, 1980).
Cushing, Peter. *An Autobiography* (Weidenfeld & Nicholson, 1986).
Cushman, Thomas, and John Rodden. *George Orwell: Into the Twenty-First Century* (Paradigm Publishers, 2004).
Edgerton, Gary R. *The Columbia History of American Television* (Columbia University Press, 2007).
Fischer, Dennis. *Science Fiction Film Directors 1895–1998 volume 1* (McFarland, 2000).

Fulton, Roger. *The Encyclopedia of TV Science Fiction* (Boxtree, 1990).
Ghiglione, Loren. *Don Hollenbeck: An Honest Reporter in the Age of McCarthyism* (Columbia University Press, 2008).
Goldberg, Fred. *The Insanity of Advertising* (Council Oak Books, 2013).
Gullo, Christopher. *In All Sincerity: Peter Cushing* (Xlibris, 2004).
Hitchens, Christopher. *Why Orwell Matters* (Basic Books, 2008).
Jacobs, Jason. *The Intimate Screen: Early British Television Drama* (Oxford Television Studies, 2000).
Jones, Simon. *London Film Location Guide* (Batsford, 2007).
Leab, Daniel J. *Orwell Subverted: The CIA and the Filming of Animal Farm* (The Pennsylvania State University Press, 2008).
Manvell, Roger. *The Animated Film* (Sylvan Press, 1954).
Meyers, Jeffrey. *Orwell: Life and Art* (University of Illinois Press, 2010).
Meyers, Jeffrey. *Orwell: Wintry Conscience of a Generation* (Norton, 2000).
Murray, Andy. *Into the Unknown: The Fantastic Life of Nigel Kneale* (Headpress, 2006).
Peary, Danny. *Guide for the Film Fanatic* (Simon & Schuster, 1986).
Peary, Danny. *Omni's Screen Flights/Screen Fantasies: The Future According to Science Fiction Cinema* (Doubleday, 1984).
Pitts, Michael R. *Columbia Pictures Horror, Science Fiction and Fantasy Films 1928–1982* (McFarland, 2010).
Redgrave, Corin. *Michael Redgrave: My Father* (Fourth Estate, 1996).
Rodden, John. *George Orwell: The Politics*

of Literary Reputation (Transaction Publishers, 2002).

Shaw, Tony. *British Cinema and the Cold War: The State, Propaganda and Consensus* (IB Taurus, 2001).

Shaw, Tony. *Hollywood's Cold War* (Edinburgh University Press, 2007).

Shelden, Michael. *George Orwell: The Authorized Biography* (Heinemann, 1991).

Stonor Saunders, Frances. *Who Paid the Piper? The CIA and the Cultural Cold War* (Granta Books, 1999).

Taylor, DJ. *Orwell: The Life* (Chatto & Windus, 2003).

Warren, Bill. *Keep Watching the Skies! American Science Fiction Movies of the Fifties* (McFarland 2d ed., 2010).

Wilkie, Bernard. *A Peculiar Effect on the BBC* (Miwk Publishing, 2015).

Index

Numbers in *bold italics* indicate pages with illustrations